I Arise!
2023

Day by day, from one heart to another

Published by: BUCJC UK, Bethel National Women's Council

Category: Christianity

Copyright: BUCJC UK, Bethel National Women's Council 2022

ISBN: 9798360849315

Cover design by: Inspirational Journals

Graphic design by: Ashani Allen & Anna-Kaye Williams

Edited by: Jackie Jacobs

Proofreading Team:

Charmaine Boora

Marie Chisnall

Lorna Lewin

Carol Lord-Paul

Beulah McKenzie

Deveen Smith

Vera Walters

Jackie Wilkinson

CONTENTS:

Acknowledgements

Introduction

Book Endorsement

Monthly Writings:

ACKNOWLEDGEMENTS

We give thanks and praise to Almighty God for His guidance with the: *"I Arise"* 2023 devotional writings project. There is nobody greater than Him.

We also give thanks to everyone who helped to make this edition happen. Whatever your contribution, we appreciate you.

We remember our pioneering mothers of the Bethel National Women's Council who laid a deep and solid foundation upon which future generations could build. You trained us well; you are not forgotten.

INTRODUCTION

Welcome to *"I Arise"* 2023, our 2nd edition of this special book for you, from you, about you.

Women of different backgrounds, age groups, statuses, nationalities, etc., have once again united to uplift and empower each other with personal life experiences, and encouragement from God's Word.

Each month has a central theme. We start 2023 with: *"A Heart for God"*, and end giving thanks for: *"The Gift of Jesus Christ"*. We recommend that you also read the suggested daily Scripture readings given in each chapter.

Our medical professionals are back to share their expertise on health subjects such as: *Autism, Alopecia, Osteoporosis*, and much more. There is something for everybody.

We recognise that sometimes life events mean we need additional support, although we don't always know where to find it. New for this year is a Support Directory with contact details of where help can be found in such seasons.

As you go from page to page, please remember to pray for the other women also reading the same - we have so much in common: Today's Eve, Jochebed, Abigail, Tamar, Vashti, Syrophoenician Woman, Rhoda, Lydia, Priscilla, Phoebe; every woman who is struggling to maintain *"Joy During Suffering"*. We are not independent of one another; it's a fact - we are stronger together.

May we continue to *"Arise!"*. Make it personal. *"Break Limitations"* and *"Move into Destiny"*.

Bethel National Women's Council

"I Arise" 2023 – Book Endorsement

In every season of life, we as women are at times required to lead, care and provide the nurturing for our families, church members, and wider community.

"I Arise" 2023 is the 2nd in this excellent series of books published by our National Women's Council. The Council is committed to encouraging all of us as women to pursue purpose and excellence in every area of our lives.

Reading the testimonies of our sisters who have experienced challenges and successes, is a lifeline of hope for women of every generation and background. From the pain and survival of divorce, to the faith needed to experience joy as we go through the tests of everyday life, *"I Arise"* 2023 will encourage you to sing and hope, always knowing that: *"Weeping endures for a night, but joy will come in the morning" (Psalm 30:5).*

"I Arise" 2023 is a wonderful addition to our daily Bible readings as we enter our private place of prayer to be renewed, revived, and restored so that we can once again Arise for another day!

First Lady Yolanda Edmund, Bethel UK

January

A Heart for God

SUNDAY 1st

(New Year's Day)

Arise, and go down to the potter's house - Jeremiah 18:2

LORD, GIVE ME A HEART LIKE YOURS - Reading: Jeremiah 18:1-6

Regularly Lady Yolanda and I will listen to a song by CeCe Winans called: *"A heart like yours"*. We are captivated, not only by CeCe's amazing voice, but by the words of the song which minister healing to us.

"A heart like yours is my desire, a heart like yours is what I'm searching for. Full of compassion, nothing wrong within. Please hear me, Lord! Give me a heart like yours. So much grace, so much kindness, so much faith, forever true, strong as the wind, soft as the shadow. If just once I could be like you".

Sisters, should not this be the theme and guiding principle of our lives, that we have the heart of God? Samuel was a great man, but he could not see the heart of Eliab, he could only see what we see. But God, in selecting a king and shepherd for His people, found a man that had His heart.

May our hearts be ever shaped by the message of our Lord Jesus Christ, who came not to be served but to serve. It is only as we have the heart of God that we will develop a heart for God.

We love you and pray that God will bless you and your family this year in Jesus' name!

Bishop Dexter Edmund & First Lady Yolanda Edmund

January 2023
Theme: A Heart for God
21 – 28 January: Cervical Cancer Prevention Week
Love Your Liver Awareness Month & National Soup Month

10

MONDAY 2nd

(Bank Holiday)

Purge me with hyssop, and I shall be clean - Psalm 51:7

PURGE ME LORD - Reading: 2 Samuel 12:1-14; Psalm 51:7

This penitent psalm was written by the famous King David, the greatest king that Israel ever had.

David was a true worshipper, a man after God's own heart, and was truly loved and admired. This great king found himself in a predicament from which only God, and God alone, could deliver him. 2 Samuel 12 captures the storyline that contributed to King David penning Psalm 51. This Psalm really expresses the heart of a king that was deeply sorrowful for his actions. In Psalm 51:7, David acknowledges that the sin he had committed against the God he so loved, could only be purged with hyssop.

In those days, hyssop was a deep cleansing plant that had the power to remove very stubborn stains. David understood that the sin he had committed against God was so deeply engrained in his heart, it was going to take something very strong to remove this stain.

Today, we have something far greater than hyssop that can remove any sin of which we are guilty, it is the efficacious blood of Jesus Christ that was shed at Calvary! God's love, care and tender mercy towards humankind has no limits, it has no boundaries. As David found forgiveness in his time of need, so can we today.

So, *"Let us therefore come boldly to the throne of grace, that we may obtain mercy and find grace to help in time of need"* (Hebrews 4:16).

Evangelist Paula Clarke
Bethel National Women's President

January 2023
Theme: A Heart for God
21 – 28 January: Cervical Cancer Prevention Week
Love Your Liver Awareness Month & National Soup Month

11

TUESDAY 3rd

Ye shall seek me, and find me, when ye search with all your heart - Jer. 29:13

HAVE YOU LOOKED PROPERLY? - Reading: Jeremiah 29:1-14

I remember being asked this question many times as a young child: *"Have you looked properly?"*.

It was asked because when I lost things, I often felt that rather than looking thoroughly, it would be easier just to ask for a replacement. Sometimes I would say that I had searched but it was obvious by the speed at which I returned with my report, that I had really not looked properly at all.

Time and effort are necessary when doing a search. What always works is to retrace one's steps, physically or mentally, to the last place where you last saw what is missing.

It is true for every Christian that at different stages of our walk with God we will feel we've lost our original connection with Him. The cause is not always easy to identify, and we may not even notice that something is missing straightaway. Mary and Joseph didn't realise that they had travelled for a whole day from Jerusalem without Jesus in their company. It then took them three days to find Him (St Luke 2:42-46).

Is Jesus still in your company? You may say that you can't find Him, but have you looked properly? He's not hiding. Search again!

JEJ

January 2023
Theme: A Heart for God
21 – 28 January: Cervical Cancer Prevention Week
Love Your Liver Awareness Month & National Soup Month

12

WEDNESDAY 4th

Arise, shine…the glory of the LORD is risen upon thee - Isaiah 60:1

I ARISE - Reading: Judges 4:13-16; Isaiah 60:1-2

I arise!
From the depth of sweetest slumber
I arise!
To be among the number
Of those who greet the dawn of day
Of those who give thanks as they say
I arise!

I arise!
Since I have been called from sleep
I arise!
To light from darkness deep
Another time to ply my trade
In this the day the Lord hath made
I arise!

I arise!
Among the living to take my stand
I arise!
Protected by God's mighty hand
To declare that He's my God and King
To lift my voice, His praise to sing
I arise!

I arise!
Though I know not what lies before me
I arise!
Trusting in God's grace and mercy
Just knowing that what e'er betides
He will direct and be my guide
I arise!

Sister Barbara Hendrickson, Nevis, WI

January 2023
Theme: A Heart for God
21 – 28 January: Cervical Cancer Prevention Week
Love Your Liver Awareness Month & National Soup Month

13

THURSDAY 5th

Who can discern their errors? Forgive my hidden faults - Psalm 19:12 (NIV)

UNKNOWN SINS - Reading: Psalm 19:12; St Matthew 18:1-6

Not all sins are on purpose; it is possible to be oblivious to a trespass which we have committed.

Most of us will easily identify with the words of this song:

"If I have wounded any soul today
If I have caused one foot to go astray
If I have walked in my own wilful way
Dear Lord, forgive

If I have uttered idle words or vain
If I have turned aside from want or pain
Lest I offend some other through the strain
Dear Lord, forgive

Forgive the sins I have confessed to Thee
Forgive the secret sins I do not see
O guide me, love me, and my keeper be
Dear Lord, forgive."

(An Evening Prayer – C Maud Battersby)

We should never be so confident in ourselves that we would dismiss the possibility that we may have hurt someone unintentionally. Sometimes, because it was not our intent to wound, we are not too bothered about the outcome; the person offended should just 'get over it'. But a stray bullet will not hurt less because the victim was not its target!

So, Lord, if by tactlessness, selfishness, or some other work of the flesh I have injured anyone or offended you as a result of a personal fault, I too, like the psalmist, will include this catch-all request in my prayers each day: *"Purge and forgive me of sins that to me are hidden"*.

JEJ

January 2023
Theme: A Heart for God
21 – 28 January: Cervical Cancer Prevention Week
Love Your Liver Awareness Month & National Soup Month

14

FRIDAY 6th

I find then a law, that when I would do good, evil is present - Romans 7:21

THE INNER STRUGGLE - Reading: Romans 7:14-25

Why did I do that? Why did I say that? Oh no!

These are questions and exclamations that born-again believers ask and say to ourselves from time-to-time. We utter them from frustration and/or disappointment that, despite loving God so much and doing our best to please Him, we still don't get everything right all of the time.

We identify that there is a constant inward war going on between the Spirit and the flesh, between good and evil. The old Adamic nature (the nature with which we are born) is always trying to dominate and conquer the new creation we now are in Christ Jesus *(2 Corinthians 5:17)*. Hence, we must constantly feed the Spirit and starve the ungodly desires of the flesh, i.e., the carnal, earthly, sin-nature part of us; control it by application of the Word, fasting and prayer.

I'm not only talking about the kinds of sins which would make readers be shocked and gasp in surprise! As well as those, I'm also referring to 'simple' things like going on fasting on a particular day. One part of us knows that we must fast to gain spiritual strength or for a specific purpose, but the other voice says leave fasting for another day.

The other law, i.e., principle, on the inside, tries to prevent us from doing what is right. We therefore draw on the strength of the Holy Spirit who dwells within us, and thereby we keep the opposing principle under subjection.

JEJ

SATURDAY 7th

If we confess our sins, He is faithful and just to forgive us our sins - 1 John 1:9

IT'S ME O LORD! - Reading: 1 John 1:1-9

We are good at observing faults in others, and easily notice when someone else says or does the wrong thing. But we often struggle to admit when we are not right and instead, try to justify our wrongdoing. This behaviour sometimes begins from childhood, for instance, telling tales of the mischief of a sibling, but a reluctance of the same child to own up that it was them who wrote on the wallpaper!

If we can but remember our desired destination, i.e., heaven, this will or should make confession of sin less difficult. Why? It is sin that will prevent any one of us from entering heaven.

With this in mind, as soon as we know that we have sinned, i.e., offended God by missing His standard of holiness, say like the Prodigal Son: *"Father, I have sinned"* *(St Luke 15:21)*. Our confession must also be followed by a sincere vow and effort not to repeat the offence.

Just as the father's reaction in the parable was totally different to what was anticipated by his son see that John says, after confession, God won't reject us but will forgive, purge and purify us from all unrighteousness.

JEJ

January 2023
Theme: A Heart for God
21 – 28 January: Cervical Cancer Prevention Week
Love Your Liver Awareness Month & National Soup Month

16

SUNDAY 8th

Lord, what will you have me to do? - Acts 9:6

GO! - Reading: Acts 9:1-16

This is the account of Saul's meeting with Jesus. Saul was his Hebrew name, but when he went into Roman territory he was known as Paul. That is how we know him today.

Saul was travelling along the Damascus Road when he met with Jesus. Imagine what he might have thought? There he was persecuting all who called upon the name of Jesus, and now here was Jesus speaking to him! Saul asked Jesus two questions: *"Who are you, Lord?" (Acts 9:5)* and then: *"What will you have me do?" (Acts 9:6).*

Saul acknowledged who Jesus was and immediately wanted to obey Him. Jesus said: *"Go!".*

As we look at this, we are reminded of the Great Commission (St Matthew 28:19) which starts with Jesus saying: *"Go!".* He expects us today to go into our world and share the Good News of Salvation with everyone we meet. Maybe our world is where we work, or maybe our unsaved family. But wherever it is, we must tell people the Good News that Jesus loves them more than they will ever know.

Marie Chisnall

MONDAY 9th

Forgive us our debts, as we forgive our debtors - St Matthew 6:12

SINCERE FORGIVENESS - Reading: St Matthew 6:1-15

When we are hurt, or owed something, it is easy to become self-righteous. Our ego and pride are impacted. We feel that what has happened must not go unrecognised; a desire for retribution feels justified.

But Jesus, teaching His disciples to pray, emphasises the complete submission of self that is necessary for the heavenly will of God to work through us. When said in sincerity, the person praying recognises how unjustified their self-righteousness is, and the similarity of their position with that of the debtor's, i.e., we all need to be forgiven.

I sometimes hear statements with the sentiment: *"I forgive you **for me"***; but *Biblical* forgiveness comes from a place of empathy, and a desire for the *offender's* soul to be right with God. We understand the depth of our own offences to God, and how guilty we are, i.e., weak and without excuse or means of restitution, facing certain judgment. But through the grace of Jesus Christ, our Advocate, we now have peace with God.

The gravity of what was our own jeopardy, and the boundless love of God, move us to compassion for the offender: *"I forgive you, even as my Heavenly Father forgave me"*.

Beulah McKenzie

January 2023
Theme: A Heart for God
21 – 28 January: Cervical Cancer Prevention Week
Love Your Liver Awareness Month & National Soup Month

18

TUESDAY 10th

Out of the abundance of the heart the mouth speaketh - St Matthew 12:34

VOICE OF THE HEART - Reading: St Matthew 12:22-37

Only God can read our heart but our speech will give the hearer, and us, an indication of its condition, especially when we are under pressure.

When we are being pressed, and don't have time to measure or tailor our response in difficult situations, we hear what is in our heart. God allows us to be presented with circumstances to alert us that we still have areas of weakness that need to be worked on and healed by the Holy Spirit. In the heat of a trial, we sometimes meet someone whom we do not know, although that person is us!

We never surprise God with our actions but we are always on a journey of discovery. Peter passionately said that he would never deny Christ, even if everyone else did. Yet later, in that same day, Peter began to curse and swear that he was not a disciple (St Matthew 26:74-75).

Jesus said it this way: *"Out of the abundance of the heart the mouth speaketh"*. That's the KJV but other versions perhaps give a clearer translation, e.g.: *"Out of the overflow of the heart the mouth speaks" (Berean Study Bible)* or: *"The mouth speaks what the heart is full of" (NIV)*.

Our words, bitter or sweet, harsh or kind, angry or calm, false or true, have their roots in our heart. Let us fill our heart with good things so that its overflow through our mouth always sounds like Christ.

JEJ

January 2023
Theme: A Heart for God
21 – 28 January: Cervical Cancer Prevention Week
Love Your Liver Awareness Month & National Soup Month

19

WEDNESDAY 11th

Draw nigh to God, and He will draw nigh to you - James 4:8

JUST FOR WHO YOU ARE - Reading: James 4:1-12

When was the last time that you pursued after God just for a deeper relationship, and not because you wanted something?

Many readers of this page will have experience of at least one relationship which felt/feels very one-sided, i.e., only hearing from a particular individual either when you take the initiative to contact them or if they need something! This can give a feeling that the other person does not care as much about you as you do about them, or that you're being used as a matter of convenience. You may by now be nodding in agreement as you reflect on such a person or persons.

While you are nodding, please read the first paragraph of today's article again.

If you were not in trouble, not seriously sick, you had the level of income necessary to meet your expenditure, all of your family members were well and saved and abiding by God's Word, if all of your brethren, work colleagues and neighbours were treating you right, would you still draw nigh to God?

God wants to hear from us without a list of repairs. He wants us to get in touch just because we love Him and desire to know Him better!

JEJ

January 2023
Theme: A Heart for God
21 – 28 January: Cervical Cancer Prevention Week
Love Your Liver Awareness Month & National Soup Month

20

THURSDAY 12th

The LORD weighs and examines the hearts - Proverbs 21:2 (AMP)

A WONDERFUL CHANGE - Reading: Proverbs 2:1-8

My conversion came not from conviction, but from frustration.

It was in the year 1963 that I attended an Evangelistic Church Service held in Trowbridge, Wiltshire, by the young Elder Gerald Edmund. He was accompanied by members from the Bethel United Church of Jesus Christ Apostolic, Bristol. I was curious about the *"Jesus Only"* doctrine that they were preaching, having been brought up from a child as a Baptist in Jamaica.

The church service was held at Trowbridge Football Club. I had no intention of getting saved or becoming a member of a Jesus Only Church. Those churches were considered by many, including me, to be an error of the truth according to the command given by Jesus and recorded in St Matthew 28:19.

As a matter of fact, I was more fascinated by the youthful looking preacher, (Elder Gerald Edmund) whose voice seemed to echo throughout the small room as he preached about God becoming a man to save man from eternal damnation. I thought within myself: *"Who is he trying to convince? Definitely not me, for sure!"*.

After what felt like hours, he stopped preaching and then referred to an Altar Call: *"Those of you who are not saved, or have not been baptised in Jesus' name, I want to invite you to come to this altar, and we will pray for you"*.

I was just about to leave the service when a woman came up to me and insisted that I walk with her to the altar for prayer. I refused and politely told her that I didn't need to be prayed for, but she would not leave me alone. I thought to myself: *"This woman is getting on my nerves, and I don't want to be rude!"*. I was so frustrated by her; I decided that the only way to get rid of her was to get up and go to the altar. As I got up from my seat, I looked at her and smirked!

Little did I know that God was waiting for me at the altar. Immediately as I knelt down, I felt as if someone knocked me on the back of my neck, and I fell forward! With tears running down my face I wept unashamedly. That night I surrendered my life to the Lord.

From frustration to conversion!

Rev. Dr. Una M. Davis

January 2023
Theme: A Heart for God
21 – 28 January: Cervical Cancer Prevention Week
Love Your Liver Awareness Month & National Soup Month

FRIDAY 13th

The LORD seeth not as man seeth; He looketh on the heart - 1 Samuel 16:7

THE REAL ME - Reading: 1 Samuel 16:1-13

There is a saying: *"You can't judge a book by its cover"*.

It is a true proverb although we have all at some stage been guilty of forming judgments about people based only on what we can see. Our opinion sometimes stems from the clothes that someone wears, where they live, or their academic qualifications. It's also very easy to be tricked into a false sense of security of an individual's sincerity based on things that they say, or even what they give, but we cannot determine the content of their heart.

In the Garden of Gethsemane, Judas kissed Jesus not as a sign of love and affection, but to betray and identify Jesus for His arrest. Sometimes a hug or embrace is given to try to camouflage a bitter heart.

The question for today is: How does God see me? Does He see me as someone who is sincere, whose external actions mirror what's on the inside? Would God be able to give the same testimony to Satan of me as He did about Job, i.e.: *"none like (Job)…blameless…upright…feareth God…turns away from evil" (Job 1:8)*?

Who then is the Real Me? The Real Me is whoever I am in my heart.

JEJ

January 2023
Theme: A Heart for God
21 – 28 January: Cervical Cancer Prevention Week
Love Your Liver Awareness Month & National Soup Month

22

SATURDAY 14th

Strengthen the things which remain, and are ready to die - Revelation 3:2

STRENGTHEN EACH OTHER - Reading: Revelation 3:1-6

God will never give up on us, indeed it is we that might give up on Him.

Jesus loves His church and speaks to them (the church in Sardis*): "Be watchful and strengthen the things which remain"* (Revelation 3:2). Be alert, be mindful and be faithful to God.

The cares of life can easily distract us, so much so that we lose focus on who we are and our purpose!

Strengthen the things which remain. YOU and I are those which remain. I will strengthen YOU by praying for you, by speaking words of life from the Word of God into your spirit. These are words that you must physically hear. I will strengthen you by fasting with you in times of great need for deliverance and healing.

But here's the thing: *"I have been crucified with Christ and I no longer live, but Christ lives in me" (Galatians 2: 20 NIV).*

It is Jesus that will strengthen us, if we allow him. SO ALLOW HIM.

Pastor Janette Watson

January 2023
Theme: A Heart for God
21 – 28 January: Cervical Cancer Prevention Week
Love Your Liver Awareness Month & National Soup Month

23

SUNDAY 15th

A new heart will I give you, and a new spirit will I put within - Ezekiel 36:25-26

CLEANSED & CHANGED - Reading: Ezekiel 36:22-38

Israel was in captivity for committing idolatry.

Despite warnings by the prophets, Israel wouldn't change. Consequently, God punished them with removal into captivity by Nebuchadnezzar. Their land laid barren and desolate; they became a 'laughing stock' to their neighbours. God used Ezekiel, himself exiled, to reassure Israel of future restoration.

God promised destruction to their enemies, but blessings for Israel. Prosperity to the land, spiritual awakening and revival for Israel. But first, a national cleansing from their wrongdoings. God Himself would sprinkle pure water on them, taking the place of Israel's priests. Sprinkling the water of separation, for purification of sin (Numbers 19:9), making Israel ceremonially clean from defilement, and sanctified back to God.

Henceforth permanently remedying backsliding tendencies by changing their heart. They would then have a new attitude, and true desires for the Holy One who had vowed to be their God, and they His people.

God would also change their spirit to have a mind to serve Him in truth wholeheartedly, not just by ritualistic duties, but with a tender obedient heart. A heart that cured them from their wanderings and stubbornness to be indeed: *"His peculiar treasure above all people" (Exodus 19:5).*

Today we are also recipients of the promise.

Sis Jx

January 2023
Theme: A Heart for God
21 – 28 January: Cervical Cancer Prevention Week
Love Your Liver Awareness Month & National Soup Month

24

MONDAY 16th

As the deer longs for streams of water, so I long for you, O God - Psalm 42:1

THIRSTY FOR GOD - Reading: Psalm 42:1-11 (NLT)

Deer pant mainly as a means of cooling down when they're hot, since they have very few sweat glands.

They yearn for fresh water during the heat of the day but will only stop to drink when they feel safe. Their surroundings must be peaceful and still. It's also thought that the water acts as an aid or means of escape by removing their scent-trail from those who seek to kill them.

Picture if you can, a deer desperately seeking for water, it will not give up until a stream or another source is found. Visualise too the deer bending its head to lap the water, feeling safe from predators. Imagine it drinking until it's fully satisfied.

Compare now the psalmist's analogy of a deer's strong desire for water with: *"So panteth my soul after Thee, O God"*. A desperate desire for the refreshing water of the Word, looking for the right place to be alone and spiritually rehydrated, safe and secure from all alarm. Such a place does exist:

"There is a place of quiet rest, near to the heart of God,
A place where sin cannot molest near to the heart of God

There is a place of comfort sweet, near to the heart of God
A place where we our Saviour meet, near to the heart of God

There is a place of full release, near to the heart of God
A place where all is joy and peace, near to the heart of God."

(Near to the Heart of God – C Boyd McAfee)

JEJ

January 2023
Theme: A Heart for God
21 – 28 January: Cervical Cancer Prevention Week
Love Your Liver Awareness Month & National Soup Month

25

TUESDAY 17th

If I regard iniquity in my heart, the LORD will not hear me - Psalm 66:18

THE BLOCKED PRAYER - Reading: Psalm 66:13-20

Many Christians have particular times during each day to pray, and often look forward to this time of communion with God.

Prayer is also when, as a songwriter penned, we: "*make all our wants and wishes known*" (*Sweet Hour of Prayer – A Jackson*).

However, before praying again, let's consider today's Scripture verse very carefully, for it may help us to understand why sometimes our prayers yield no results.

To assist with our learning, we will use a combination of other Scripture versions alongside the KJV of Psalm 66:18: "*If I know that I have sin in my heart and do nothing about it; if I have malice in my heart; if I have ignored my sins; if I have cherished sin or harboured wickedness in in my heart - God will not listen*".

It's not always another prayer that is needed. **Before** we make requests, we must have a clean heart otherwise our words are going nowhere.

JEJ

January 2023
Theme: A Heart for God
21 – 28 January: Cervical Cancer Prevention Week
Love Your Liver Awareness Month & National Soup Month

26

WEDNESDAY 18th

Search me, O God, and know my heart: try me…- Psalm 139:23

LORD SEARCH MY HEART - Reading: 1 Samuel 16:1-13; Psalm 139:23

Whenever we want to learn more about any piece of equipment, we consult the manufacturer's manual. The manufacturer has expert knowledge because they are the creator.

David recognised God as his Creator, the One who sees and knows all things including the most hidden and secret thoughts of the heart. In 1 Samuel 16:7, we remember God saying that while man looks at the outward appearance, He looks at the heart.

Every dark spot within our heart can be illuminated by the light of Jesus Christ if we ask Him to search us. He knows the desires and intents of our heart, even before they become known to us. Sometimes, we are ashamed or afraid to ask the Lord to search our hearts because we know that there are bad thoughts within us; but He is already reading our hearts. Still, He wants us to ask Him for help. Just like David, go to Him in prayer and confess our sins.

His Word reminds us in 1 John 1:9 that: *"If we truly repent, He will always forgive and cleanse us"*.

Cherely Simons, Fl. USA

January 2023
Theme: A Heart for God
21 – 28 January: Cervical Cancer Prevention Week
Love Your Liver Awareness Month & National Soup Month

27

THURSDAY 19th

I delight to do thy will, O my God: yea, thy law is within my heart - Psalm 40:8

SUBMIT YOUR WILL - Reading: Acts 9:1-19

Here's the chorus of a song which you may know very well:

"Jesus use me and, O Lord, don't refuse me,
Surely there's a work that I can do!
And even though it's humble, Lord, help my will to crumble
Though the cost be great I'll work for you"
(Jesus Use Me - Jack Campbell)

Sometimes we don't fully understand or perhaps are not conscious of what we're singing, or what we read or recite. The writer of today's psalm writes that they *"take joy"*, *"take pleasure in"*, and *"love"* to do God's will. That's easy to say when the will of God doesn't cost anything - or not much; when it does not move me away from my Comfort Zone or ask me to give up something or someone that I love.

Abraham was prepared to offer up Isaac, the son for whom he had waited and was born to Abraham when he was 100 years old (Genesis 21:5). God said to Abraham: *"Give me your son, your only son, the one that you love" (Genesis 22:2)*. Abraham saddled his ass and took Isaac with him to Mount Moriah, prepared in his mind to do the will of God.

Jack Campbell understood when he wrote: *"Jesus Use Me"* that the hardest thing to crumble is my will, and until that happens, God can't fully use me. My will can be a hindrance and in opposition to God's will. So, pray today: *"Lord, help my will to crumble"!*

JEJ

January 2023
Theme: A Heart for God
21 – 28 January: Cervical Cancer Prevention Week
Love Your Liver Awareness Month & National Soup Month

28

FRIDAY 20th

LORD, who shall abide in thy tabernacle? - Psalm 15:1-2

DO I QUALIFY? - Reading: Psalm 15:1-5

Have you ever seen something that you wanted, and wondered how you could get it? It may have been a job advertised, and you made enquiries of how or if you qualified to apply.

Jesus outlined in St John 4:24 the criteria for spiritual worship, i.e., *"God is a Spirit and they that worship Him must worship Him in Spirit and in truth"*. David, whilst musing upon the holiness of God in Psalm 15, considered the characteristics of those whose worship would be accepted by Him. He contemplated the qualities necessary to gain entry not just to the sacred tent or tabernacle of God, and a permanent place to stay in His holy mountain, but how to get access into the presence of God. Look at this: *"blameless"*, *"does what is right"* *"speaks the truth from their heart"*, *"does not backbite or slander"*, *"does no evil to anyone"*; *"they keep their word"*, *"they cannot be bribed"*, *"will not testify falsely against the innocent"*.

The above list is not exhaustive. The standard set by God is very high. The requirements reflect who He is.

JEJ

January 2023
Theme: A Heart for God
21 – 28 January: Cervical Cancer Prevention Week
Love Your Liver Awareness Month & National Soup Month

29

*SATURDAY 21ˢᵗ

Who knows (if God) will revoke your sentence...? - Joel 2:14 (AMP)

A MERCIFUL GOD - Reading: Joel 2:12-14; St Luke 15:18-32

One definition of mercy is to not get what we deserve.

If we are ever struggling to think of a reason to be thankful, we can at least thank God for His mercies. When we recall to mind some of the times when and how we offended God, the memory can cause us to feel ashamed, but it should also simultaneously bring with it a feeling of marvel and gratitude.

We don't marvel because we got away with our wrongdoing, for no sin goes unpunished, but we are humbled that even when God was angry, in His wrath He still remembered mercy *(Habakkuk 3:2)*. He did not cut us off forever. Our chastiser is also the one who sustains us.

Judah was in captivity in Babylon for 70 years as judgment for their sins. Yet in the midst of their penalty came a Word of Hope to them from God: *"For I know the thoughts that I think towards you, saith the LORD, thoughts of peace, and not of evil, to give you an expected end" (Jeremiah 29:11).*

God can choose to bestow a blessing upon us when it's least expected, and certainly at a time when we, and others, know it is absolutely undeserved!

JEJ

*International Hug Day

January 2023
Theme: A Heart for God
21 – 28 January: Cervical Cancer Prevention Week
Love Your Liver Awareness Month & National Soup Month

30

SUNDAY 22nd

That which cometh out of the mouth, this defileth a man - St Matthew 15:11

THE CAUSE OF DEFILEMENT - Reading: St Matthew 15:1-20

Many of us are very concerned about our diet and lifestyle. The doctors, dieticians, herbalists, and others spend a great deal of time telling us what is good to consume and what is not.

Upon closer examination, we find that many of these experts actually contradict each other with the instructions given. Their expertise can create chaos in our lives if we are not careful, but I will never advocate that we should throw out everything they say and be careless with our health.

The analogy in St Matthew 15:11 is that, as we eat physically and our body reacts to what we have eaten, so too our soul reacts to what we eat spiritually. The things that we see and hear take up an integral part of our lives so we must take care to ensure that we gravitate to what is good and right.

Let the right things be absorbed through our very pores and become part of us. This is what will dictate what comes out of our mouths, and show to the world our level of purity. God wants us to manifest His love unto others. Our purpose must be to guide souls to Christ and not drive them away by our 'defiled' speech.

Let us be as fanatical today with words, i.e., speaking words of life, as we are with eating a healthy diet.

Pastor Londy Esdaille, Nevis, WI

January 2023
Theme: A Heart for God
21 – 28 January: Cervical Cancer Prevention Week
Love Your Liver Awareness Month & National Soup Month

31

MONDAY 23rd

And the LORD God called unto Adam, "Where art thou?" - Genesis 3:9

IS GOD MISSING YOU? - Reading: Genesis 3:1-10

Do you know that God looks forward to His time with you?

Even when you've sinned, His desire is that you will not try to hide but come to Him with a repented heart, confess, and then move on.

Sin automatically brings separation from God because He is holy, also sin comes with consequences. But God is always willing to restore and bring us back into fellowship and relationship. If that wasn't so, He would not have reached out for Adam when he and Eve sinned; God would not have called out: *"Where are you?"*.

There's a song that says: *"When gloom and sadness whisper, you've sinned no use to pray! I look away to Jesus and He tells me to say: I see a crimson stream of blood, it flows from Calvary, it's waves which reach the throne of God, are sweeping over me"* (I See a Crimson Stream of Blood - G T Haywood).

You may have disappointed yourself by something wrong that you thought, did or said but our God never says: *"Go away"*! Instead, He calls out our name: *"Come now, and let us reason together....: though your sins be as scarlet, they shall be white as snow; though they be red like crimson, they shall be as wool"* (Isaiah 1:18).

JEJ

January 2023
Theme: A Heart for God
21 – 28 January: Cervical Cancer Prevention Week
Love Your Liver Awareness Month & National Soup Month

32

TUESDAY 24th

But seek ye first the kingdom of God, and his righteousness - St Matthew 6:33

THE LORD IS MY HELPER - Reading: Psalm 121:1-7

When I was going to buy my house, the bank said that because I was the only one working, they could only lend me £50,000. My husband is retired.

I went to a mortgage consultant who tried to get a better deal for me, but when each company looked at my circumstances, all of them said the same thing, i.e., they could not lend me more. I said to myself, I'm going to Convocation and will ring them again when I'm back. I put it to the Lord in prayer.

Afterwards, I received another appointment to see our mortgage broker but my husband said that he didn't want to come with me. He said that I wouldn't get the amount needed, so I went on my own.

My mortgage consultant found a mortgage for me with the same bank that he had tried before! *"I will lift up mine eyes unto the hills from whence cometh my help. My help cometh from the LORD…" (Psalm 121:1-2).*

Name withheld

January 2023
Theme: A Heart for God
21 – 28 January: Cervical Cancer Prevention Week
Love Your Liver Awareness Month & National Soup Month

33

WEDNESDAY 25th

I travail until Christ be formed in you - Galatians 4:19

THE HOUR IS COME - Reading: Galatians 4:8-20

Travail has to do with toil, labour-pains, along with suffering as it is experienced.

It often describes childbirth which is similar to Jesus' analogy in St John 16:21-22: *"A woman when she is in travail hath sorrow because her hour is come...",* but is hopeful of joyful results.

Paul's choice of expression *"travail in birth"* was no trivial matter as the turning away of the Galatians from what he had taught them, caused his hour to come. Labour pains again! Yes, until Christ is formed in them (Galatians 4:19).

Look at Ephesians 1:12: *"In whom ye also trusted, after that ye heard the word of truth, the gospel of your salvation: in whom also after that ye believed, ye were sealed with that Holy Spirit of promise".*

True faith cometh by hearing. We must therefore endeavour to hear truth accurately, and believe it wholeheartedly. What we believe does matter; our belief will either move us from or towards our ultimate God-ordained destiny - to be conformed to the image of Christ.

Sadly, many are rapidly turning away from complete faith and continual trust in the person and teaching of Christ, thus signalling our hour is come to travail in birth again until Christ is formed. See the joyful hope of change in labouring again.

Pastor Josephine Lewis

January 2023
Theme: A Heart for God
21 – 28 January: Cervical Cancer Prevention Week
Love Your Liver Awareness Month & National Soup Month

34

THURSDAY 26th

What is anyone profited, if they gain all and lose their soul? - St Matt 16:26

RUN OUT OF TIME - Reading: St Matthew 16:21-28

I spent some time at the cemetery today
And no one spoke a word.
Yet every single lesson they had conveyed
Was oh so poignantly heard!

One young man spoke of heartbreak
He just could never forgive.
He held them guilty forever
And decided that's how he would live.

A young girl spoke of charmers
Whose flowers always made her feel good.
Yet none had been to see her
Or clear the old flowers, they promised they would!

One had been too tired
Of all this praying, and living, and fasting.
They never knew just how long now
This 'resting in peace' would be lasting!

One had blurbed-lips of complaining!
Never stopped to think just how blessed,
And now there was no one to listen
To the testimonies they had gained from their tests.

A businessman wealthy and thriving
Had worked himself to the ground,
And just like when he had been living
Not aware of his family all around.

The woman always looking at another,
And never satisfied with what she had got,
Now she owned this patch to be proud of
A name, a number, a plot!

The dreamer never woke from their dreaming
To do anything with their plans;
Procrastination had finally killed him
With his dreams clasped tight in his hands.

January 2023
Theme: A Heart for God
21 – 28 January: Cervical Cancer Prevention Week
Love Your Liver Awareness Month & National Soup Month

Hear the sound of the pleading,
Do the things you have on your heart!
Don't stand here too long in the silence,
Live your life while you've got a head-start.

If you listen to the sound of their chorus,
Hear their voices in the wind chime,
I thought I would be here forever
Never knew I would run out of time!

Joy Lear-Bernard

January 2023
Theme: A Heart for God
21 – 28 January: Cervical Cancer Prevention Week
Love Your Liver Awareness Month & National Soup Month

36

FRIDAY 27th

Those (ruled by) the flesh set their minds on the things of the flesh - Rom. 8:5

DOMINATED BY THE SPIRIT OR THE FLESH? - Reading: Romans 8:1-9 (NKJV)

The starting-point to live according to the Spirit is to first have the Spirit of Christ living within.

Paul to the church in Rome also says: *"Now if any (person) does not have the Spirit of Christ, he is none of His" (Romans 8:9).* But even when we are Spirit-filled, we must allow the Spirit to work in us, and not let it be quenched.

If you were to do an honest introspection, which of these would you conclude dominates you? Which one receives more of your attention, the flesh or the Spirit? They are direct opponents and both want control.

Do you live a life that is all about self-gratification? Do you seek to please yourself first rather than God? In your quiet time, what do you meditate upon most? If you were to prepare a list of things that you would like to achieve during the remainder of your lifetime, how many desires would be for God?

Finally, does everything seem expensive when it comes to the things of God but not when it's for the things of the flesh? For instance, if you had a limited amount of spare cash this month, and were given a choice between attending a Bible seminar, versus having a luxurious facial, which would you choose? Either of these can be done later in the year when funds allow; which one would you put on hold for now?

JEJ

January 2023
Theme: A Heart for God
21 – 28 January: Cervical Cancer Prevention Week
Love Your Liver Awareness Month & National Soup Month

37

SATURDAY 28th

Keep your heart with all diligence; for out of it are the issues of life - Prov. 4:23

GUARD YOUR HEART - Reading: Proverbs 4:14-23

We are often cautioned about heart health, i.e., the dos and don'ts to maintain a healthy heart.

That's because if our heart stops, life stops! As with the natural so with the spiritual. Our spiritual strength is contingent upon the condition of the inner core of our being which drives us, the part which can only be seen by God, our heart. We must therefore be careful what we ingest by sight or sound, because what we consume will affect how we function.

If we participate in hours of gossip yet spend only a few minutes daily listening to Bible teachings or an audio Bible, this will of course impact our spiritual development. If we watch hours of soap operas and endless chat shows, and then spend five minutes reading the Word before falling asleep with no prayers, we will become weak and have no strength to stand against the wiles of the devil.

Furthermore, with no Word in our heart, we will not know whether or not we're pleasing God, nor what He requires. How we speak and behave tells a story of our heart's condition, if it is well or sick.

So, the psalmist says: *"Keep your heart"* meaning: *"Guard your heart"*. Guard it from impure thoughts, contaminated conversations, and unclean visual images. Guard it from spiritual starvation and thirst, i.e., lack of the Word. Also choose your company and friends wisely in order to shield your heart.

JEJ

January 2023
Theme: A Heart for God
21 – 28 January: Cervical Cancer Prevention Week
Love Your Liver Awareness Month & National Soup Month

38

SUNDAY 29th

Every one that loveth is born of God - 1 John 4:7

WHAT KIND OF HEART PLEASES GOD? - Reading: 1 John 4: 7-11

God's desire is to see Himself reflected in our hearts, our worship, and our adoration of Him.

David is generally described as: 'a man after God's own heart' because of his faith and obedience to God.

Songwriter Kevin LeVar encapsulates for me the qualities of a heart that pleases God:

"I want a heart that forgives, a heart full of love
One with compassion just like yours above
One that overcomes evil with goodness and love
Like it never happened, never holding a grudge

I want a heart that forgives those lives and lets live
One that keeps loving over and over again
One that men can't offend because your Word is within
One that loves without price like you Lord Jesus Christ
I want a heart that loves everybody, even my enemies…"

(A Heart that Forgives – K LeVar)

A heart that pleases God, is one just is like His own!

Christine Knight

January 2023
Theme: A Heart for God
21 – 28 January: Cervical Cancer Prevention Week
Love Your Liver Awareness Month & National Soup Month

39

Create in me a clean heart, O God: and renew a right spirit in me - Psalm 51:10

CREATE IN ME A CLEAN HEART - Reading: Psalm 51:10-19

Here we find King David arriving at a place of acknowledgement that, unless his spiritual heart condition is dealt with, he will continually be prey to the enemy of his soul.

He desperately cries out to God who he knows is able to supply his prayerful requests: *"Create in me a clean heart…renew a right spirit within me" (Psalm 51:10).* David's petition is not just for a clean heart, but the creation of this clean heart by the Lord. He desires the making of, the designing of, the patterning of a new heart totally unlike the heart which led him to commit the sinful acts for which he was now repentant.

To 'create' means: 'to cause something to exist which was not there before'. David's internal yearning was to bring about a renewal of his spirit through which he would communicate with God.

Renewal would bring about the restoration of this man after God's own heart - a return to a former state of mind, the new creation of his spiritual man - bringing him to a place of total surrender from a wayward will, to God's will for his life.

Evangelist Viv Lear

January 2023
Theme: A Heart for God
21 – 28 January: Cervical Cancer Prevention Week
Love Your Liver Awareness Month & National Soup Month

40

*TUESDAY 31st

Think of yourselves as dead to the power of sin - Romans 6:11 (CEV)

DEAD TO SIN - Reading: Romans 6:1-14

"Likewise reckon ye also yourselves to be dead indeed unto sin, but alive unto God through Jesus Christ our Lord" (Romans 6:11).

The Holy Ghost through Paul is reminding believers that our sinful nature is dead, it has been nailed to the cross once and for all. Believers are not called to crucify the old fleshy nature, but to count it dead. This sin-nature inherited from Adam, no longer reigns in our bodies, we are set apart from sin and free from it.

Through the work of sanctification, we become obedient to the new man and have the desire to please and honour God. The Holy Ghost teaches, guides, enables the understanding of His Word, His truth, and all things about His nature and character.

Believers are adopted into the family of God and given the same ID as Jesus Christ. Through His death on the cross, we are alive in Jesus Christ.

The old nature is gone, and Christ lives within us. The believer can sing the victory song: *"I am free, no more chains holding me".* Only the believer in Christ is set free from sin. People who are not converted are free to sin, and cannot live righteously because the inherent sin nature reigns within.

Believers are required to: *"Delight in the law of the LORD" (Psalm 1:2).* This is not only the five books of the Pentateuch, but in every Word of God written in God's instruction manual, the Bible.

Missionary Audrey Simpson

*Hot Chocolate Day

URINARY INCONTINENCE

Urinary incontinence is the unintentional passing of urine. It's a common problem thought to affect millions of people, including both men and women but more frequently in women.

There are several types of urinary incontinence, namely:
• stress incontinence – urine leaks out at times when your bladder is under pressure; for example, when you cough, laugh, sneeze or during heavy lifting. It is not related to feeling stressed!
• urge incontinence – urine leaks as you feel a sudden, intense urge to urinate or soon afterwards. You're unable to delay going to the toilet - you have to go when you have to go!
• Mixed incontinence is when you have symptoms of both stress and urge incontinence as above.
• overflow incontinence, also called chronic urinary retention, occurs when you're unable to fully empty your bladder, which causes frequent leaking. This may result in passing small trickles of urine very often. It may also feel as though your bladder is never fully empty and you cannot empty it even when you try.
• total incontinence – occurs when your bladder cannot store any urine at all, which causes you to pass urine constantly or have frequent leaking

Causes of urinary incontinence
Stress incontinence is usually the result of the weakening of or damage to the pelvic floor muscles and / or those controlling the opening and closing of the bladder.

Urge incontinence tends to be the result of overactivity of the muscles, which control the bladder.

Overflow incontinence is often caused by an obstruction or blockage in your bladder, which prevents it from emptying fully.

Total incontinence may be caused by a problem with the bladder from birth, a spinal injury, or from a fistula - small hole that can form between the bladder and a nearby area.

Other factors that may increase the chances of urinary incontinence, include:

• pregnancy and vaginal birth
• obesity
• a family history of incontinence
• increasing age – although incontinence is not an inevitable part of ageing
• inadvertent damage to the bladder or nearby area during surgery.
• neurological conditions such as Parkinson's Disease or Multiple Sclerosis
• certain medications

Treating urinary incontinence:
1. Non-surgical treatments
Initially, your GP may suggest some simple measures to help improve your symptoms.
These may include:
• lifestyle changes such as losing weight, reducing caffeine and alcohol intake
• pelvic floor exercises
• bladder training - learn ways to wait longer between the urge to urinate and passing urine
• the use of incontinence products such as absorbent pads and handheld urinals.
• medications may be recommended

2. Surgical treatments
Surgery may also be considered. The procedures that are suitable for you will depend on the type of incontinence you have.

Preventing urinary incontinence
It's not always possible to prevent urinary incontinence, but there are some steps you can take that may help reduce the chance of it happening.
These include practising the lifestyle changes as noted above (in the non- surgical treatments), staying active – in particular, doing exercises to ensure that your pelvic floor muscles are strong; including during pregnancy, avoid lifting, avoiding and / or treating constipation promptly.

When to seek medical advice
You are advised to see a GP if you have any type of urinary incontinence. Do not feel embarrassed talking to your doctor about your symptoms. This can also be the first step towards finding a way to effectively manage the problem.

Your GP, who will ask about your symptoms and may do a pelvic or rectal exam. You may also be asked to keep a bladder diary and undergo additional tests to assist with diagnosing the problem correctly.

For more information, check out the NHS and / or Patient UK websites.

Submitted by: Dr Carol S. Ighofose GP, Author
BSC (Hons); MBChB; MRCGP

February

True Love

WEDNESDAY 1st

Each day the LORD pours His unfailing love upon me - Psalm 42:8 (NLT)

GOD'S LOVE - Reading: Psalm 73: 24-28

God's love is like an ocean, limitless.

Can you imagine diving into an ocean where you will never get to the bottom, nor to the sides, it is so immense? That's God's love!

Psalm 73, particularly verses 24 and 25, has been my Scripture for 32 years now. *"Why?",* you might ask. It's because when Jesus called me, I was in a really dark place, but His love was like an ocean surrounding me, and His light penetrated through the darkness.

In the years that I have been saved, I've had some real lows, but this Scripture always comes back to me. I then remember what Jesus has done for me. He truly is the strength of my life.

I know that I can depend upon Him for He is the source which can supply everything I need.

Marie Chisnall

February 2023
Theme: True Love
National Heart Month (British Heart Foundation)
7 – 14 February is National Marriage Week

46

*THURSDAY 2nd

If I don't love others, I'm nothing more than a noisy gong - 1 Cor. 13: 1 (CEV)

MOTIVATED BY LOVE - Reading: 1 Corinthians 13:1-13

The church in Corinth was very similar to many of our churches today. If you read Paul's letter to the Corinthians, you might think that he was writing to a church you know.

The Corinthian brethren, though gifted, were deficient in love. They focused more on their spiritual gifts and deeds rather than their motives. God examines our motivations just as much as the things we do. We can do things for God and each other out of duty, or because everyone else is doing it, or even to out-do someone or make a name for ourselves, but love is not the true driving force. Please read St Luke 18:10-14 for a clear example of fasting and giving for the wrong reasons and in the wrong way.

Paul in 1 Corinthians 13, explains to us the futility, or pointlessness, of doing anything without love being at the centre. He describes the Christian operating outside of love as, *"a noisy gong or a clanging cymbal"*. In other words, empty.

It's worth examining then whether we are motivated into action by love or driven by self.

JEJ

*Time to Talk Day

*FRIDAY 3rd

Peace and love be multiplied - Jude verse 2

LOVE TESTED - Reading: Book of Jude

In his salutation to Jewish Christians the apostle Jude pronounced, in the only chapter of his book: *"Peace and love be multiplied"*. A multiplication of peace and love was necessary for the time in which they were living.

So concerned was Jude about the spiritual climate, that it seems he adjusted the sermon which he had planned to preach about *"the common salvation"* to a message to admonish the believers to *"earnestly contend for the Faith" (Jude verse 3)*.

What then is the relevance of peace and love being multiplied in this context? Jesus said: *"If you love me, keep my commandments" (St John 14:15)*. *"Commandments"* refers not only to the ten listed in Exodus 20, but all of God's commands and the teachings of the Bible. Love for God makes pleasing Him a delight, not burdensome *(1 John 5:3)*.

As the attack of heresies, i.e., false teachings, increases towards the end of the Church Age, so must our peace and love for God be more. Peace and love are also qualities of the fruit of the Spirit *(Galatians 5:22-23)*.

Just like when Jude wrote his letter, many Christians today who are not grounded have become uncertain of what they believe. May our love for God be or become enough to make us want to shape our lives according to His Word, rather than wanting to mould the Word to accomodate our lifestyles.

JEJ

Carrot Cake Day

SATURDAY 4ᵗʰ

(God's) kindness shall not depart from thee - Isaiah 54:10

GOD WILL TAKE CARE OF YOU - Reading: Isaiah 54:7-10; Philippians 4:19

My testimony is of God as a provider.

Paul reminds us in Philippians 4:19 that: *"…God will supply all your need according to His riches in glory by Christ Jesus"*. It is hardly ever 'a walk in the park' when you emigrate to another country. However, with our recent experiences, my husband and I have seen the providential hand of God all over our lives.

It has been amazing when we look at how He made the way for us in providing a home, food, vehicles and other amenities, all at either low cost or no cost to us. We have seen Him provide money to do the necessary applications, school admissions, etc. We have watched Him release destiny-helpers and these persons would come and offer their time and resources in helping us to achieve specific objectives.

This has encouraged us in our walk and cemented this fact that indeed, God is a loving Father, way maker and miracle worker. He always takes care of His children.

Cherely Simons, Fl., USA

February 2023
Theme: True Love
National Heart Month (British Heart Foundation)
7 – 14 February is National Marriage Week

49

*SUNDAY 5ᵗʰ

God is love - 1 John 4:8

DIVE IN! CAPSIZED INTO LOVE - Reading: 1 John 4:7-10

Enjoying a recent kayaking experience, I observed how more skilled participants manoeuvred around the water. I, a complete novice, found the adventure much bigger and stronger than me. The longer I stayed in the water, the wetter I became!

Isn't that's just like God's love! It is bigger and stronger than us; bigger than any of our emotions, and the longer we stay surrendered to it, the more we emerge soaked by His love.

Do we somehow resist being capsized, maintaining our own will, never really looking like we've been 'in the water' of God's love? This is why John so boldly said: *"He that loveth not, knoweth not God; for God is love" (1 John 4:8).*

"Knowing" here is not the familiar encounter we have seen in the Rich Young Ruler, the parable of one looking in the mirror and walking away without change, even Judas! No, they didn't KNOW Him. They paddled around but maintained the control, holding the paddles of flesh.

Many people saw Jesus, but never became like Him, even though they got close to Him every day. That is still true for today, seeing is not knowing. Knowing Jesus is connecting in sweet abandon. Knowing, in biblical terms, speaks of intimacy. Intimacy produces offspring that looks just like daddy! This is the kind of knowing John speaks of.

When we dive intimately into prayer, and are submerged in His Word, we will change. Love changes us! Love is life altering! God's love means a chance to be loved, and to become love, but only if we are unrestrained and ready to dive in!

Joy Lear-Bernard

*British Yorkshire Pudding Day

February 2023
Theme: True Love
National Heart Month (British Heart Foundation)
7 – 14 February is National Marriage Week

MONDAY 6ᵗʰ

If you love me, keep my commandments - St John 14:15

GOD'S AGAPE LOVE - Reading: St John 13:1-17, 33-35

Before the above statement in our focus verse today, Jesus had recently shown His disciples how much He loved them by washing their feet. If His disciples loved Him, they should not have any issues keeping the commandments.

Jesus was affirming *"one another"* principles to His disciples, which today we are commanded to adopt. He charged them to wash one another's feet *(St John 13:14-15)*. He charged them to love one another using His template of love *(St John 13:35)*.

Keeping the commandments of God speaks to the heart of the individual, based on *"Agape"*, which is the richest and deepest form of love. It is unconditional, it has no strings attached. Believers must imitate Jesus Christ and adopt this kind of love for God and one another.

God tells us that His commandments are not burdensome. Believers are born again and given a new heart which has the desire to please God. The New Covenant that is written in Jesus' blood, writes the laws on the heart of every believer.

When we are born of God there is nothing that we cannot do, even displaying Agape to those who we would find difficult to love with our own kind of love. Jesus is our perfect example. Jesus was an overcomer - we too are overcomers.

Missionary Audrey Simpson

TUESDAY 7th

He who loveth God love his brother also - 1 John 4:21

THE GOD STANDARD OF LOVE - Reading: 1 John 4:15-21

Isn't it so interesting that God by His love draws us to Him, and we have a **choice** to respond to His love.

But once we have experienced His love, and proclaim that we love Him, we are now **commanded** to love others. Dear reader, welcome to the God-standard of love, where the only appropriate response to His love, is love. The God-standard of love is the highest expression of love because it requires an outward flow and manifestation.

God's love for us never stopped at just a thought, or profound words, but in an expression so abundant, so pure, and so real, that Jesus Christ became that tangible, atoning sacrifice of love. We too are required to love others in a way that is tangible, real, and profitable, especially those who we may find difficult to love.

Loving others to the God-standard of love is a command, but the beautiful thing is that, with humility, it begins to feel like an honour and not a command to love others.

Minister Kay Dawkins

February 2023
Theme: True Love
National Heart Month (British Heart Foundation)
7 – 14 February is National Marriage Week

52

WEDNESDAY 8th

Above all, have fervent and unfailing love for one another - 1 Peter 4:8 (AMP)

LOVE COVERS IT - Reading: 1 Peter 4:7-19

In this day and age, it is not difficult to find someone that is offended by something or other. It is so easy to make mistakes, even when we mean well, and sometimes we inadvertently cause deep and painful wounds.

If we are the ones who have been wounded, it can be so tempting to act or react to our hurts. But we do have a choice! We can deliberately overlook the offence, just like Jesus did when He hung upon the cross and shed His blood for the remission of our sins. We too have the choice to cover the faults of others with love, and 'let it go'.

Loving each other and releasing past hurts, helps us to build each other up, especially when someone has fallen.

Doing this will take practice, we will have to work hard, but the reward is great. It will help us to stand out in the glory of God and allow our light to shine.

And, best of all, we will be doing what the Lord requires.

Sis Esther Kelly-Levy

February 2023
Theme: True Love
National Heart Month (British Heart Foundation)
7 – 14 February is National Marriage Week

53

THURSDAY 9th

The LORD God is abundant in goodness - Exodus 34:6

THE GREAT PHYSICIAN - Reading: Exodus 34:6; St Matthew 8:1-13

A long while back I experienced remarkable healing.

I had a very bad headache on the right side of my head. I could hear my own head beating inside. When the pain came on, if I opened my mouth, I could not close it! If the pain came on and my mouth was closed, I could not open it! To get a bit of relief, I used to roll on the floor whilst holding my head.

One day I was at work and the pain began again. I ran out of the hospital ward where I was working, jumped over a low wall, got home, threw my bag on the floor, ran upstairs and rolled on the floor.

Then one Sunday evening I heard that a member of the community had died suddenly of a brain haemorrhage. I was afraid! The doctors were not helping me at all. I said to Jesus: *"Jesus I can't die now; I have got young children to care for. I have no family in this country to take over the care of my children. I don't want them to go into the Childcare System, as good as it may be. Jesus, please heal my head".*

As time went on, I no longer felt the pain. I did not notice immediately that the pain had gone but I was no longer in pain and until this day, which is several years later, the pain has never come back.

Jesus healed me! I am still thanking Him, my Great Physician, the Sympathising Jesus.

Missionary M Fraser

February 2023
Theme: True Love
National Heart Month (British Heart Foundation)
7 – 14 February is National Marriage Week

FRIDAY 10th

Love covereth all sins - Proverbs 10:12

STRIFE: HATRED STRIKES A MATCH - Reading: Proverbs 10:1-32

A saying said that if there is a fire, always look for the person leaving the scene that lit the match!

Proverbs 10 brims with truth and wisdom. It offers an anchor in our perplexed world. Proverbs is both soothing and challenging for today's world.

Strife: discord, contention and conflict. Where we see this then at its root is hatred. Love covers, it forgives and makes wise decisions about where and when to speak. Love is a catalyst and so is hate.

When I oppose wrongdoing, am I stoked by the powerful source of love or by fruits of the flesh rooted in hate? God's Word always empowers us to truly live in love once we allow it to divide, cut and dissect the things in us that are sinful. God's beautiful Word heals and soothes us as perfectly as it cuts. Today we can ask if our presence, at any stage of the day, lit a match of strife and contention, and if so, where is the hatred in me that God's perfect love comes to cleanse.

At times we hate the reflection of ourselves in others, we hate the challenge we see to do better, or the flaws in ourselves that we loathe but live with unrepentantly. Yet wasn't this the very thing that Jesus took upon himself? He took every kind of our sins so that we could reflect peace rather than strife.

The book of Proverbs is an ocean of wisdom, and a mirror allowing us to see if we are strife-builders, or just how much we need God's love to make us new.

Joy Lear-Bernard

February 2023
Theme: True Love
National Heart Month (British Heart Foundation)
7 – 14 February is National Marriage Week

55

SATURDAY 11ᵗʰ

We love Him, because He first loved us - 1 John 4:19

THE BLESSING OF A PRAYING WIFE - Reading: 1 John 4:10-13,19

Ultimate and unlimited praise belongs to the King Eternal.

It's not always easy to wait patiently, but how many know that having God's indwelling presence, His peace, and His overcoming power will allow us to do what is totally unnatural for us to do, that is, take a Selah moment?

"Selah" is a Hebrew word referring to a voluntary and intentional pause for reflection. Often in times of pausing, God gives us a revelation that transforms our perspective, bringing us closer to Him. Selah positions us to hear His voice and be in His presence. And this is just what the Lord wanted, i.e., my complete focus and attention on Him and not my situation.

I must say that having to wait 21 years for my husband to accept Jesus as his personal Saviour allowed the Lord to shepherd me into many midnight solitary prayers, JAM meetings (Jesus and Me).

There truly were times when I felt lonely and asked God why my husband couldn't just 'get the revelation' and fall in love with Jesus in the way that I had! There were countless occasions when I felt inward sadness that my husband had not caught sight of the Saviour and committed his life. Here I was with this powerful testimony of God's healing virtue on my life, and I felt the person closest to me couldn't see what God had done. I'm reminded of Philippians 2:12: *"Wherefore, my beloved, as ye have always obeyed, not as in my presence only, but now much more in my absence, work out your own salvation with fear and trembling".*

After many moments of tears, I finally realised that my husband was on his own journey and, most importantly, I couldn't save him! I just needed to trust God, pray and leave him to the Lord. He is the one that saves.

Having this realisation, I decided that I would try my best to pray for my husband continually and be a loving wife. In all honesty, there were many occasions where I felt a bit weary, but God would always send someone, one of the mothers or sisters to say: *"Don't give up praying because…"* or: *"I'm praying with you".* These little nuggets of encouragement always came at the right time when I needed some strength for the journey. God is an on-time God! I would always let my husband know that I and the brethren were praying for him to be saved.

One night I was weeping openly before God for my husband to be saved, and after I had cried and cried out to God, I received a telephone call from a prayer partner

February 2023
Theme: True Love
National Heart Month (British Heart Foundation)
7 – 14 February is National Marriage Week

advising me that I had come up before her in prayer. She said she felt my tears and we both would fast and pray for my husband to accept the Lord Jesus.

One week later on Sunday 15th May 2016, after 21 years to be exact, as I arose early, my husband said he thought he would come to church with me. I remained very calm outwardly, but inside I was rejoicing and giving God thanks. We went to church together that Sunday, and as we drove, he suddenly turned to me and said: *"You know, Susan, I think believing in God is a leap of faith..."!* I'd never **ever** heard him talk about faith!

On this occasion, unlike countless others, my husband was convicted. He made his decision to accept the Lord Jesus after the message was preached that day by Elder Robert Murray. He was baptised later during the night service.

What a rejoicing in Bethel, 2 Gibson Road! Our beloved Bishop Dunn was there to witness this momentous occasion. He welcomed him into the body of Christ as Brother Rupert Higgins went the Water Way and took on the precious name of Jesus.

To every sister who is longing for her husband to be saved, please don't give up. Keep on praying, believing, and trusting Almighty God.

Missionary Susan Higgins

SUNDAY 12th

How excellent is thy loving kindness, O God! - Psalm 36:7

GOD OF A SECOND CHANCE - Reading: Psalm 36:1-12

God is my strength and He is my redeemer. He made me in His own image, has been ever present in my life from the day that I was born until now, and I know He will be with me to the very end.

My first encounter which I recall with my Lord and Saviour was at 3 years old. When His wounded hand touched me, I lay gravely ill. I remember that the hand touched my forehead, and a voice told me to ask my grandmother for a drink of water.

When I told my grandmother about this encounter in my childlike way, she said: *"It was Jesus who touched you and returned you to my care"*. Granny told me when I was 5 years old that the doctor told her that I was very sick, and I had little time left with her. But Granny, who was a woman of faith, said she prayed and fasted for my recovery.

At 16 years old, I was baptised and again encountered the man with the wounded hand. He placed His hand on my head, and said: *"Worship always!"*, but after a while I left the church and went my own way.

However, in August 1994, the Lord once again made His presence known to me. I was in my house when I heard a voice calling my name. During this experience not only did He call my name, but His presence shook my house from the four corners. I answered His call and now I worship Him for who He is.

Name withheld

MONDAY 13th

God's love has been poured out into our hearts - Romans 5:5 (NIV)

HOPE THAT WILL NOT BE DISAPPOINTED - Reading: Romans 5:1-11

"And hope maketh not ashamed, because the love of God is shed abroad in our hearts by the Holy Ghost which is given unto us" (Romans 5:5).

Our God is the God of Hope, this is the Greek word *"Elpis"* which means a desire for good with an expectation of obtaining it.

The word *"Hope"* in the natural sense is based on a belief in things expected. Without hope, humankind feels helpless, hopeless, and lost. In the spiritual sense, Hope is the Word of God, confirming with certainty to all believers a bright future, even if it's not in this life *(1 Corinthians 15:19)*, and assures with confidence the promise of eternal life through our faith and belief in Him.

Jesus so loved humankind, even to death that yes, He died to remit the sins of the whole world and was confirmed dead on the cross and then buried. But hallelujah! This was not the end of the story. Three days later He was resurrected from the dead.

We too have this hope and will not be ashamed or disappointed. Jesus is the only one who has ever had the power to come back to life, but believers with the New Birth in two parts experience *(St John 3:5)*, will also rise from the dead when Jesus returns, had they fallen asleep before The Rapture. They, and those who are still alive, will be caught up together to meet Christ in the air.

We have the promise of everlasting life and are assured of transformation from mortal to immortality. We will receive a glorified body. To continue His everlasting love toward us, He sent the Comforter, which is the Holy Ghost, to always be with us until the end of our Christian journey on earth.

Missionary Audrey Simpson

TUESDAY 14th

I found him whom my soul loveth - Song of Solomon 3:4

FRIENDSHIP WITH JESUS - Reading: Song of Solomon 3:1-4

Friends even when I let Him down

Risen, so I that can rise someday

I can always trust Him

Encouraging, me when I feel low

Never leaves me alone

Died so that I might live

Shields me from all harm

He is my confidante

Intervenes when I need Him the most

Patient, even when I am not listening

When I am afraid, He hears my cry

I've never had a friend like Jesus

Thankful I have a friend like Him

He is my Rock when no-one else can be found

Jesus, the sweetest friend I know

Enlightens me when I do not understand

Stands by me no matter what

Understands my fears and gives me strength

Soon coming King.

Sister Jennifer Miller

February 2023
Theme: True Love
National Heart Month (British Heart Foundation)
7 – 14 February is National Marriage Week

60

WEDNESDAY 15th

There is no fear in love - 1 John 4:18

FEARLESS LOVE - Reading: 1 John 4:17-19

When fear is present, it's often an indication that a relationship is not yet strong, and there is a level of insecurity. It shows a lack of trust. We cannot be bold and fearful at the same time. We will therefore be likely, through fear, to miss out on many benefits to which we are entitled.

Fear limits and stunts our spiritual development as we remain frozen at one level, sometimes for years. Peter demonstrated fearless love when Jesus called him to step out of his fishing boat, and walk on water, during a storm. It was knowing Jesus' voice: *"It is I, be not afraid" (St Matthew 14:27)*, and knowing Jesus, the person, that prompted Peter to come out of the boat. Peter's confident love for Jesus said: *"Lord, if it's you, bid me come unto thee on the water" (v28)*.

As with any kind of relationship, our relationship with God will only develop as we spend more time with Him. Our love and trust will then be built upon personal experiences and revelations, not just what we read or from hearing the testimonies of others.

JEJ

February 2023
Theme: True Love
National Heart Month (British Heart Foundation)
7 – 14 February is National Marriage Week

61

THURSDAY 16th

Love ties everything completely together - Colossians 3:14 (CEV)

GOD'S PERFECT LOVE - Reading: Colossians 3:1-17

Colossians 3:14 *"And above all these things* put on *charity, which is the bond of perfectness"*

The love of God is perfect...why? Because God is love. We know that the opposite of love is hate!

Hate goes against God's first commandment which declares: *"Thou shalt love the Lord thy God, with all thy heart, and with all thy soul, and with all thy mind. The second is like unto it, thou shalt love thy neighbour as thyself" (St Mathew 22:37-39).*

When we are clothed in God's love, it will make us give out of His love in a selfless way.

God's love is perfectly pure; you will find no malice, no hate, no jealousy, no covetousness, no unforgiveness in His love. The strength of God's perfect love is so strong, it's airtight, and gives inseparable bonding which connects and brings us closer together. This perfect love is unconditional and measureless.

Let's have poured into us God's perfect love and in so doing, others will experience the perfect love of God in their lives.

Evangelist Maureen Morris

February 2023
Theme: True Love
National Heart Month (British Heart Foundation)
7 – 14 February is National Marriage Week

FRIDAY 17th

God is indeed…the faithful God who keeps his covenant - Deut. 7:9 (NLT)

GOD IS A FAITHFUL COVENANT-KEEPING GOD - Reading: Deut. 7:1-10

Deuteronomy 7:9 gives us insight into who God is.

What a mighty God we serve, from everlasting to everlasting He is God. Abba Father, our loving and faithful God. The true and only God who loves us so unconditionally and lavishly. He seeks to find us daily to whisper into our ears how much he loves us.

God's love toward His children is so pure and sure, there is nothing that can stop the divine flow of the love that God has for us. Our loving Father is a promise-keeper, His words are true and unfailing.

Our God cannot lie. Whatever He has said in His Word, that He will surely do for those who call upon his name.

Thank you for loving me, Jesus!

Minister Geraldine Parker-Smith

February 2023
Theme: True Love
National Heart Month (British Heart Foundation)
7 – 14 February is National Marriage Week

63

SATURDAY 18th

I have loved you with an everlasting love - Jeremiah 31:3

EVERLASTING LOVE - Reading: Jeremiah 31:1-11

It's not difficult to keep on loving someone who gives you no trouble, brings no heartache or inflicts no pain. But to love those who hate you, and people who are just plain difficult, to show a consistent demonstration of pure love to them can be challenging.

Have you ever taken time-out to thank God for loving you, and for putting up with you for so long despite all of your faults and the numberless times that you've failed Him?

God's love is absolutely amazing! Described in today's focus verse as *"everlasting"*, everlasting here does not only refer to never ending, but unchanging! Love often changes in relationships as a result of one party failing to live up to the expectations of the other. Not with God. We often miss the mark, i.e., sin. We disappoint Him again and again, and still He says: *"I have loved you with an everlasting love"*!

We cannot get love like this from anyone else. Nobody has the capacity to love us like Jesus.

JEJ

February 2023
Theme: True Love
National Heart Month (British Heart Foundation)
7 – 14 February is National Marriage Week

SUNDAY 19th

Who will go for us? Then said I, Here am I; send me - Isaiah 6:8

WILL YOU GO FOR ME? - Reading: Isaiah 6:1-13

In October 1974, my husband received a telephone call from Bishop Sydney Dunn to say that the Lord had laid it on his heart to send us to start a church in Brooklyn, New York.

But long before then, I remember my husband saying during a church service in Wellington, England, that whatever God wants him to do, he is willing, and wherever God wants him to go he would be willing to go. He said we must all be flexible in the hands of God. When I heard him say this, I said *"Amen"* to the will of God; I would not stand in my husband's way as long as God did not send us to anywhere that has snakes!

The funny thing was that Elder Barnes, as he was known then, did not like America. He once returned from a Convocation in Baltimore and said to me: *"I would never live in America, and even if I did, New York is out of it"!*

Before our assignment I visited New York for a vacation. I recall singing this song while I was here, not knowing what God had planned for us:

1. *The Lord said stand up Paul and dry your tears*
   You must preach the gospel for many long years
   Go down to Damascus, a street that's called Straight
   My servant will tell you the road you must take

2. *I'll send you to the Gentiles, I'll send you to Rome*
   And Paul you will suffer, 'til I call you home
   You will sleep in the desert, be shipwrecked at sea
   Just go right on preaching the gospel for me

   Refrain:
   I counted on Adam, and counted on Cain
   I counted on Jonas but he was the same
   I counted on Judas but he proved untrue
   Go telling the world, Brother Paul, I'm counting on you.
   (Paul's Ministry – Kitty Wells)

When Bishop Dunn phoned and shared his vision, I said that I will give my husband my full support. We had lived in England for 15 years and I loved it there, but I was willing to follow the leading of the Lord.

Our final service at Wellington church was so very sad. We had been pastoring there for many years, and we had a close relationship with all of the brethren, but we had to do what God wanted us to do. My son was young at the time. He thought that we were going to New York only for a vacation, not to stay! But our children soon settled into their new school and home.

When I look at the church in Brooklyn today, there is no doubt in my mind that we were sent here by God. Our obedience was better than any of the sacrifices that we had to make.

Mother Etta Barnes, Brooklyn, NY, USA

MONDAY 20th

For God so loved the world, that He gave His only begotten Son - St John 3:16

LOVED! - Reading: St John 3:13-21

This Scripture means so much to me. It's very close to my heart to know that God loved us when we weren't thinking of Him, doing our own thing, not acknowledging Him.

Romans 5:8 says: *"But God commendeth (demonstrates) His love towards us, in that, while we were yet sinners, Christ died for us".*

When we have received and experienced God's love in our hearts, we will appreciate the fact that we must have love for one another as Christ has loved us.

St John 13:34-35 says: *"A new commandment I give unto you, that ye love one another; as I have loved you, that ye also love one another. By this shall all men know that ye are my disciples, if ye have love one to another".*

If you welcome God's love into your heart, then you will be able to love like God loves too.

Clovette Simmonds

TUESDAY 21st

In all these things we are more than conquerors through Him - Romans 8:37

MORE THAN CONQUERORS - Reading: Romans 8:31-39

Isn't it amazing how we can read the same verse of Scripture multiple times and each time there's a different and awesome revelation?

As God illuminates His Word and expresses Himself to the believer, we stand in awe of Him and His Word which is spirit and life.

In Romans 8:37, Paul wrote: *"Nay, in all these things we are more than conquerors through him that loved us".*

Whenever I have read this Scripture, I've focused on the things that could distract us and cause us to lose focus as born again believers. It is very easy to get caught up with the cares of everyday life and as a result, miss numerous opportunities to commune with God. However, God gives us constant reminders that believers have to face hardships in many forms, e.g., persecution, illness, imprisonment for doing and saying what is right, and even death. But by standing firm in our faith, it is impossible to be separated from Him.

Most importantly, God wants us to understand that we are more than conquerors over sin through the power of the Holy Ghost which gives victory over sin and purity within.

Minister Andrene McLeod

WEDNESDAY 22nd

See what great love the Father has lavished on us - 1 John 3:1 (The Message)

GOD'S FAMILY - Reading: 1 John 3:1-10

It's often been said that we cannot choose our family; we can only choose our friends.

God choosing us entitles you and I to be members of His family. This choice came out of God's plan of salvation, ignited by His love for humankind. The Scripture in St John 3:16 tell us: *"For God so loved the world, that He gave his only begotten Son, that whosoever believeth in him should not perish, but have everlasting life".*

Once we accept, believe, and take on the name of Jesus, we must be confident in knowing that we have been accepted into God's family…we are the children of God! We are His chosen people, His royal priesthood, and a peculiar people. This love bestowed or lavished upon us has been made perfect. So, we are entitled to be members of God's family.

He loves us, and sent his Son to become sin for us, that through Jesus' death, burial, and resurrection we are victorious over death and sin. This theme of God's family is resounded many times over in the Scriptures, giving us the confidence and affirmation of His love for us. St John 1:12 tells us: *"But as many as received Him, to them gave He power to become the sons of God, even to them that believe on His name".*

Welcome to God's family!

Hedy Edmund

*THURSDAY 23rd

Patiently put up with each other and love each other - Ephesians 4:2 (CEV)

RESTORATIVE POWER - Reading: Psalm 23:3; Ephesian 4:1-3

He restores my soul....

My husband and I separated then eventually divorced, backslid, and left the Lord, over 20 years ago.

That, however, is not where the story ends!

Ephesians 2:4 says: *"But God, who is rich in mercy, for His great love wherewith He loved us…"*. In His great love and mercy to us, God drew us both back to Himself at separate times, then to church, then to each other, and we remarried some twenty years after being apart!

I give God praise! He's taking us one day at a time. It's not always easy but we know that God has a plan and purpose for our lives. The enemy knows this too and is also trying...BUT GOD...! He is greater than the enemy.

God has brought us this far; His perfect will shall be done in our lives to the honour and praise of our Lord Jesus Christ. To Him be all the glory. Amen and Amen!

Name withheld

*National Toast Day

FRIDAY 24th

Love your enemies, bless them that curse you - St Matthew 5:44

ENCOURAGEMENT FOR KINGDOM WOMEN - Reading: St Matthew 5:43-48

Special greetings in the precious name of Jesus Christ.

When Jesus said we are to love our enemies, He was declaring a new standard for human relationships. He proclaimed in the Sermon on the Mount the command to love our neighbour, this was a law of God (Leviticus 19:18).

Jesus also amends the statement of the Scribes and Pharisees which said: *"Thou shalt love thy neighbour and hate thine enemy" (St Matthew 5:43-44).* But Jesus says unto us: *"Love your enemies".* The substance of this very hard saying is based on the fact that: *"God so loved the world that He gave His only begotten Son that whosoever believeth in him should not perish, but have everlasting life" (St John 3:16).*

God's nature is LOVE; He loved us when we were unlovable.

To love everyone is an un-negotiable obligation. We have to love those who hate us, and pray for them that despitefully use us. This doesn't come naturally but can be achieved through the power of God's spirit.

As we encourage each other my beloved women: *"Let us not love in word, neither in tongue; but in deed and truth" (1 John 3:18).*

Minister S Campbell

February 2023
Theme: True Love
National Heart Month (British Heart Foundation)
7 – 14 February is National Marriage Week

71

SATURDAY 25th

Those whom I love I rebuke and discipline - Revelation 3:19 (NIV)

REBUKE & DISCIPLINE - Reading: Revelation 3:14-22

What does the word 'love' signify to you?

Does it mean always having your own way, and getting what you ask for? Or never being told that you are wrong? Or is it always being showered with gifts, and being pampered and repeatedly told: *"I love you"*?

Of the seven churches in Asia to whom Jesus sent a letter through John the Divine, the majority received a letter containing a rebuke. Not because Jesus hated them, but because He loved them and wanted them to repent and do better. God knew that if the churches followed His prescription of correction, their relationship with Him would be restored.

Note that it is only because of love why God rebukes and disciplines. We as recipients don't like chastisement for it is painful, but neither does the chastiser enjoy executing punishment, they wish that they didn't have to do it. God chastises us now for future service: *"Afterwards (it produces) a peaceful harvest of right living for those who are trained in this way" (Hebrews 12:11 - NLT)*. Unfortunately, it's not always enough just to rebuke verbally, sometimes sharp words need to be coupled with discipline. After many years of rebuke, Judah entered into their discipline of Babylonian captivity for seventy years.

Rebuke and discipline can be painful, but they are both necessary.

JEJ

When I said, "my foot slippeth"; thy (love) O LORD held me up - Psalm 94:18

THOU HAST BEEN MY HELP - Reading: Psalm 94:1-23

The psalmist of today's focus verse said to himself: *"my foot slippeth"*!

They felt that they were just about to fall, but (and thank God for but) God's love held him up. God's love *"is able to keep us from falling" (Jude:24)*.

You too must be able to recall times when you almost fell under the load you were carrying. You cried out: *"Lord, how much more? I can't take my situation any longer"*! Perhaps like Jonah under the juniper tree you said, *"Let me die" (Jonah 4:3)* or similar to Elijah in his discouragement said: *"I alone am left" (1 Kings 18:22)*, or like Peter when he began to sink you cried: *"Lord, save me" (St Matthew 14:30)*.

But each of us can echo David from Psalm 27:9: *"Thou hast been my help"*. Maybe you were just about to backslide, just about to lose your home or your job, or given only days to live. Perhaps you were accused of something which you did not do, or you were at the wrong place at the wrong time.

Whatever the problem, the conclusion afterwards was: *"Thy mercy, Thy love O LORD, held me up"*!

JEJ

MONDAY 27th

Thou shalt love thy neighbour as thyself - St Mark 12:31

COMMANDED TO LOVE YOURSELF - Reading: St Mark 12:28-34

Can we really love others if we do not love ourselves?

We may have conditioned our minds to believe that self-neglect, and lack of self-love, is humility. However, Jesus in today's focus verse says that my love for others should be like how I love me.

If I can't see any good in me, it's likely that I will struggle to see the good in other people. If I am constantly critical of me, I will naturally always find fault in others. If I am hesitant to spend any money on myself, I will definitely over-think whether any funds to be spent on someone else is necessary.

Psalm 139:14: "I will praise thee; for I am fearfully and wonderfully made". I will only praise God like this when I have learned to love me as me, not wishing that I was more like someone else. I can admire the beauty that I see in other women, comfortable that I too am beautiful. I will compliment another woman when she looks chic in a nice choice of colours, outfit, hairstyle or pair of shoes. I don't have to know her; I can just walk up to her and say: *"You're looking lovely today!".* Without being jealous, I can be inspired by other women to improve how I carry and present me; I can strive not to be better than them, but to be the best woman that I can be.

JEJ

February 2023
Theme: True Love
National Heart Month (British Heart Foundation)
7 – 14 February is National Marriage Week

74

TUESDAY 28th

Because thy lovingkindness is better than life, (I'll) praise thee - Psalm 63:3

LIFE CHOICES - Reading: Psalm 63:1-11

"*If I could just make it to 5 years*" she thought, as she stood by the window with an absent-minded stare through the glass pane.

A sense of helplessness overwhelmed her thoughts as she remembered the word that seemed to echo in her mind: "*Submit!*". Dismayed and confused, she replayed this word over in her mind. She had been prayed for yet felt no solace within. She repented yet the inner struggle continued; feelings were so profound. Dejection, emotionally sore, spiritually wounded. She felt trapped in pressure, this is not what she expected.

The pre-marital counselling worked in theory but what about behind closed doors? More thoughts raced through her mind. All the red flags that were once dismissed as prideful thoughts, in hindsight were warnings. She had been warned not to go through with it but was persuaded. It was too soon to conclude defeat; this marriage has got to work. It's until death do us part. She encouraged herself in the Lord again, she must humble herself and try again.

God does send answers to prayer, He does. The tragedy occurs when His answer is not understood – sometimes missed by excitement, attraction, or sometimes the spiritual radar is lowered. Apart from salvation, getting married is considered one of the most important decisions to be made. Becoming one with another is to link destiny and purpose. It is to be responsible, mature, to lay down your life in a selfless loving relationship, to share, to trust, to support, to (God willing) raise children as a heritage to the Lord.

Seek God, wait, pray again, wait, seek confirmation. Though it's pointless to pray for God to lead on this matter when the mind is already made up, sometimes influenced by ideas of romance. The decision to marry is to be ready to demonstrate the love of God to one another in a solitary covenant relationship. To represent Christ and the Church. He laid down his life for the bride because of His love. He's gone to prepare a place and is coming back for His bride because of His love. It's vitally important to get it right for our soul's sake. To get it wrong then the pain can become seventy times seven. The stigma of a broken marriage, the trauma of a wounded soul, a broken spirit can drive us out from God's presence by our own feelings of guilt and/or shame.

Oh, but in God there is no variableness! He does not abandon us, and He remains true to His Word. Truly, He has been present through the internal and the external crises. *"Through seasons of distress and grief, my soul has often found relief…"*. He has been and is my protection; He is faithful, He's my friend and lover of my soul. I have proven the Lord Jesus to be constant, every time.

I still hold that marriage is beautiful, after all it is God-made.

Just be careful handling Life Choices.

Name withheld

SHARING THE GIFT OF LOVE

Before my husband and I got married, we spoke about having children and were excited about the thought of also fostering because we had so much love to give. We have two children of our own and have been fostering from when they were babies.

Being a foster carer is not easy, it is a calling. A child coming into your home as a complete stranger needs time to adjust to their new surroundings. These children are often emotionally, physically, and mentally damaged by the situation that they're coming from, yet no matter how unhealthy the environment they left behind was, it would be considered the norm for them.

When our children were much younger, I would worry about what we were exposing them to by fostering because, at times, the fostered children's behaviour could be very challenging. This was difficult because our own children didn't understand why the children whom we took in were damaged and sometimes needed more attention than them.

Our children sometimes found it difficult having to share us, their parents, so we constantly talked to them explaining that the foster children are missing their own parents and need not only the love and support from us, as foster parents, but the reassurance that we are not going to leave them. As Christians, we would pray with our children and foster children.

We have been Foster Carers for 25 years and have fostered many children, some we are still in touch with. We've looked after the children in our care in the same way that we take care of our own; we make them feel a part of our whole family not just our immediate family.

We network with other carers; we support each other and keep everything confidential. It is comforting to speak with professionals who have similar experiences to yours. They offer empathy plus good advice and encouragement.

When a child is first placed with you there are a lot of tears but as time goes by and they start to feel a part of your family, their behaviour begins to settle and mirror yours. It's nice when their birth parents finally sort themselves out and the child can return to a safe, loving environment but unfortunately, in our 25 years of fostering, this has only happened once. Childhood is special and is only for a short period of time so if we can make a difference to a child's life, that makes us extremely happy.

Fostering is not easy, ministry never is! However, we sincerely believe that God has given us the strength, enthusiasm, energy, and love to take up the challenge.

Sharon and Harley Miller

February 2023
Theme: True Love
National Heart Month (British Heart Foundation)
7 – 14 February is National Marriage Week

March

Joy During Suffering

WEDNESDAY 1st

Count it all joy when you fall into various trials - James 1:2 NKJV

THE COUNTING EXPERIENCE - Reading: James 1:1-18

James 1:2 paraphrased strongly encourages us to count it all joy, *not if* but *when; not after* but *when* we enter, *unexpectedly* into divers temptations.

The word *"count"* has a mathematical flare similar to *"reckon"*. It has the idea of weighing up, calculating as to understand.

So how is your counting? Are you arriving at joy?

When we go through all kinds of temptations (testing) for the name of Jesus Christ and His Word, be intentional in experiencing joy in this process – to do this, just add divine purpose. This is a winning attitude in warring a good warfare.

Experiencing divers testing helps our character to develop and conform to Christ's image, our ultimate goal. Here is a perfect example: consider Jesus. In Hebrews 12:2, He experienced unimaginable pain and shame. However, He remained focused on His purpose - our deliverance; afflicted with grief yet inspired by the joy set before Him.

Joy goes deep, unlike happiness with its fleeting-like moments and ripple effects. True purpose inspires joy! In the process of reckoning, we count the correlation between pain and purpose. Oh yes! There is inter-connectivity, we should therefore reach this calculation, i.e., *"What's ahead is far greater in worth"*. So, count it all joy!

Pastor Josephine Lewis

THURSDAY 2nd

Weeping may endure for a night, but joy cometh in the morning - Psalm 30:5

MORNING IS ON THE WAY - Reading: Psalm 30:1-12

With a shout of joy, we will praise Thee Oh LORD
Thanking you for your favour which is life assured
Knowing there is hope when trusting in Thee
You give us your light in this dark world that we may see

LORD Jesus we are encouraged to know you are always with us
In the times of trials and tribulations, in you we put our trust
You give us grace when in the mist of unrelenting hurt and sorrows
Your Word, love and your faithfulness sees us through to the morrow

Remembering of this great hope in the promises of you our God
That the morning is already on the way, filled with joy and love
Sorrow will not have the last word in our times of mourning
For weeping may endure for a night, but joy cometh in the morning.

Thank you, Jesus!

Name withheld

*FRIDAY 3rd

For the joy that was set before Him, endured the cross - Hebrews 12:2

SUPPORTERS FROM THE PAST - Reading: Hebrews 12:1-3

If you're going to end the Christian race in the same lane in which you started, you've got to focus on what is beyond the finishing line.

You can be encouraged by *"so great a cloud of witnesses" (Hebrews 12:1)* who have already run and completed the race that we are currently in. Through their files of perseverance and stamina kept in Scripture, we draw strength and hope; their testimonies spur us on. Those who by faith: *"wrought righteousness, obtained promises, stopped the mouths of lions, quenched the violence of fire, out of weakness were made strong, women received their dead raised to life again…"* *(Hebrews 11:33-35).*

Whether it was Abraham when he offered Isaac, or the three Hebrew boys in the fiery furnace, or Daniel who was thrown into a lion's den, or you can picture Moses at the great Red Sea. Perhaps you should imagine Jesus when He walked upon the water during a storm, or hear Paul and Silas in jail singing praises to God.

It doesn't matter whom you choose as your inspiration from the Cloud of Witnesses, because a songwriter said: *"They all came out victorious in my dream of the Bible days".*

JEJ

*World Day of Prayer

SATURDAY 4th

Think it not strange concerning the fiery trial which is to try you - 1 Peter 4:12

A CHANGE IN OUR HOME - Reading: 1 Peter 4:7-19

My husband got saved before I did.

I remember how he loved the house of God. He had one suit and would wear the same suit to church every Sunday. The pride in me just could not understand. I was still going to parties, and he would take our daughter to church. The thought that came to me then was that my husband was seeing a woman in the church; why else would he be going every Sunday wearing the same suit?

I decided to follow him to church, but when I walked into the building, I saw myself for the first time in my life, a messed-up sinner! The women were modestly dressed and looked glorious. I shamefully sat at the back of the church but after the service, the women came to me smiling, greeting me, and expressing how wonderful and exciting it was to meet me. I felt so much love that Sunday I decided I wanted more so I went back every Sunday. Each time I received the same warm welcome.

One Sunday I sat in church and the pastor was calling souls to the altar. I realised that I needed Jesus, but I was very scared so decided I was not going to go up there. But then I felt as if I was floating, as if someone was carrying me to the altar. Afterwards the question came: *"Do you want to be baptised in Jesus' name?"*. With tears rolling down my cheeks I shouted: *"Yes! Yes!"*.

The following week I was baptised in the name of Jesus Christ. The church sisters' generosity even until today still has me in awe. They saw that my clothing was not really suitable for church, so they gave me what I needed, and I was not too proud to accept their gifts.

But there was still a void in my life, and my marriage was falling apart. So, I started to seek God on a higher level. I needed the Holy Ghost, and it was urgent. I would pray earnestly to be filled.

Not long after I was baptised, I returned from the altar and sat down. The pastor raised a song that made me look back in my life; I saw where Jesus brought me from. I started to thank God, and I began to love-on Him. Then suddenly the fire came down from heaven! My first utterance was: *"Hallelujah!"*. It came from the bottom of my belly. The heavenly language started to pour out of me. I kicked my shoes off and began to run around the church speaking in other tongues, with the pastor behind me and the rostrum associates following.

When we got home and I opened the door to our apartment, I began to see all the demons that had held us bound for years. I rebuked them in the name of Jesus and commanded them to leave.

Along with our blessings, there were many challenges and obstacles within our marriage. My husband was not interested in God as he used to be, and it became very hard to live with him because he was not filled with the Holy Spirit. He was double-minded and started to commit adultery. With the help of the Holy Ghost, I have kept my integrity through prayer and fasting.

I would encourage every woman to pray for her home. She should not be so proud that, if she is physically able, she cannot bend her knees in prayer. Pray that our homes will reflect the beauty of Jesus Christ.

Name withheld

SUNDAY 5th

When I am weak, then am I strong - 2 Corinthians 12:10

MAINTAIN JOY DURING SUFFERING - Reading: 2 Timothy 2:1-13

I reflected over a time in my life when I spent years suffering in what felt like mental torture. I wondered how I maintained joy during those challenging times which were not always joyful! What kept me going was the 'hope' that one day it would all be over.

Joy during suffering is to remember that no matter how bad a situation, there is hope, and also: *"If we suffer, we shall also reign with him: ..." (2 Timothy 2:12).*

You see ladies, my hope transcended my circumstance and I discovered that by maintaining hope, it gave me joy. Satan tries to rob our joy by presenting pure negativity, especially during our times of distress, but we must focus on hope and the positives in life.

"If in this life only we have hope in Christ, we are of all men most miserable" (1 Corinthians 15:19)

Lady Pam Lewin

MONDAY 6th

In the tenth month…the tops of the mountains were seen - Genesis 8:5

WHAT CAN YOU SEE? - Reading: Genesis 7:17-24; 8:1-5

We often pray for change yet do not always acknowledge when change has begun.

I've read with interest the detailed account of the time which Noah spent in the ark. Yes, it was a place of safety during the flood, but it was also a measured space of indefinite confinement and restrictions, no doubt with many inconveniences. The only way that Noah could tell how close he was to coming out, was to keep looking through the ark's only window *(Genesis 6:16),* and documenting changes - comparing his notes of the present with writings of what was now past.

See that Noah records when the rain started *(Gen.7:11-12)*, but also notes when the rain stopped *(Gen. 8:1-3)*. He records the time when the ark floated on swollen waters *(Gen.7:17-18)*, but also when the ark rested *(Gen. 8:4)*. He records when the hills and mountains were submerged under water *(Gen. 7:19-20)*, but also makes mention of the month and day on which: *"the tops of the mountains could be seen" (Gen. 8:5)*.

We sometimes feel that our prayers are not answered if the result is not immediate or does not happen all at one time. However, change can be gradual. I believe that Noah thanked God for each slight change seen, although he was still 'boxed-in'.

Elijah had a servant who needed to take note of small changes. He kept on saying: *"there is nothing" (1 Kings 18:43-45)*. I do wonder if the cloud which was the size of a man's hand, was there the first time that he went to view, but he thought it was too insignificant to mention. Maybe it took seven times to correct the servant's perception. A little cloud - during a drought? Bless His name! Change has begun!

JEJ

TUESDAY 7th

Many are the afflictions of the righteous: but the LORD...- Psalm 34:19

GOD IS ALWAYS ON TIME - Reading: Joshua 6:17, 23-24; Psalm 34:17-22

You've probably 'been there', i.e., as soon as one trial is over, along comes another.

Or sometimes you may have to deal with several perplexing situations all at the same time. How do you cope when your afflictions are many? By trusting God. We trust that He has the solution to every problem, and He will deliver in His way and His time.

Rahab received a true token from the spies to assure her that deliverance for her and family would come *(Joshua 2:12-21)*. It was only a scarlet cord that she was given. She had to keep the same red thread hanging from her window and believe that, as simple or foolish as it seemed, it was enough to identify the house to which help should be sent before the complete destruction of Jericho. We don't know how long it took for the spies to come to rescue Rahab, but they returned on time.

Maybe your situation is so bad that it's rotten! You're wondering: *"Where's Jesus?"*. Like Martha you say: *"Lord…(it) stinketh!" (St John 11:39)*. This may well be a cliché, but it's relevant and definitely true: *"God may not come when you want Him, but He is always on time"*.

JEJ

*WEDNESDAY 8th

Though the righteous fall seven times, they rise again - Proverbs 24:16 (NIV)

DON'T WORRY & DO NOT FEAR - Reading: Psalm 27:1, 14; Proverbs 24:16

Why do we fear when we have Jesus, and He is our light and our salvation?

We should give our troubles to Him, there is no need to try and sort them out ourselves. If we would just leave our cares with Him, we would not worry so much.

"Wait on the LORD: be of good courage, and He shall strengthen thine heart; wait I say on the LORD".

Waiting is something we struggle with because patience is not one of our strong points! But Jesus never lets us down, whatever we ask for He will grant it in His own time. We must be courageous whilst being patient. He will come through with an answer, just in time.

We waste so much time worrying when we must only FEAR NOT and WAIT!

Sister Jennifer Miller

*International Women's Day

*THURSDAY 9th

Fear thou not, for I am with thee... for I am thy God - Isaiah 41:10

PRESSED OUT OF MEASURE AND INTO SHAPE - Reading: Isaiah 41:1-29

My relationship with the invisible God defines my hope, desire, and future.

He is the divine instrument who shaped me by allowing my trials to change my perspective on this journey from fear to faith and glory to glory. I've discovered that grapes exposed to the harshest elements frequently produce the best wine.

My life, women of a great God, has become like the proverbial English tea bag; when hot water hits it, it reaches its full potential. This is the season when faith in the supernatural will allow us to step out in faith and become the women of purpose that God intends for us to be.

We are more than the title we may have that sometimes limits our ability to function outside of our paradigm. God has established my going out so that I can now cultivate the spiritual call and business acumen (Brynels: Etsy, Amazon & www.brynels.co.uk/Amazon: Lolonyo Products & Bethanifaith) that has always been there.

However, we often need that pressing moment to release the anointing already in us, so that we can be pressed into God's shape as destiny and time come together.

Sister Vivean Pomell

World Kidney Day

FRIDAY 10th

Thou hast been a refuge from the storm, a shadow from the heat - Isaiah 25:4

QUIET REFLECTIONS - Reading: Isaiah 25:1-12

It is good to quietly reflect upon God's goodness.

As women, we are often busy from the moment we awake until we go to sleep. But today, let's pause for a while. Our reflections may help to change our perspective on difficult situations that we're currently in.

Our archives will show that during times when we were weak, weak from dealing with one pressure, trouble, or sickness after another, we survived by a divine infusion of strength. When we faced financial hardships, we proved that God not only provided for Abraham, but He is our on-time provider too. We learned that our God who sees, also *"sees to it"*, whatever our *"it"* may be!

A refuge from the storm. We've heard of an institution called: 'Women's Refuge'. It's a safe place where women in danger have security from someone who means them harm. Ladies, we can remember particular storms that have blown into our lives the strength of which could have wiped us out permanently!

But we found a shelter in the Lover of our Soul, a Hiding Place in which to dwell until the storm had passed, and a Heavenly Coolant when we were in the furnace of affliction. Any one of us reading the key Scripture verse today could easily have written the same.

JEJ

SATURDAY 11th

I will bless the LORD at all times: His praise shall continually...Psalm 34:1

I WILL BLESS THE LORD - Reading: Psalm 34:1-22

This is a Psalm of David regarding the time that he pretended to be insane in front of Abimelech, who sent him away.

"Bless": meaning to adore, praise, exalt, worship

Even whilst hiding in a cave David realized that despite his failures, God had been gracious to him. In every circumstance, David was determined to express humble adoration to God.

The reason why we can bless the LORD at all times is because our praise is not based upon our emotions or how we are feeling at a particular time. It is knowing and understanding who God is and what he has done for us. We therefore submit our will and focus on the Creator.

However, it is not enough to just adore the LORD from within, we must verbalize it, our mouths must speak the praises of God! Nothing disturbs the enemy like when he sees a child of God, who according to what they're going through, should be cast down, but instead they are opening their mouth and exalting the LORD. That soul's adoration bursts through the gloomy circumstances with the raising of the hands, or a shout of *"Hallelujah"*!

The more we spend time in God's presence in prayer and studying the Word, the greater we will discover the benefits of blessing the LORD at all times.

Evangelist Marjorie Burgess

SUNDAY 12th

Hope thou in God: for I shall yet praise Him - Psalm 42:5

HOPE IN GOD - Reading: Psalm 42:1-11

You believe in God; you know He cares for you
You love Him because He first loved you
You sing about His goodness despite your daily trials
Yet the joy of your soul is turning into sorrow
And your soul is sinking in the quicksand of depression.

Now is the time to let your faith rise up and counsel your dejected soul against hopelessness
Let your faith persuade your soul to Hope in the LORD, her creator and sustainer
Why? Because Hope in God is the anchor that keeps your soul stalwart during life's trials
Because Hope in God is the helmet that protects the mind from doubts and fears
Because Hope in God keeps your soul in a peaceable state
Finally, because the eye of the Lord is upon them that hope in His mercy.

So, Hope in God and let it propel you into God's presence, where your sorrows will be turned into joy and your whole being will be united in Praises unto the LORD.

MT

MONDAY 13th

When thou passest through the waters, I will be with thee - Isaiah 43:2

I AM WITH YOU! - Reading: Isaiah 43:1-13

As blood washed believers we are bound to face many trials. These trials can bring a lot of fear into our hearts. Sometimes we don't know what to do after we have prayed and there seems to be silence!

Isaiah 43:2 is one of my many favourite Bible verses because I have been through so much, and these precious powerful words have brought me through in Jesus' name.

During trials, we can feel lonely and sometimes scared that our world is falling apart, but with God we can face and overcome anything because He gives us strength. One can feel like they are drowning with cares of life, and can easily drown without Christ, so these words are a lifeline unto us.

No wonder David cried out in Psalm 69:1 (NIV): *"Save me, O God; for the waters have come up to my neck"*. He was echoing what many of us feel when we find ourselves in those dreadful situations we cannot manage alone. My words of encouragement are that when we are in trouble, cry out aloud to God! God is with us throughout our trying times and hard seasons, even if it may look like He is not there.

Call upon Him, meditate upon His Word, day, and night. Do not stop until your answer and change come!

Sis EM

TUESDAY 14th

None of these things move me that I might finish my course - Acts 20:24

STAND FIRM - Reading: Acts 20:13-24

Teachers at any further education institution will confirm that student numbers decrease as the term progresses.

They may have a full classroom at the beginning such that other applicants are declined and placed on a waiting list. But staff know that as time goes by, pupils will fall away. Reasons vary why they can't continue with the course; it may be due to sickness, change in circumstances, loss of interest, not keen on the teacher, etc., the result is that their seat becomes empty.

It is necessary to remain motivated to complete a course, the main motivation being the benefits you'll receive when the course ends. Each of us has been given a specific Divine Assignment by God to be completed within an allotted space of time. The course requires effort and is much more difficult in places than we could have ever imagined.

Sadly, some of those who started their course at the same time as we did have given up, but that hasn't stopped us. We have started and are determined to finish.

JEJ

WEDNESDAY 15th

Our God whom we serve is able to deliver us - Daniel 3:17

OUR PROTECTOR - Reading: Daniel 3:1-30

It is clear that we are living in dangerous times when the forces of evil seek to discourage and destroy the child of God.

The Bible offers us hope and reminds us that the Lord Jesus Christ is our source of protection and deliverance in a wicked and evil world. The Scriptures use a number of metaphors in reference to God's protection for His people. He is our shield, fortress, hiding place, keeper, refuge, rock, shade, shelter, and stronghold.

His presence and the power of His anointing become a force field of protection, making us inaccessible to the enemy, no matter what the circumstances. Just like Shadrach, Meshach, and Abednego in Daniel 3:17, if we abide under the shadow of the Almighty, we need not be afraid.

There are physical dangers and there are satanic perils, but out of them all our God will deliver us. We have the assurance that those who walk with God can depend upon His deliverance.

Missionary Monique S. Lewis, Kingston, JA

THURSDAY 16th

Rejoice not against me, O mine enemy: when I fall, I will arise - Micah 7:8

IT'S NOT OVER UNTIL GOD SAY SO - Reading: Micah 7: 1-10

Wouldn't it be nice if everyone in our lives meant us good and wished for us only what they would want for themselves?

However, life is not like that. Sometimes hidden snares are deliberately planted in our way to make us fall. Or when our enemies hear that we have met upon hard times and misfortunes, they hope that will be our end.

It is confidence in God that allows us to challenge how circumstances appear. Our trust in Him who knows the end from the beginning gives us the boldness to silence and oust the premature rejoicing of the adversary. Why? Because we are women of purpose! So even when we fall, a purpose is in the fall. When we are in darkness that too is on purpose, for we are developed not in the sunshine but in a dark space.

There isn't a moment in our lives that is not divinely orchestrated when lived in the will of God: *"The steps of a good (person) are ordered by the LORD" (Psalm 37:23).* Sometimes those steps lead us into lonely places, into tunnels which seem to have no end. But though it's a long experience, it is not for ever.

Therefore, pass on either or both of these messages to the enemy and his friends: *"I will arise and am coming out of this trial stronger than when I went in";* or/and: *"You started to rejoice too soon. I'm getting up and will be back"*!

JEJ

*FRIDAY 17th

Yet I will rejoice in the LORD, I will joy in… - Habakkuk 3:18

JOY IN THE LORD - Reading: Habakkuk 3:1-19

Life is unpredictable and sometimes overwhelming.

We would 'prefer' to have only one thing going-on at a time, rather than manifold temptations coming at us from every direction. You may even occasionally wonder whether you've been given a portion of someone else's troubles as well as your own!

During these seasons, be comforted that if God allowed it, you can manage it. The Word says: *"God is faithful, and will not allow you to be (tested) beyond your strength" (1 Corinthians 10:13 ISV).*

When surrounded by things and people that are failing, fading health, help from others being withdrawn, a personal season of isolation, drought, and famine - pause! Right at that moment, make a conscious decision: *"I'm going to rejoice"*; *"I will triumph".*

Understand that your rejoicing is not about what you're going through, but it's in God who will work on your behalf. Our joy is often misplaced for it is in people and things that change and decay. But joy in, rejoice in, the God in whom there is no shadow of turning. Jesus Christ the same, yesterday today and forever.

JEJ

*World Sleep Day

SATURDAY 18th

Rejoicing in hope; patient in tribulation - Romans 12:12

HOPE TO BE THERE - Reading: St Matthew 6:19-21; Romans 12:12

We'll soon be done with troubles and trials.

We are confident that one day soon we will have our last temptation, our final disagreement, pay our last bill, have our last hospital appointment.

During the darkest of times, what make us joyful is hope. Hope speaks of expectation and walks alongside faith.

Paul, whilst in prison, wrote to Philemon and asked that he prepare him a room in readiness for when he was freed. Paul knew that the saints had been praying for his release. He envisioned himself no longer incarcerated even though he had not yet been given a discharge date.

We become despondent if we live without expectation of change. No wonder Paul also said that: *"If our hope in Christ is good only for this life, we are worse off than anyone else" (1 Corinthians 15:19 CEV)*. We must therefore raise our expectations and build our hopes on things that are eternal, on things which we have not yet seen. We expect to one day be: *"where moth and rust no longer destroy our treasures, where there are no thieves who break in and steal" (St Matthew 6:19-20 NKJV)*.

Some call that place, *"Beulah Land"*. Others say it's *"The Glory Land"*. Some say they have *"A Mansion Over the Hill Top"*. But whatever you call it, don't lose hope, expect to be there!

JEJ

*SUNDAY 19th

Who passing through the valley of Baca make it a well - Psalm 84:6

NO NEVER ALONE - Reading: Psalm 84:1-12

In my dream, a man was walking with me on a long journey.

He said: *"This is the valley of Baca".* Valley of Baca - a place of experience during my Christian journey. The journey was very challenging, but I survived because I was not on my own. While travelling this journey, (my road of Baca) there were many obstacles to face! The road was rough, but the Lord promised never to leave me alone.

The man and I in the dream sang the song: *"Never Alone".* One of the verses says:
When in affliction's valley, I'm treading the road of care,
My Saviour helps me to carry my cross when heavy to bear
My feet, entangled with briers ready to cast me down,
My Saviour whispers His promise: 'I never will leave thee alone'
(Author unknown)

The mention of the well is the Lord sustaining us through our valley experiences. During my time of sickness, the Lord gave me this Scripture to comfort my heart. I have used it as a testimony to encourage others as well as to strengthen myself.

The battle is hard, but the Lord will never leave us alone. Everyone who trusts in the Lord will find comfort and encouragement in His words.

Mother Vangie Eunice Spence

*Mothering Sunday (UK)

MONDAY 20th

We glory in tribulations also: knowing that (it) worketh patience - Romans 5:3

THE TREADMILL - Reading: Romans 5:1-5

The initial visit to a gym often involves a fitness instructor preparing an exercise programme to follow to achieve your desired result.

To begin with you may struggle to keep up with the exercises listed, but you continue because your trainer gives assurance that there's an athlete in you!

After a while, exercises which once seemed so difficult become more comfortable and less challenging. At that stage your coach will change your routine to further heighten and improve your fitness. They will tell you that, although some exercise is better than none, a repetitive programme is not the best for you.

It is the same spiritually. We would all choose to have easy-to-solve problems, but elementary-level trials will keep us as weak, immature Christians. So, God places us on His special treadmill, and He sets the pace. We sometimes feel like the incline of the hills is too steep and the time is too long. We feel out of breath and pressured with manifold temptations coming at us from all directions. We wish that we could press the stop button and have a rest.

But God, who is our instructor, tells us to carry on. He wants the tests of life to work (produce) endurance. And they will, as long as we remain hydrated with God's Word.

JEJ

*TUESDAY 21ˢᵗ

Do not cast away your confidence, which has a great reward - Hebrews 10:35

LET NO ONE TAKE YOUR CROWN - Reading: 2 Tim. 4:8; Heb. 10:35; Rev. 3:11

Keep your eyes on the Crown of Righteousness which I promised as a reward for those who diligently seek me and long for my appearing.

Continue to make me the center of your interests, your attraction and give me your full heart.

To secure your crown; keep focusing on my Word, my truth and grace. *"Hope thou in me"!*

Do not cast away your confidence which carries such a great reward but hold fast to that which you have; my return is imminent!

There is no time now to slip, lose focus or get distracted. *"Let no man take your crown!"*

The victor's crown awaits in your name, so continue to refresh yourself in my presence. If you do this, your steps will remain safely secure and ordered by Me.

Sister Veronica Linton

*World Down Syndrome Day

WEDNESDAY 22nd

Let us not be weary in well doing - Galatians 6:9

DON'T LOSE HEART - Reading: Galatians 6:1-10

Today's main Scripture verse should be an encouragement to every reader.

Weariness or discouragement is something that we all experience, even when we're doing what we love and doing what is right.

Sometimes we feel weary because our best efforts yield no results, or less than what we had hoped for. We can also become discouraged in the presence of criticism and absence of encouragement. But don't stop doing what is right, and never stop doing what you have been called to do.

We must remind ourselves that every reward will not be in this life. Every deed that we do can never be noticed by man. But God is an excellent record keeper, He misses not a thing! When this life is over and we see Jesus and receive our crowns, we will wish that we had done even more for Him. A songwriter penned: *"It will be worth it all when we see Jesus, life's trials will seem so small when we see Christ. One glimpse of His dear face, all sorrows will erase. So bravely run the race, 'til we see Christ"*.

Paul writing to the brethren in Galatia does not say, *"we may reap"*, he says, *"we shall reap"*… but only if we don't give up!

JEJ

THURSDAY 23rd

The LORD knoweth the way of the righteous - Psalm 1:6

LET GOD PROTECT YOU - Reading: Psalm 1:1-6

We don't need to say as much as we do - not all the time. God is always willing to intervene, it's just that we have difficulty waiting on His timing.

We would have a better outcome in our circumstances if we would allow God space to speak for us, space to act for us. But we can be so 'quick off the mark' that we often make matters worse, and add to our initial problem, before God has a chance to do anything.

Dear Reader, I've learned the value of remaining silent even when I am **bursting** to defend myself! What happens as I 'swallow my words' is that God moves in ways which of course I could never do for myself. He uses people and methods that I would never have considered to fight my case. He positions angels to protect me from traps set to make me fall.

As women we can be fiercely independent, can't we, sometimes unnecessarily so! When we fully grasp that: *"The LORD knoweth the way of the righteous"*, then the worry to constantly defend and take care of ourselves is at last replaced with a feeling of peace that God is in control.

JEJ

FRIDAY 24th

Preserve me, O God: for in thee do I put my trust - Psalm 16:1

KEEP ME LORD - Psalm 16:1-11

The Psalms are grouped into five divisions preserving ancient Jewish tradition.

Psalm 16 (first division) entitled Michtam: a prayer/ meditation. Considered as golden in value, it may have been engraved on tablets for preservation.

The introduction of this psalm is loaded with the intensity of David's reliance on God.

"Preserve me…": keep, support, guard or defend me.

David's petition reveals complete confidence in God's protection. Imagine running like a fugitive from an evil possessed King Saul. David's complete reliance on God was proof of his relationship. We too can attest to God's protection of us.

"O God...": David called on God as **El**… Omnipotent one, unlimited in power, has unlimited ability! He recognised God as El Shaddai, the Breasted One (Psalm 91).

"For in thee do I put my trust": firm belief, reliability.

Beloved saints, this psalm demonstrates faith. We declare our trust is in God, there is no other Spiritual Rock but the Lord Jesus Christ! Shalom.

Evg. Charmaine D Boora

SATURDAY 25th

I will glory in my infirmities - 2 Corinthians 12:9

GENERAL LIFE LESSONS - Reading: 2 Corinthians 12: 1-10

The bottom line is that following God will at some point involve challenges. The question is not whether we will experience challenges, but how we'll respond to them.

God often uses challenges to mould us into the influencers He has called us to be. God is more interested in our spiritual growth than our gifts.

Being women of influence, we will always face criticism which sometimes makes us doubt ourselves, questioning our abilities, our qualifications, our positions, particularly in comparison to others.

But it's important that we understand God has created us for a unique purpose. We often fail to comprehend this truth, i.e., if we are to fulfil our purpose, God will first have to break us, and then mould us to be conformed to His image.

Many of our biblical heroes of faith experienced brokenness, and defeat before being victorious! Brokenness doesn't disqualify us from ministry. Being aware of God's grace in our own lives makes us more humble, compassionate, merciful, and gracious to others.

"Don't work for the applause, but for the cause!"

Rev. Dr. Una M. Davis

*SUNDAY 26th

The LORD has done great things for us - Psalm 126:3

MY HEALER - Reading: Psalm 126:1-6

The week beginning 3rd May 2021 started like any other week.

I was going into work with a mild headache, but thought I'd be able to push through as usual. By the Wednesday, my headache had turned into a migraine which was still not unusual; I just thought I needed to stay home until it passed. My family is used to living in darkness for a few days when I have a migraine, so we joked about it.

On the Friday, my head was not getting any better, so my husband got me some more migraine tablets. I had forgotten which order I needed to take the tablets in so tried to read the instructions. I realised then that I did not understand the words and I could not read! I did not tell my husband but thought: *"Oh gosh Sian, this is a bad one, you really need to sleep"*, so I tried to get some more sleep.

It was Bethel's Central District Convocation that weekend. On the Saturday, my family went, and my sister came to check on me. She contacted 111 who asked a series of questions that I should have been able to answer but was unable to do so. My sister took me to the hospital during which time I was falling in and out of consciousness. I have no memory of that part of the evening, but my sister said that she stayed with me while I was taken down to have a brain scan.

I remember being in a side room and a doctor introducing herself to me. She said that the scan showed I had a brain tumour. I asked her if I was going to die and she said she did not think so, they may have caught it in time. She went on to tell me that my husband was on his way, and I needed to be strong for him and my children.

Information concerning my condition was conveyed to the Central District Convocation, and urgent prayer was requested on my behalf. I just remember lying on the bed and saying to God: *"Into thy hands I commend my spirit"*. I was not worried or afraid, I just knew that whatever was going to happen to me, God was in control.

Although the hospital was still operating under Covid-19 rules, they allowed my husband to come in and see me. We spoke for a little while before he had to go, and they placed me onto a ward. I was in so much pain! I struggled to even open my eyes and move my head. I had been placed on a lot of medication.

When I woke up the next day, I realised that I had forgotten my full name, where I lived, my date of birth, my children's names, and so much more. I had lost the ability to read, to write, and my vision was not clear. This was quite scary but, thank God

March 2023
Theme: Joy During Suffering
Women's History Month & Ovarian Cancer Awareness Month

106

that I was still able to remember and recite scriptures and songs to encourage me that God was with me, that I had nothing to fear.

The following days were a blur of scans, assessments, medications, and tests. On day three, a consultant came to speak to me. He said: *"I have come to talk to you about the blood clot you have had"*. I interrupted him and said: *"I thought I had a brain tumour"*. He responded that I did not have a brain tumour and insinuated that diagnosis was never given!

Immediately, I knew that God had worked a miracle because I know the diagnosis that was given not just to me, but my husband separately also. The doctors were baffled! They were trying to figure out what had happened and why. I had so many scans that I had to sometimes wait a day or two in between them because of the radiation risk.

Slowly but surely, my clot began to decrease, and I began to feel a little better each day. I was in hospital for ten days, much of which I have only vague recollections.

It has been just over a year since this all happened. I have regained some memories that were lost, and I've learned how to read and write again. I have chronic fatigue, and often feel a little out-of-sorts.

I still have a long road to full recovery but cannot thank God enough for being my healer! Every day that I wake up I am reminded of the miracle my God performed in my life, and how he continues to do remarkable things through me!

I also thank Him for my husband, children, and family. I am a living, breathing, walking, talking miracle, and I want the world to know what God has done for me!

Sian Campbell

*Neighbour Day & Clocks go forward UK

MONDAY 27th

I believe God that it shall be even as it was told me - Acts 27:25

ANSWER BACK! - Reading: Acts 27:13-37

There's no denying that some of us find faith to be a challenge, at least sometimes. Faith is seeing what is not there, what has not yet manifested. Faith partners with trust.

In today's focus verse Paul, and other passengers, are in the midst of a storm called Euroclydon (Acts 27:14). They had seen neither stars nor the sun for many days. But in the midst of this, God gave Paul assurance in a dream that they would reach their intended destination.

Paul, strong in faith, made it known to his fellow passengers that everything was going to be alright. It was a ship full of prisoners so there was nobody on board to say *"Amen"* and, in the prevailing circumstances, Paul probably looked like a fool. Believing God can sometimes seem foolish to onlookers, and even to ourselves.

Beyond the black clouds and howling gusts of the Euroclydon, Paul saw himself standing before Caesar like the angel had said. As the tempest continued, if he was at any time challenged for proof that they would not all drown, Paul would say: *"I believe God that it shall be even as it was told me" (Acts 27:25).*

We need to adopt that same attitude and not let Satan and doubters cause our faith to fail. When the enemy talks to you (yes, he talks to all of us) don't stay silent and absorb his lies and threats. Open your mouth and answer back: *"I believe God!"*. Chase the devil off with your faith!

JEJ

TUESDAY 28th

I will never leave thee, nor forsake thee - Hebrews 13:5

LET YOUR CONVERSATION BE…- Reading: Hebrews 13:1-17

The fatherly letter in Hebrews 13 is one of challenge and wisdom. The writer begins this writing on relationships, from how we encounter strangers right through to the closeness of marriage. Seems God is concerned with all our relationships.

The writer of Hebrews gives us a reminder about not being covetous, (wanting what others possess) and shows us how easily human engagement strikes up jealousy and comparison. But look at how he tells us to deal with it!

He talks about the power of our words. Don't speak about your covetousness in ways that give volume to that sin.

He models the type of speech that should replace covetous conversation: *"The Lord is my helper"; "He will never leave me nor forsake me"; "consider the Word of God that has been spoken unto you".*

The power of words is most critically established in Genesis, and though we are not God, we too have power in the words we share amongst women to nurture truth and grace. Every conversation is not a grace-filled one. We just bring grace with us from our time spent with God.

How beautiful when women share truth with one another as simultaneously as we share burdens. Let's speak grace, truth, challenge, and love, and always bring the focus back to God.

Joy Lear-Bernard

WEDNESDAY 29th

God is always at work for the good of (those) who love him – Rom. 8:28 (CEV)

JOY DURING SUFFERING - Reading: Romans 8:18-30

Many years ago, God gave me a Scripture: Romans 8:28.

I kept reading and re-reading it, and wondered why this Scripture? Some months later all was revealed as my little world was turned upside down. The pain was unbearable at times, but this verse just kept coming back to me: *"For we know that all things work together for good...".*

Because of this Bible verse I was able to bear the pain and know that God loved me, and everything was going to work out for my good. Yes, I suffered loss, but His comfort and love brought me through. My family and friends only saw the joy in me as I trusted in God.

Sometime later, I realised that my little world had finally turned the right-way-up. What a God we serve!

Marie Chisnall

THURSDAY 30th

Hold tight what you have - Revelation 3:11 (AMP)

HOLD FAST - Reading: Galatians 1:6-10; Revelation 3:11

There used to be an advertisement years ago which said: *"Watch out! There's thief about!"*.

One style of theft is for a criminal to grab suddenly, and with force, what they've seen and want. It's done so quicky that by the time the victim realises what has happened, the thief is running away into the crowd or has disappeared.

The church in Philadelphia was cautioned to *"Hold fast"* or *"Hold tight"* what they had received. The warning is the same to us today. Holding the Word of God only loosely will cost us our heavenly reward. There are many temptations which we must overcome each day, many difficult situations and awkward people along the way. We need to take another grip onto the treasure of the Word.

Bear in mind that Satan is hosting an intense End Times Campaign right now; its purpose is to grab, to seize, to snatch the peace and joy of Christians; to steal our faith and the Word from our hearts.

Let us not allow ourselves to be drawn into pointless arguments. Don't become distracted by circumstances. Be wise. Be alert. Hold firmly on to your crown!

JEJ

FRIDAY 31st

If we suffer as a Christian, let us not be ashamed; but glorify God - 1 Peter 4:16

IT'S GOING TO BE WORTH IT - Reading: 1 Peter 4:7-19

With the reopening of health spas and gyms after the Covid-19 pandemic, I'm reminded of many a quest to keep fit!

It may have been your own resolution as it has been mine to feel the burn! We press hard through the 'suffering' of exercising because we feel that our outcome IS going to be worth it, or why suffer at all?

How do we as Christians remain unashamed when we are going through suffering for our faith? The preluding verses to 1 Peter 4:16 rouse a certain glory for the suffering believer. The reading suggests that suffering is our lot. All but verse 15 which suggests something a little different: *"Let none of you suffer as a murderer, thief, evil doer or busy body"*. Our mistakes will cause us to suffer as will our godless decisions, but there's no glory in that, only pain upon pain. Why would we wallow in a place that has no reward?

For one to find glory in suffering as a Christian, we must pause to view a prize worthy of the sacrifice, ridicule, pain, or tears.

When you go through, bear down with the knowledge that God's spirit is resting upon you. That will give you a reason and focus in the hardest fight. God is glorying in you.

If I must go through this, God don't let me finish empty handed. I want to come out shining in your glory and able to say: *"I knew it! This indeed was worth it!"*.

Joy Lear-Bernard

OVARIAN CANCER

Ovarian cancer is the 6th most common cancer in women, where approximately 7,500 women are diagnosed each year (Cancer Research UK).

It occurs when abnormal cells develop and grow in the ovary which multiply if untreated and may spread to other nearby organs of the body.

The ovaries, which house our female eggs and produce the female hormones Oestrogen and Progesterone, are part of the female reproductive system linked to the fallopian tubes and uterus (womb). But the reproductive system is in the pelvis which is near the abdominal organs such as the bowel, bladder, kidneys, liver, pancreas and even the base of the spine and base of the lungs.

The most common age group to develop ovarian cancer is the Over-50s, but greatest in 75 to 79-year-olds.

A woman is at increased risk of developing ovarian cancer if: there is family history (genetics) e.g., mother or sister with ovarian cancer; if a woman has herself had breast cancer (or BRCA 1 or BRCA 2 genes); if a woman uses HRT to manage the symptoms of menopause; has never used hormonal contraception; by smoking; having endometriosis or diabetes; being overweight.

The symptoms of ovarian cancer can be quite vague, e.g., abdominal bloating, weight loss, pain in the pelvis between the hips, needing to urinate urgently or more often. However all of these symptoms can be common in many other situations, so if you are concerned, SEE YOUR GP so that you can have tests and investigations as required.

Treating ovarian cancer varies greatly, depending on how aggressive and how widespread it is, so IF IN DOUBT, CHECK IT OUT!

Sis Elaine Richards (RGN, RM, Dip HE, RHV)

For further information, check out:

Cancer Research – www.cancerresearchuk.org

Ovarian Cancer Action – www.ovarian.org.uk

NHS – www.nhs.uk

April

A Prayerful Life

SATURDAY 1st

Lord, teach us to pray - St Luke 11:1

PRAYER LESSONS - Reading: St Luke 11:1-13

It is good to be ambitious in all aspects of our lives, but this should all be secondary to prayer.

We read that the apostles: *"gave themselves continually to prayer, and to ministry of the Word" (Acts 6:4)*. Note the order, i.e., we must build our prayer lives before anything else.

Are you seeking for a solution to a problem? What did Moses do about the query raised by the daughters of Zelophead? He prayed (Numbers 27:5-7). Are you being tempted to backslide from your steadfastness? What did Daniel do when he was faced with the Lion's Den? He prayed (Daniel 6:10-11). Are you locked into a situation with no obvious route of escape? What did the Church do when Peter was in prison? They prayed (Acts 12:5). Do you have an important decision to make? What did Jesus, our perfect example, do before choosing His twelve disciples? He spent all night in prayer (St Luke 6:12-13). Are you struggling to bring your will into submission to the will of God? What did Jesus do? He prayed more earnestly until His sweat became as drops of blood (St Luke 22:40-44).

We put ourselves at risk if we:

- put ministry before prayer
- 'solve' problems without prayer
- enter int our Lion's Den without prayer
- make choices without prayer

Sermons don't move God for He is the Word. Our intelligence won't move Him either for He is all-knowing. Nothing moves God like sincere prayer.

JEJ

*SUNDAY 2ⁿᵈ

We know not what we should pray for - Romans 8:26

INTERCESSION FOR OUR INFIRMITIES - Reading: Romans 8:18-30

To get a true sense of what Romans 8:26 is conveying, I had to also read verse 25:

"But if we hope for that we see not, then do we with patience wait for it. Likewise, the Spirit also helpeth our infirmities: for we know not what we should pray for as we ought: but the Spirit itself maketh intercession for us with groanings which cannot be uttered".

Because of the hope that we have in Christ Jesus, and we know He loves us, that we are the apple of His eyes, the sheep of His pasture, sons of God and joint-heirs with Him…, knowing all of this helps to anchor and hold our faith and trust in a faithful God. We know who He is and who we are.

Standing on the Solid Rock and being connected to the True Vine, gives me hope. The Holy Spirit working in and through every challenge you and I face each day will ensure we become what He wants us to be.

It is the Spirit, the dunamis power, that sustains and helps us. When we feel like we have no strength and want to give up, God's strength kicks-in, and His strength becomes perfect in our weaknesses. Each of us has experience of infirmities, i.e., a condition of being feeble, frail, diseased, or having a personal failing, but when despite any or all of these we humble ourselves and recognise it is not by power or might but by His spirit, we can rest in Jesus.

It is the spirit of God that intercedes for us. We are not able to maintain the pressure at times, but God's hand holds us.

Evangelist June Johnson

*World Autism Day

MONDAY 3rd

Pray without ceasing - 1 Thessalonians 5:17

A PRAYERFUL LIFESTYLE - Reading: 1 Thessalonians 5:14-28

In Paul's encouragement to the saints in the Thessalonian church, he tells them what a prayerful lifestyle looks like - here are just three principles:

- Rejoice evermore
- Pray without ceasing
- In everything give thanks

To pray effectively, we must also rejoice and give thanks. Each of these builds on the other. So, rejoice! Pray! Give Thanks!

Paul was completely sold out on consistency: don't just rejoice sometimes, rejoice all the time! Don't just pray sometimes, pray all the time! Don't just give thanks for some things, give thanks in every thing! This level of consistency can take a lifetime to accomplish, so that we don't just do those things, but we actually become those things, and embody those principles.

So, LORD, teach me not just how to pray, but how to *become* a prayer in Jesus' name! And if whilst I'm praying, I'm rejoicing, and whilst I'm praying, I'm giving thanks, I will indeed be *"praying without ceasing"*.

Min. Jo Earle

TUESDAY 4th

Keep on praying and never give up - St Luke 18:1 (CEV)

PRAYER IS THE KEY TO GOD'S HEART - Reading: St Luke 18:1-14

We have a most awesome God, who never turns away when we pray sincerely.

His ear is always tuned in to listen to the humble petitions of His people, and the more we pray, the more He tunes in! The apostle Paul advises us to: *"Pray without ceasing" (1 Thessalonians 5:17).* This doesn't mean we're literally on our knees all the time, but that we keep God on our minds as we go about our daily business. Doing this leaves no room for unhelpful and unedifying tittle-tattle.

It's our duty to fear (revere) Him and keep His commandments. When we do this, He promises never to leave or forsake us; He will lead and hold us up so that we will not fall (or faint).

"Let's not be weary in well doing" (Galatians 6:9), because the harvest that we reap will be straight from God's Garden!

Sister Elaine

WEDNESDAY 5th

And being in an agony, (Jesus) prayed more earnestly - St Luke 22:44

PRAY YOUR WAY THROUGH - Reading: St Luke 22:39-46

Have you ever been in agony? Agony means to be in anguish or great pain, and can be physical or emotional.

In times of anguish, we wish that there was a way to escape, that there was a button we could press to make the painful situation go away. But unfortunately, just like being in a tunnel, it's less dangerous to carry on than turn back; we have to go through in order to get out.

We read in today's lesson of Jesus in the Garden of Gethsemane, He was about to be betrayed and would soon be crucified. In His humanity He prayed, *"If it be possible, let this cup pass from me" (St Matthew 26:39),* but later concluded that, *"If this cup will not pass unless I drink it, Thy will be done" (v. 42).*

If you have ever given birth, you will know that at the peak of your contractions you are encouraged by the midwife to *"push!".* Although you would prefer to run home and leave the pain behind, you have to stay and keep courage until the labour is over.

Our verse today could have read as: *"When Jesus was in agony, He gave up",* but instead it says, *"He prayed more earnestly".* How will the script read for you at the end of your current test? Will it say: *"She gave up"* or: *"She prayed more earnestly"*?

JEJ

THURSDAY 6th

Nevertheless, not as I will, but as thou wilt - St Matthew 26:39

A DIFFICULT PRAYER - Reading: St Matthew 26:36-46

Some prayers are difficult to pray; our main Scripture verse today proves that.

It takes a total surrender of will to be able to say: *"Lord, do whatever you choose to do and I'll accept it"*. We hear: 'God knows best', but there are times when our words and actions suggest that we know better than God, or that God has made His first mistake. In those instances we may call for an urgent prayer meeting, do an extended fast, round up a number of Prayer Warriors to 'storm heaven', to try and reverse God's decision.

Like Jesus, our prayer will at some stage need to change from: *"If it be possible, let this cup pass from me…"* to: *"Not as I will, but as thou wilt"*. You may soak your pillow with tears as your flesh battles with God's will, similar to a child who resists a parent's final word. Your prayer may be for a loved one who is terminally ill. It may be that God wants you to relocate to another place to do His work. It could be to accept that you will remain single, or never give birth to children of your own. It could be to agree that the promotion or position you so desire is better suited for someone else.

We all have difficult prayers to pray. Let us not pray to try and change God's mind, but instead that we will lay aside our will in order to accept His.

JEJ

FRIDAY 7th

(Good Friday)

He offered up prayer… yet learned… by the things He suffered - Hebrews 5:7-8

LEARNING THROUGH SUFFERING -Reading: Hebrews 5:1-10

In case you're wondering who the writer of Hebrews is referring to in today's focus verses, he's talking about Jesus.

I say it like that because it may help us to understand how much Jesus understands. Picture when Jesus was praying in the Garden of Gethsemane. Whilst praying, He was crying, not quietly but loudly. We could accurately say that Jesus was bawling! When He thought of what He was about to face in His humanity, His flesh cried out to God for help, and **was** heard, but Salvation's Plan could not be changed. Jesus still had to say yes to the cross.

May we today really feel the inner anguish of Jesus Christ as we, by faith, hear His loud crying even before nails were driven into His hands and feet, even before the crown of thorns was placed upon His head and the spear plunged into His side. Screaming out to be saved from crucifixion, but then submitting: *"…being found in appearance as a man, He humbled Himself and became obedient to the point of death, even the death of the cross" (Philippians 2:8 NKJV),* for you and for me.

May we also learn that there are some things which we can only learn through suffering; some things we cannot pray away.

JEJ

SATURDAY 8th

I have prayed that your faith will be strong - St Luke 22:32 (CEV)

THE COVERING OF PRAYER - Reading: St Luke 22:31-38

I love that, although God has so many children, He knows each of us personally.

Jesus, speaking to Peter and the other disciples, alerted them to what was about to befall them. Satan desired to have and destroy them. If his desire had come to pass, and they had been *"sifted"*, how would the gospel be spread worldwide (St Mark 16:15)? Satan would have cancelled the plan of God.

Jesus is always way ahead of the devil. He prayed in advance that when the hour of temptation came, the disciples' faith would withstand the pressure. However, Peter, confident in himself, felt that Jesus had nothing to worry about: *"Lord I am ready to go with thee, both into prison and to death" (St Luke 22:33)*. If only he knew what was coming!

It is dangerous, and perhaps somewhat naïve, to believe that certain things could never happen to you, those things only happen to other people! The truth is, anything that can happen could happen to you, and sometimes with no warning (2 Kings 4:27). Hence, we need the covering of prayer from one another so that when the unthinkable comes, our faith will not fail.

JEJ

SUNDAY 9th

(Easter Sunday)

After three days I will rise again - St Matthew 27:63

VICTORIOUS! - Reading: St Matthew 27:62-66; 28:1-7

The words that Jesus spoke were profoundly intriguing and often left His disciples bewildered at His sayings.

Just before He went to the cross, and was crucified, He told His disciples: *"For as Jonah was three days and nights in the whale's belly; so shall the Son of man be three days and three nights in the heart of the earth" (St Matthew 12:40).*

The Easter story is one of triumph and victorious hope. The powers of death, and the darkness of the grave, were not able to hold Jesus captive. For three days and three nights, death, the grave, and corruption, struggled relentlessly but their efforts were futile! Death was defeated and eventually surrendered its power to Jesus who rose victoriously, and triumphed over death and the grave. Mockingly, He made an open show of them both, declaring: *"O death, where is thy sting? O grave where is thy victory?" (1 Corinthians 15:55).* Jesus Christ *"became the firstfruits of those who slept" (1 Corinthians 15:20).*

There are a lot of things going on in our world today, but there is good news for those who have a personal relationship with God. It is good to know that death has no power over the blood-washed saints. Death, for the child of God, is just a cessation from worldly toils.

Paul reminds us: *"There remains therefore a rest to the people of God. For he that is entered into his rest, he also hath ceased from his own works, as God did from His" (Hebrews 4: 9-10).*

Rev. Dr. Una M. Davis

*MONDAY 10th

(Bank Holiday)

(Jesus) took bread, and blessed it, and broke, and gave to them - St Luke 24:30

THE BEAUTY OF JESUS - Reading: St Luke 24:13-35

Today's focus verse is part of an account of something remarkable which happened shortly after Jesus rose from the dead.

As two disciples were on their way to a village called Emmaus someone, who they thought was a stranger, drew near to them and listened to their conversation. They did not recognise that it was Jesus, even when He joined the discussion and started to expound in much depth from the Scriptures, beginning with Moses and the prophets.

What removed the veil from their eyes regarding who was in their company was when, having invited Jesus into their home, before eating, He took the bread and broke it and gave it to them (St Luke 24:35). Jesus then disappeared. Their response was, no wonder we were feeling like we were on fire: *"Did not our heart burn within us?" (St Luke 24:30-32).*

It should not always be necessary for us to have to tell those with whom we mingle that we are a child of God. There should be something different about us.

Who knows what could happen on the inside of the person with whom you will talk today at the bus stop, in the supermarket, or at the doctor's surgery? They should sense and feel a difference, and want to ask you what it is!

JEJ

*Siblings Day

TUESDAY 11ᵗʰ

Hear my cry, O God; attend unto my prayer - Psalm 61:1

GOD DOES KNOW - Reading: Job 23:1-10; Psalm 61:1-3

When we have something important to say, we may check that our audience can hear us and we have their full attention. We want to be heard.

Although we know that God hears and is everywhere, circumstances can arise to make us think otherwise. Job said that he could not perceive God in whichever direction he chose - he was not able to pick up a Divine Signal from heaven. Job felt that God was not on his left nor his right, neither was He in front of him or behind. Even in places that he would usually find God, Job could not perceive Him. He therefore concluded that God was hiding (Job 23:8-9).

Life can sometimes cause us to feel like God isn't listening, or has no awareness of the depth of our troubles. In those moments, if possible, we should pray more earnestly. Jesus being in agony, prayed more earnestly (St Luke 22:44).

David in Psalm 61 interchanges between a cry and a prayer. We feel his desperation between the lines of the text: *"Lord, help! Give me your full attention! When I call, please hear me! It's urgent!"*. David also says in Psalm 27:7: *"Hear O LORD when I cry with my voice, have mercy also upon me, and answer me"*.

Please pause for a moment and absorb this: Believe that God has heard you, even if He has not yet spoken. Believe that you have His attention, even if He has not yet turned.

JEJ

WEDNESDAY 12th

In the morning will I direct my prayer unto thee, and will look up - Psalm 5:3

MORNING PRAYER - Reading: Psalm 5:1-12

Listen to my voice in the morning Lord.

Each morning I bring my request to you and wait expectantly. Lord, at the start of my day you hear my voice and pay attention to my supplication as I speak to you.

I pray to you because you alone are my help, the one in whom I hope as I expectantly wait on your direction and guidance.

Father, I am thankful and grateful that when I call upon your name you will answer and you will be with me as I face the challenges that life brings my way. You give me wisdom for how to deal with each situation.

Thank you, Lord, that your peace keeps me grounded and takes away anxiety and fear.

I rest in you as you instruct, teach and guide me.

Sis. Thelma Stanley

THURSDAY 13th

After this manner therefore pray ye - St Matthew 6:9

DO THIS LIKE ME! - Reading: St Matthew 6:5-15

Isn't Matthew 6:9 a beautiful text, where Jesus literally teaches His disciples how to pray.

I love that Jesus teaches the positioning of our prayers should always be God-facing when we begin. Jesus role-models that we should gaze at Him as a wonderful father and also a holy (hallowed) God.

The prescription for prayer is taught so tenderly. He shows us how to be sorry and how to petition for the things we need. And still at the end draws everything back to God's sovereignty and worship: *"Thine is the kingdom, the power and the glory" (St Matthew 6:13).*

So many faiths in our world are as prescriptive, if not more. They announce times of prayer, recitals, positions they must take physically in order to pray. But here, Jesus was modelling the very heart of the prayer.

Jesus was regular and focused in His prayers. He went early to pray and set aside 40 days at a certain time. We experience the grace of God so wonderfully that we can easily dismiss the simultaneous reverence of God through prayer.

We have a template of power in Christ to pray regularly, fervently, humbly and yet boldly. As we share the gospel, prayer should be taught often; that reverence and communication with God is paramount.

If we are truly impassioned beyond mere words at the prospect of being completely His, then we must be tenacious and focused in spending every humble opportunity in His Word and prayer.

Joy Lear-Bernard

FRIDAY 14th

Hannah (prayed) in her heart...her voice was not heard - 1 Samuel 1:13

PRAY ANOTHER WAY - Reading: 1 Samuel 1:1-20

We all have heard the saying: *"There's a time for everything"*. This is true and even applies to the kinds of prayers that we pray.

There is a time to pray out loud and there's also a time for silent prayer, it depends on where you are when praying. We must learn that it's not the pitch or volume of our prayer that makes it effective, it is that we are praying from a pure heart and praying in faith.

Sometimes a prayer request is so personal that we would not even dare to whisper it at the altar during a service, in case it is overheard by the wrong person. Or sometimes we may feel so weak physically or spiritually that we cannot lift up our voice.

Notice that Eli first assumed Hannah's style of prayer that day in the temple was because she was drunk, but it was not so. She was just silently and desperately pouring out to God from her heart in a way that was different to 'the norm'! Eli observed her because she was not doing 'the norm' and finally said: *"Go in peace: and the God of Israel grant you your petition that you have asked of Him"* (1 Samuel 1:17).

It is good to allow the Spirit to lead us into prayer another way!

JEJ

SATURDAY 15th

What things soever ye desire, when ye pray, believe - St Mark 11:24

A TESTIMONY OF HEALING - Reading: St Mark 11:11-26; Revelation 12:11

Revelation 12:11 says that: *"They overcame him by the blood of the Lamb and by the word of their testimony…"*. Believers are victorious because of the blood of Jesus Christ.

I testify today of God's faithfulness to us. In May 2017, just two months after I came back from being abroad, my mum was found on the bathroom floor after having a bath. The ambulance was called and they said that she had suffered a stroke. She was taken to Salford Royal Infirmary.

Prior to this she was not on any medication and had no GP. She had suffered a bleed to her brain and was shut down temporarily, and we were also told that she would not be resuscitated because of her age; the medical staff called us to come and say our goodbyes. Mum had changed colour and was in a coma for three days.

But after the prayer warriors and intercessors were called to pray, both day and night, my mother came back to life! And though she suffered paralysis on her right side for a couple of months, today she has regained all of the use of her right side, plus her memory, and she is alive praising and worshipping God!

My mother is alive today because of the awesome power of our great God. Hallelujah! This can only be God!

Sis EM

SUNDAY 16th

Pray in the Spirit at all times and on every occasion - Ephesians 6:18 (NLT)

PRAY AND BE PATIENT - Reading: Psalm 27:1-14

I know that prayer really works when we pray and believe.

To me prayer is wonderful because God answers me. He does not always answer straightaway, we must give Him time and wait. The Bible says: *"Wait on the LORD: be of good courage, and he shall strengthen thine heart: wait I say on the LORD"* (Psalm 27:14).

I've noticed that I don't need to keep on repeating the same prayers over and over again. I believe that God will answer me in His own time. God is not in a hurry because He knows what we are in need of, even before we ask. I just believe God because He has never let me down yet; I have proven the Word of God for myself.

Prayer is essential, just like food. I always pray and give God thanks first thing in the morning; I do nothing else before I pray! Wait on God, don't push Him. It is amazing that God can speak to us for a long time to do something and we take no notice, but as soon as we ask God for anything, we want Him to act immediately!

Jesus said: *"If you ask anything in my name, I will do it" (St John 14:14)*, as long as we abide in Him. He said that He will do it, but did not say when!

We must be in communion with God all of the time.

(as spoken by a Senior Mother of Bethel UK)

MONDAY 17th

(Elisha) went in, and shut the door, and prayed unto the LORD - 2 Kings 4:33

CLOSE ALL DOORS - Reading: 2 Kings 4:32-37

Prayer time is an intimate time with the Lord.

We want no distractions or interruptions as we start our communion with Him. If we are in a shared dwelling, we will often shut the door of our room to make others aware that we do not want to be disturbed.

However, closing a bedroom door, or any door in the house, is the easy part! As we position ourselves for prayer, our mind can go on several journeys although our body goes nowhere. This is one reason why our prayers shouldn't be rushed, i.e., because it takes time to get our mind to settle and focus on God. As we battle to mentally shut out and shut down what happened during the day, or yesterday, or even years ago, or what might happen tomorrow, we recognise that this is the first stage of prayer.

To stand a chance of making a connection with heaven, and getting our prayers through, we must first close all of the doors.

JEJ

TUESDAY 18th

I pray...that thou shouldest keep them from the evil - St John 17:15

ON JESUS' PRAYER LIST - Reading: St John 17:1-15

Whenever I read this chapter, I marvel that Jesus would be thinking of us on His way to Calvary to be crucified. He was about to experience a cruel execution, a humiliating death naked on a cross, yet He had us on His prayer list. How selfless and loving was He!

We can all learn something from Jesus' prayer in St John 17. Often when we are going through hard times, we become totally consumed by what's happening to us, such that we do not consider others who are also suffering and still need our encouragement and prayers. Can we perhaps train ourselves to continue to pray for someone else, even when we are in a crisis?

We should also note that Jesus' prayer for us wasn't that we should not be tested, He prayed that we would not be overcome by the evil of this world. When we pray, we usually pray to get out of our problems, but Jesus prayed for our preservation not for our escape. We should therefore pray like David in Psalm 16:1: *"Preserve me O God, for in Thee do I put my trust".*

JEJ

WEDNESDAY 19th

Peter was in prison: but prayer was made without ceasing - Acts 12:5

PRAYER WORKS - Reading: Acts 12:1-19

Herod, an agent of Satan, attacked The Church. James was killed and the strategic plan was to kill Peter also.

The authorities felt threatened by The Church that had turned their communities *"upside down"*. Old systems and religiosity were in question. An insurgence, a Holy Ghost invasion, was rampant as lives changed and churches emerged and were established. Believers were an unstoppable powerful force in spreading the gospel. Evidently the enemy was disturbed and uneasy!

Since war was declared (Genesis 3:15), hostilities against the Kingdom of Light had raged. Nevertheless, *"The weapons of our warfare are not carnal, but mighty through God for pulling down strongholds" (2 Corinthians 10:4)*. We fight spiritual battles with the arsenals God ordained.

Hence, The Church engaged in full-on warfare on the battlefield of a prayer meeting for Peter. Earnest, intense supplication brings results. Peter though chained, heavily guarded and secured in prison, this was no deterrent to the move of God. Holy Ghost power-filled prayers intercepted despite the might of man. What a remarkable demonstration of the efficacy of fervent prayers in righteousness at work! Burning, passionate, or simple prayers of faith, change things; the prayers of the saints will always accomplish much.

Prayer worked back then and prayer still works today. Saints don't stop praying.

Sis Jx

THURSDAY 20th

Never stop praying – 1 Thessalonians 5:17 (CEV)

KEEP PRAYING - Reading: St Luke 11:5-13

Paul encourages us in 1 Thessalonians 5:17 to: *"Pray without ceasing"*. Sometimes we pray and because we don't see results within the timeframe we would expect, we get discouraged and give up.

J.T. Latta wrote: *"Keep praying, toiling, praying toiling on; there soon will dawn a brighter day, keep praying, toiling on"*. Praying without ceasing requires being persistent and consistent. It takes determination, perseverance, and commitment.

The heartfelt and persistent prayer of a believer yields great rewards (James 5:16). Elisha prayed intensely for no rain, and God answered his prayer and the rain ceased for three and a half years. He prayed again for the rain to return, and it rained allowing crops to produce (James 5:17-18).

Daniel highly esteemed prayer, to the extent that he continued to pray three times a day openly, without fear of being thrown into a den of lions (Daniel 6). Hannah's sincere prayer for a son, and her vow to dedicate him to God, ended her time of barrenness (1 Samuel 1:9-20).

Jesus told a parable about a persistent widow seeking fair treatment against a heartless judge to illustrate the importance of continuing to pray and never giving up (St Luke 18:1-8). Keep praying and don't stop!

LEL

*FRIDAY 21ˢᵗ

Pray to your Father in private - St Matthew 6:6 (CEV)

A PRAYER CLOSET - Reading: St Matthew 6:1-8

It is really important that each of us has a private place where we can have an open conversation with God.

By 'open conversation' I mean where we can bawl if we need to, where we pour out the contents of our heart without restraint or fear of disturbing anyone, and nobody can hear and repeat what was said. One of the good things about these kinds of prayers is that God does not change His opinion of us, or dilute His love because of what He heard. He knew what we were going to say anyway!

A private place is not only for us to pour out, but also where God pours back into us the things in which we have become depleted. He ministers to us. He speaks and tells us things that He would not say when we have company.

Your prayer space may not be in your bedroom. If you live in a busy household where there's always lots of noise, and people coming and going, your room alone may have to be in the garage at the back of the garden, or a room at your workplace during your lunchbreak. But we must all be able to get alone somewhere with God.

"Alone with God, the world forbidden. Alone with God, O blessed retreat. Alone with God and in Him hidden, to hold with Him communion sweet". (Alone With God – J Oatman)

JEJ

*National Tea Day

SATURDAY 22nd

If we ask consistent with His plan, He hears us - 1 John 5:14 (AMP)

PRAY ACCORDING TO GOD'S WILL - Reading 1 John 5:1-21

Have confidence that God hears and answers our prayers when they are according to His will.

When we abide in His Word (St John 15:7) and know God's Word, we can then pray for His will to be done, e.g., *"It is God's will to give us the kingdom" (St Luke 12:32)*. It is God's will to give us the Holy Ghost (Acts 2:38-39). It is God's will to give us our daily bread, both spiritual and temporal (St Matthew 6:11).

Believe that He is a healer and the supplier of our needs.

Evangelist Cherry Smith

SUNDAY 23rd

(Jesus) went out into a mountain to pray, and continued all night - St Luke 6:12

THANK YOU FOR PRAYING! - Reading: St Luke 6:6-16

Prayer is our daily food. When we pray, we not only ask for things but give God thanks for His goodness.

I think of the recent sicknesses and sufferings that I have been through. My family saw the pain that I was in and tears fell from their eyes as they watched me in agony. They prayed for me and by the time that an ambulance came, the pain had gone. The ambulance staff still took me to the hospital although maybe wondering if it was necessary, but I was kept in for three days for tests.

After being discharged, I had only been home for a few days before I was admitted into hospital again for something else, and spent nine days in there. But the petition and fervent prayers of the saints ascended to heaven on my behalf. When I see what God has done, He has brought back my soul from the grave, must I not give Him thanks?

"I will extol thee, O LORD; for thou hast lifted me up, and hast not made my foes to rejoice over me. O LORD my God, I cried unto thee, and thou hast healed me. O LORD, thou hast brought up my soul from the grave: thou hast kept me alive, that I should not go down to the pit. Sing unto the LORD, O ye saints of his, and give thanks…" (Psalm 30:1-4).

I have no other gift to give God but my praises and thanks.

Mother Cherry Redman

MONDAY 24th

If I shut up heaven...if my people humble themselves...- 2 Chronicles 7:13-14

IF - Reading: 2 Chronicles 7:11-22

In 2 Chronicles 7:13-14, the word *"if"* is mentioned four times. *"If"* means that a thing is conditional, it will only happen when/after something else happens. *"If"* can also be interchanged with *"supposing that"*.

When quoting 2 Chronicles 7:14, I've noticed that it is almost always recited in isolation but, to really get its full essence, we must also include verse 13. The semi-colon at the end of verse 13 shows that verse 14 is a continuation of the previous verse:

"If (supposing that) I shut up heaven that there be no rain, or if (supposing that) I command the locusts to devour the land, or if (supposing that) I send pestilence among my people; if (supposing that) my people, which are called by my name, shall humble themselves, and pray, and seek my face, and turn from their wicked ways; then will I hear from heaven, and forgive their sin, and will heal their land" 2 Chronicles 7:13-14.

Verse 14 shows the power of prayer when certain conditions are met. The drought through lack of rain (v13), the famine caused by the locusts and dry conditions, the pestilence or plagues among the cattle and the people just as in the ten plagues in Egypt - God says: *"Supposing that my people humble, pray, seek, turn..."*! If all of these criteria are met, then: *"I will hear, I will forgive and I will heal"*. Everything is dependent on *"if"*!

JEJ

TUESDAY 25th

Is anyone among you suffering? Let him pray - James 5:13 (NKJV)

WE HAVE GOT TO PRAY - Reading: James 5:13-18

Whilst writing this brief page, I am wondering at what stage do we start to pray when we're suffering or in trouble?

What I mean is, do we talk about our problems with everyone else first, and pray later? Who is the first name that comes to mind to contact when we are experiencing affliction?

James is not saying that we should not talk with each other, or to those who may be able to help, but he gives a clear statement and reminder that we have got to pray!

JEJ

WEDNESDAY 26th

No matter how unimportant they seemed, you did it for me – Matt. 25:40 (CEV)

LIFELINE - Reading: St Matthew 25:31-46

During the Covid-19 pandemic in 2020, in the UK we were repeatedly told to: *"Stay at home and save lives"*. An old hymn came to mind: *"Throw Out the Lifeline"* by ES Ufford.

A lifeline can be prayer, words of encouragement, a 'listening ear'. Never believe that, because of a person's class or status, a lifeline is not needed.

Paul, the apostle, wrote a large portion of the New Testament. From his anointed writings, we could easily assume that he had an inexhaustible supply of strength. But, on different occasions, Paul appealed to the Saints for a lifeline of their prayers: *"Praying always…for me that utterance may be given unto me…" (Ephesians 6:18-19); "Now I beseech you brethren…that ye strive together (be a partner) with me in your prayers to God for me" (Romans 15:30)*.

Jesus, just before Calvary, told His disciples that: *"…my soul is exceeding sorrowful…watch with me" (St Matthew 26:38)*. He asked them to stay awake with Him, to be there for Him whilst His soul was in anguish as He approached death on the cross. But they all fell asleep!

Will you listen silently to somebody? Hold the hand of somebody? Pray earnestly for somebody? Fast for somebody? Weep with somebody? Send a message of hope to somebody? Be patient with somebody? Stay awake with somebody? Try to understand people better so that you can help anybody?

Throw out a lifeline and save lives!

JEJ

THURSDAY 27th

Let my prayer be counted as incense before you - Psalm 141:2 (AMP)

SWEET-SMELLING SAVOUR - Reading: Psalm 141:1-10

Often as a child coming home from school, yards from the red council house door, I'd smile and skip, knowing my conversation starter: *"Good evening, Mother!".*

I would be welcomed with the aroma of bread baking, bringing the feeling of warmth, togetherness and anticipation. I knew seven children would soon be feasting on hot buttered bread rolls creatively designed by mum and dad; the smell of food creating an atmosphere to explore the events of our day.

Just as our fellowship with one another is enhanced when we eat spiritual or natural food together, so communing with God can bring the pleasure, peace and assurance we crave: *"Let my prayer be set forth before thee as incense; and the lifting up of my hands as the evening sacrifice" (Psalm 141:2).*

As we prepare ourselves at the start of this day, let's offer honour, thanksgiving, petitions and ceaseless praise. The yielding of ourselves to God equates to burning that brings the aromatic fragrance of a sweet-smelling savour on the altar of sacrifice.

"Lord, I offer myself to you today!"

Sister Dorcas (nee Simmonds)

FRIDAY 28th

Rejoicing...; patient in tribulation; continuing instant in prayer - Rom. 12:12

DEVOTED TO PRAYER - Reading: Romans 12:1-15

"Oh, the pure delight of a single hour that before Thy throne I spend..." (FJ Crosby)

Prayer is a two-way communication between us and God. It should not be squeezed in between doing something else, or be words spoken as we rush to catch our bus or train, or while we're waiting for the traffic lights to change from red to green! God wants our full attention when we're in conversation with Him, just as we do when someone is talking to us.

We sometimes make prayer difficult for ourselves by setting goals which, when we can't meet them, we become discouraged and give up on prayer altogether. For example, we may say that from today I'm going to pray for an hour each morning. After ten minutes you've run out of words, you open your eyes to look at the clock and realise that there are still fifty minutes to go!

Since communication is key to any relationship, and usually grows over time, rather than saying today you're going to pray for an hour, perhaps say that this morning you will pray for ten minutes.

As your relationship with God develops, ten minutes of prayer won't be anywhere near enough! One day you will look at the clock and be surprised that you've gone over an hour. Prayer is now part of you and your favourite time of the day.

JEJ

SATURDAY 29th

The LORD...hears the prayer of the righteous - Proverbs 15:29

PRAYER OF THE RIGHTEOUS - Reading: Proverbs 15:21-33

'Wicked!' A disdainful word describing displeasing behaviour, yet the word in Scripture speaks of more than the depravity of actions, it also describes thinking.

It is with our minds that we serve Christ. Our prayer is the face-to-face conversation where we agree for God's desires to happen. It is not just the regular thing we do on occasion, but rather refers to the very pure communication with the Holy God as He intended. Every time we pray it reaffirms our commitment to God's plan.

We often don't know exactly what to pray, but God sees our deep desire to please Him. He works upon the good desires of the heart, not the mouth only.

Jesus also said first when we pray, acknowledge Him as Father, because we are His and should be like Him: *"Hallowed be thy name, thy kingdom come, thy will be done...." (St Luke 11:2).*

In order for us to pray the words of heaven, we must adopt the mind of Christ. Our thoughts can be cleansed from depravity and corruption, and be aligned with the God who loves us and promises to make us new, only when we accept His holiness and allow it to cleanse our thoughts.

Beyond our physical posture in prayers, it is our overall mindset that must first kneel before we begin and then, He will hear us.

Joy Lear-Bernard

SUNDAY 30th

Don't be worried about anything; pray about everything - Philippians 4:6 (NLT)

PRAYER, PRAISE & THANKSGIVING - Reading: Philippians 4:1-9

Paul encourages the brethren in Philippi by expressing his gratitude and affection.

They were reminded to pray about everything and bring all their concerns to Jesus. Your life may be filled with worries and anxieties. However, upon reading this Scripture, I can encourage and assure you of the profound truth in the Word: *"Be careful for nothing; but in every thing by prayer and supplication with thanksgiving let your requests be made known unto God".*

Prayer can eradicate anxiety and bring peace of mind and protection to the believer who humbly pleads their cause, and casts all their cares upon the Lord.

God promises that if we turn to Him in difficult times, He will give us a peace beyond all human understanding. Not the peace that the world gives, but the peace of God.

Why worry when you can pray? Don't worry, instead, let your petitions and praises change your worries and anxieties into prayer.

Prayer builds faith and reveals the glory and authority of God when He answers.

Evangelist Dezrene Beezer

AUTISM

Chances are, we all know someone, child or adult, with autism. Approximately 1 in 100 children has autism; that's at least one child or young person in every school.

Children and adults with autism have the same difficulties, i.e., making friends and building relationships, displaying certain repetitive behaviours, having highly developed interests and skills, insisting on routine and sameness, and displaying differences in perception of light, touch, sound or taste.

Children may present with a delay in learning to talk and/or with a delay in their learning. Adults may present with friendship or relational difficulties, anxiety, or mental health issues.

As the Body of Christ, we can embrace people with autism and other disabilities by ensuring that our Sunday school classes and services for both children and adults are inclusive and flexible, and ensure that we are open to doing Ministry in a creative way. For example, people with autism might be distressed by loud music, loud drumming or loud preaching. On the other hand, they might absolutely love it; flexibility is key. One thing they will never be distressed by is the anointing of God; because the anointing makes the difference!

For more information on working in ministry with children and adults with additional needs, please contact:

Dr Jo Brooks FRCPCH Consultant Community Paediatrician and Lead for Children and Young People with Special Educational Needs
Joanne.Brooks13@nhs.net

May

The Christian Hope

MONDAY 1st

(Bank Holiday)

Looking for that blessed hope, and the glorious appearing… - Titus 2:13

ENJOY THE JOURNEY - Reading: Titus 2: 1-15

Whenever we plan a holiday or vacation, we start to look forward to it straightaway.

When the day arrives, we want to make the journey part of the enjoyment. Of course, there may be traffic jams, queues at the airport, and other niggly things that could upset us, but we are determined to relax and not to allow anything to spoil our journey.

I see that in our Christian Journey and walk with God too: *"Looking for that blessed hope…"*, life's trials cannot get us down. They are only light afflictions that are just for a moment.

Be encouraged to enjoy the journey as we look forward to the glorious appearing of our Saviour, Jesus Christ.

Marriette Bell

May 2023
Theme: The Christian Hope
National Walking Month & Stroke Awareness Month
29th May - National Barbecue Week begins

148

*TUESDAY 2nd

I will come again, and receive you unto myself - St John 14:3

THE CHRISTIAN HOPE - Reading: St John 14:1-3

The Christian Hope: Life tries to crush it. Fear tries to extinguish it. Disappointment tries to strangle it.

But our hope is in God, not in ourselves or other people. So whatever direction the assault comes from, our Hope cannot die; it lives forevermore. When Hope seems to have got up and gone, like King David, we must encourage ourselves in the LORD (1 Samuel 30:6).

In Psalm 43:5, the psalmist asked the question: *"Why art thou cast down, O my soul? and why art thou disquieted within me? hope in God: for I shall yet praise him, who is the health of my countenance, and my God".*

We cannot depend on others to encourage us. We must draw from the well of salvation with joy, and allow its refreshing waters to restore, replenish and reinvigorate the Hope that we cherish not in vain.

That Hope tells us that someday, we will go where Jesus is, and we will be caught up to meet Him in the air! HALLELUJAH!

Min. Jo Earle

*World Asthma Day

May 2023
Theme: The Christian Hope
National Walking Month & Stroke Awareness Month
29th May - National Barbecue Week begins

149

WEDNESDAY 3rd

The day of the Lord so cometh as a thief in the night - 1 Thessalonians 5:1-2

CHRIST'S COMING IS CERTAIN - Reading: 1 Thessalonians 5:1-11

We spend much of our time, energy and finances guarding and protecting against thieves.

We have multiple locks, grills and bars, motion detectors, cameras and alarms, neighbourhood watches, and so many other things in place as deterrents. With all that we have, yet still, the news headlines report of another burglary and sometimes death occurs in the commission of this crime. It happens because the thieves do come, and our plans are not fool-proof. This is the reality of earth.

There is another reality of which we are all aware. Some of us are preparing for this day and others are blissfully unconcerned! There is coming a day when our Lord shall return. We believe this intrinsically but believe that we have time. Time to say, *"please forgive me!"*. Time to say: *"I love you"*. Time to say: *"Lord, I surrender!"*.

That time is now! Like the coming of the thief that is undeterred by all of our security measures, the Lord is undeterred by our final wishes. He will come at the appointed time, and sadly many of us will be caught unprepared.

The same way in which we prepare for the potential coming of the thief, let us prepare for the certain coming of the Lord. Be hidden in God.

Pastor Londy Esdaille, Nevis, WI

May 2023
Theme: The Christian Hope
National Walking Month & Stroke Awareness Month
29th May - National Barbecue Week begins

150

THURSDAY 4th

If our hope in Christ is good only for this life... - 1 Cor. 15:19 (CEV)

HOPE IS NOT JUST IN THIS LIFE - Reading: 1 Corinthians 15:12-19

Hope only in this life means that we plan just for now. But when we keep in memory Christ's life, death and resurrection, we continue to live in confidence in Him, although this is not without pains and struggles.

I am confident that if we live according to the will of God a sanctified, holy life, *"which is our reasonable service",* (Romans 12:1-2), we will have abundant life with Jesus Christ. Holy living gives us hope in the resurrection, knowing *"we may obtain mercy and grace to help in time of need"* (Hebrews 4:16). We also recognise that our disappointments are God's appointments.

In St John 14:1-3, Jesus said he has gone to prepare a mansion for us. We look forward to this, to the return of Jesus Christ. He will guide and keep us daily, and give us hope and comfort of everlasting life, that where He is, there we may be also. Those of us who believe, have hope in this life and also in the life to come as we pass through death into life (St John 5:24).

Lady Michelle Williams

May 2023
Theme: The Christian Hope
National Walking Month & Stroke Awareness Month
29th May - National Barbecue Week begins

151

*FRIDAY 5th

Before his translation Enoch had this testimony…he pleased God – Heb. 11:5

WHAT A TESTIMONY! - Reading: Genesis 5:21-24; Hebrews 11:5

L C Hall writing: *"Deeper"* was so right: *"Daily must I seek to please Him, whether it brings joy or pain".*

Seeking to please God means sacrifice, not just in a monetary sense, but giving up of self in order to please Him. That can be easy or difficult, depending on what God is asking for.

We often look forward to the day when we see Jesus, and receive our reward, and will hear: 'Well done'. But it's really important to know from now that our lives are *"holy, acceptable unto God…" (Romans 12:1)*. It is the advance divine approval which will determine where we spend eternity.

Such was the commitment and faithfulness of Enoch that he did not see death; he walked with God for 300 years until one day he disappeared. There was no point searching for him. Like Elijah, who was caught up into heaven by a whirlwind (2 Kings 2:11), Enoch too was snatched from earth, never to come back here again.

If we are still alive at the time of The Rapture, we will have the same experience as Enoch when *"he was not" (Genesis 5:24)*. However, being translated is entirely dependent upon having a testimony before then *"that (we) pleased God"*.

JEJ

*International Midwives Day

May 2023
Theme: The Christian Hope
National Walking Month & Stroke Awareness Month
29th May - National Barbecue Week begins

152

SATURDAY 6th

Lift up your heads; for your redemption draweth nigh - St Luke 21:28

HE'S COMING SOON - Reading: St Luke 21:25-33

We are seeing the fulfilment of certain activities known as signs of the closing days of time. There have been warnings so don't be shaken in mind, slacken nor lose hope. We are warned in 1 Thessalonians 5:6: *"Let's not sleep".*

Actually, it's high time (about time) to awake and take action. Look up, and lift up your head! Behold and contemplate your position. Arise and change to a posture of alertness. Be vigilant, watchful, sober, not intoxicated with the spirit of the age. Move from slouching or crouching, and stand in readiness for the final victory march observing and knowing the season.

It's a period for self-examination, and a last chance to turn from a relaxed, casual, carefree attitude, to a more serious state of being. Let's be mindful of His coming, and fully prepared for His appearing, in urgency. Consider past and present occurrences which convey significant evidence of the season, and discern with understanding what's happening in the spiritual realm.

You will see that it's not the day to be getting ready, but about time to be ready waiting and anticipating, with joyous expectancy. For the ransom paid is approaching the monumental event of eminent deliverance.

Sis Jx

May 2023
Theme: The Christian Hope
National Walking Month & Stroke Awareness Month
29th May - National Barbecue Week begins

153

*SUNDAY 7th

I go to prepare a place for you - St John 14:2

THE CHURCH IS GOING HOME! - Reading: Revelation 4:1-11

On 31 July 2022, England won the UEFA Women's Euro 2022 final against Germany.

Approximately 87,000 people watched the game at Wembley stadium, and around 7,000 gathered in Trafalgar Square the next day to celebrate the first time England has won the Women's Championship title, and a major football title since 1966. The slogan that rang out during and after the tournament was: *"Football's coming home"*.

Jesus said more than 2,000 years ago that He will return to bring the Church home. He said in St John 14:2-3: *"I go to prepare a place for you, and if I go and prepare a place for you, I will come again, and receive you unto myself; that where I am there ye may be also".*

Many football fans lost hope in England ever winning a major title again, yet it happened after 56 years. Many have lost hope in Jesus' return, yet the promises of God are guaranteed; what Jesus promised, He will do (2 Corinthians 1:20; 2 Peter 3:9). Paul wrote in the second epistle of Thessalonians that: *"The dead in Christ and those who are alive and remain shall be caught up together to meet Jesus in the clouds and live with Him forever" (2 Thessalonians 4:15-18).*

The Church is going home! Are you ready to be part of the greatest gathering and celebration there will ever be? *"Eye have not seen, nor ear heard, nor have entered into the heart of man the things which God has prepared for those who love Him"* (1 Corinthians 2:9 NKJV).

LEL

*Lemonade Day & World Laughter Day

May 2023
Theme: The Christian Hope
National Walking Month & Stroke Awareness Month
29th May - National Barbecue Week begins

154

MONDAY 8th

Behold the bridegroom cometh; go ye out to meet him - St Matthew 25:6

A LITTLE MORE OIL IN MY LAMP - Reading: St Matthew 25:1-13

To fully understand the parable of The Ten Virgins, it needs to be considered from the standpoint of an ancient Jewish wedding - very different to weddings in Western Culture.

The five foolish virgins (bridesmaids), although honoured to be asked to be part of the Bridal Party, made no preparation for the wedding: *"They that were foolish took their lamps, and took no oil with them" (St Matt. 25:3)*. Their lamps were meant to illuminate the pathway of the bridegroom back to his father's house with his bride for the marriage banquet. A lamp with no oil was therefore pointless and only an accessory. Diligent preparation would have identified an empty lamp and reminded those women to bring some oil in their vessels with their lamps.

The wise may have sounded selfish by refusing to share their oil, but had they shared theirs, it's possible that the parable would have been called The Ten Foolish Virgins. Wisdom said: *"Not so, in case there isn't enough for us and you...go and buy for yourselves" (St Matt. 25:9)*.

The virgins had to be ready to go out to meet the bridegroom; the Church needs to be ready to go up to meet Him (1 Thessalonians 4:17). Are you looking forward to that day? And, more importantly, are you fully prepared? Do you have sufficient oil in your lamp for it to burn until the break of day?

JEJ

May 2023
Theme: The Christian Hope
National Walking Month & Stroke Awareness Month
29th May - National Barbecue Week begins

155

TUESDAY 9th

The coming of the Son of Man will be like lightning - St Matthew 24:27 (CEV)

SUDDEN APPEARANCE OF CHRIST - Reading: St Matthew 24:23-35

The Word of God tells us that Christ's return will be as quick as the lighting that flashes from the east to the west.

Lightning is fast, dazzling and instantly visible even in the remotest of places (ref Cambridge Bible for Schools and College). Jesus will be visible in all His glory and power where *"every eye shall behold Him, even those that pierced Him and all the kindred of the earth shall wail because of Him, even so Amen" (Revelation 1:7).*

Scriptures also tell us that as in the days of Noah, so shall also the coming of the Lord be. People were eating, drinking, marrying and giving in marriage up, lovers of worldly pleasure, until the day that the rain began.

As Christians, we must not be distracted by the things of this world, but should be watching and praying as we do not know the moment when Jesus shall appear. Try to imagine His appearance - rapid and unexpected! Not even the angels in heaven know the date on which Jesus will come back for His people (St Matthew 24:36).

It behoves Christians to be ready and waiting, not like the five foolish virgins who ran out of oil and only realised when it was too late.

Missionary M Fraser

May 2023
Theme: The Christian Hope
National Walking Month & Stroke Awareness Month
29th May - National Barbecue Week begins

156

WEDNESDAY 10th

But of that day and hour knows no man, no not the angels - St Mark 13:32

PERMANENTLY READY - Reading: St Mark 13:32-37

Sometimes the more time that we have to get ready for an occasion, the more likely we are to be late.

If the event starts at 6pm, we may plan to do lots of things in the morning, e.g., go to the hairdressers, quickly go shopping, do a quick tidy up of the house, make a quick phone call, and then get dressed.

Unfortunately, what often happens is that time runs away. We look at the clock only to realise that it's 5pm and, instead of being able to get ready at a leisurely pace, it's a last-minute rush.

When we finally leave the house, we sometimes have to return home because we left something of importance behind. We then sit in our transport wondering whether we switched off the iron, turned off the oven, closed the window, locked the door, and so on. We identify now that having our clothes on is not the only part of being ready!

The coming of the Lord is near, how near we do not know. It's going to be a splendid event but we have no date or time. Since that information has been withheld, we have to remain permanently ready! Let's use the time now to do our last checks of things that we need to get right before Jesus comes.

JEJ

May 2023
Theme: The Christian Hope
National Walking Month & Stroke Awareness Month
29th May - National Barbecue Week begins

157

*THURSDAY 11th

There is laid up for me a crown of righteousness - 2 Timothy 4:8

THE CROWN OF RIGHTEOUSNESS - Reading: 2 Timothy 4:1-8

Paul wrote letters to Timothy charging him to uphold and defend the truth of The Gospel.

This isn't a passive exercise: Paul used the metaphors of sport and war to illustrate the self-discipline, drive, pain, sacrifice, and even danger that disciples of Christ will experience.

It's important not to see this verse in isolation. This letter was written by a man who experienced rejection, literal storms and, at the time of writing, was imprisoned in Rome awaiting his own execution. But he had the unshakable belief that all he had suffered was worth it to gain Christ and a heavenly reward. In verse 7, Paul believed three things qualified him to receive the Crown of Righteousness: he had fought a good fight, he finished the race, he kept the faith. This Crown represents victory – a champion's reward for all the training, overcoming opposition and obstruction, and finishing *well*. To be partakers of the same, we must have the same qualifications: to *reign* with Christ, we must also *suffer* with Him.

Paul's convictions challenge us to pour out *everything* for Christ, to live with unwavering intensity and dedication, and commit every part of our being to run, to fight, to win. In our unashamed profession of His gospel, and the passionate pursuit of His Kingdom, we will – as joint-heirs with Jesus – gain the same glorious reward.

Beulah McKenzie

Eat What You Want Day

May 2023
Theme: The Christian Hope
National Walking Month & Stroke Awareness Month
29th May - National Barbecue Week begins

158

*FRIDAY 12th

Listen to the Spirit and understand what he is saying – Rev. 3:22 (NLT)

WHAT IS THE SPIRIT SAYING? - Reading: Revelation 3:14-22

We usually listen to the weather forecast, and respond by preparing for the weather based on what we've heard.

If hot weather is expected, we will ensure that we have appropriate clothing, sunglasses, sun-cream, and a supply of water to stay hydrated. If we dismiss the forecast, there are likely to be consequences to our health.

Likewise, Christians are called to give attention to the messages that Jesus sent to the churches. Jesus is aware of the threat of believers losing their first love and being afraid of persecution. He knows that believers may fall into a state of apostasy, be deceived by false doctrines, yield to temptations, and become so materialistic that they lose consciousness of their spiritual needs.

When focus is primarily on temporal things, e.g., beautiful church building, homes, and things that can be purchased with money (Revelation 3:17), the spiritual aspects are likely to be ignored, leading to lukewarmness and failure to hold fast to the faith. Jesus, in showing His unfailing love and care, invites us to arise from mediocracy to a place of fulfilment in Him.

If we listen attentively, seek to understand, and respond to what the Spirit is saying to us today, we can be overcomers in Christ.

J Henry

*International Nurses Day

SATURDAY 13th

Behold, he cometh... and every eye will see him - Revelation 1:7

LOOK! HE'S COMING! - Reading: Revelation 1:4-8

The proclamation: *"Behold, He cometh" (Revelation 1:7)* reminds me of the parable of the Ten Virgins: *"Behold the bridegroom cometh" (St Matthew 25:6)*.

What an announcement! A joyful call; one that you've been longing for if you're ready, but a sad occasion for those who are not.

May we encourage one another, and others who have not yet made a decision, to prepare for eternity. Time will soon be no more.

JEJ

May 2023
Theme: The Christian Hope
National Walking Month & Stroke Awareness Month
29th May - National Barbecue Week begins

160

SUNDAY 14th

My reward is with me, and I will give to each person - Revelation 22:12 (NIV)

GLORIOUS PAY DAY - Reading: Revelation 22:7-12

Those of us who are in paid employment usually have a set date each month on which we are paid. Pay Day is Reward Day!

"According to what they have done" (Revelation 22:12) means that we will each be paid based upon what we did in the Lord's service. If we have been sluggish, that will be reflected in our pay, and if we were enthusiastic, committed and loyal, we will be rewarded accordingly.

On God's Pay Day, nobody will receive more, or less, than they deserve. We will be rewarded even for those good things which we did privately and told no one; God has our records.

It's going to be a day that will make the toils of life worthwhile, we will be glad that we held out to the end. And the greatest reward of all will be to *"ever be with the Lord" (1 Thessalonians 4:17).*

JEJ

*MONDAY 15th

Whosoever liveth and believeth in me shall never die - St John 11:26

REUNITED - Reading: St John 11:11-27

Death never comes at the right time. We would always choose to postpone our death or loss of a loved one for later.

For those who were in Christ when they died, we are comforted to know that they're only asleep. One day they will awake to be caught up with those who are alive at the time of The Rapture, and we will be together again.

We do not mourn and pine because we doubt where our saved family and friends are gone, but we miss their presence. In moments when the acute pain of grief grips our heart, we do not always first remember that they are just sleeping. We long for simple things like hearing their voice, their laughter, asking for their opinion, sharing our achievements with them, and so on.

Jesus said to Martha: *"Whosoever liveth and believeth in me, shall never die. Believest thou this?" (St John 11:26)*. It's a relevant question to each of us: *"Believest thou this?"*:

"For we believe that Jesus died and rose again, and so we believe that God will bring with Jesus those who have fallen asleep in him. According to the Lord's word, we tell you that we who are still alive, who are left until the coming of the Lord, will certainly not precede those who have fallen asleep. For the Lord himself will come down from heaven, with a loud command, with the voice of the archangel and with the trumpet call of God, and the dead in Christ will rise first. After that, we who are still alive and are left will be caught up together with them in the clouds to meet the Lord in the air. And so we will be with the Lord forever. Therefore encourage one another with these words" (1 Thessalonians 4:14-18 NIV).

JEJ

*International Day of Families

May 2023
Theme: The Christian Hope
National Walking Month & Stroke Awareness Month
29th May - National Barbecue Week begins

162

TUESDAY 16th

Then we which are alive and remain shall be caught up - 1 Thessalonians 4:17

WE WHICH ARE ALIVE - Reading: 1 Thessalonians 4:13-18

Imagine if today were the day of Christ's return penned, and your eyes are cast across this writing. You would be among those mentioned in Scripture as: *"They that are alive and remain".*

It's sobering to think that many prophecies of the last days were pointing at us. It's as if the *"they"* that the Bible refers to unveiled a vast screen with all our faces... *"they".*

Should Christ's return happen in our lifetime, we will never *"sleep"* prior to His appearance. We will have outlived life on earth and be spontaneously *"caught up"*, dividing humankind with those that sleep.

Some pass away with the hope of Christ in their hearts, and others who planned for Christ in their future ran out of time. How serious a thought. All are silently paused until that day. But you and I are still surveying the Land of the Living with hopes, dreams and time to live fully with readiness and purpose.

I wonder what Paul and other writers might say to us about our remaining days? What echo of instruction might they spear through time and space?

We know Paul would say: *"Press! Keep going towards the mark for the prize of the high calling in Christ Jesus" (Philippians 3:13).* Or: *"Don't be weary in doing well, your reward is coming, just don't faint, don't give up" (Galatians 6:9). "Go, make others disciples to be ready too" (St Matthew 28:19)!*

Christ would say: *"I'm with you" (St Matthew 28:20).*

Joy Lear-Bernard

WEDNESDAY 17th

This same Jesus... shall so come in like manner - Acts 1:11

YOUR RECORD WILL SPEAK FOR ITSELF - Reading: Acts 1:1-11

According to Romans 5:5, our hope does not cause us to be ashamed because the love of God is shed abroad in our hearts by the Holy Ghost

So, I ask myself, what do we have to be ashamed of? This walk with the Lord is obviously not an event per se, but rather a journey with many ups and downs. Luke's gospel writings began with the assertion that everyone requires salvation. Keep in mind the message that Brother Zacchaeus heard: *"Today salvation has arrived to this house, for this man too is a son of Abraham" (St Luke 19:9)*. When Luke wrote to his friend Theophilus, about the things Jesus started doing and saying, he brought the records once more together.

Beloved, our optimism rests on the knowledge that we too have a personal treatise (record) of every instance in which Jesus has come to our aid. Because the Holy Spirit resides inside us, we have the assurance that we will see the King soon and very soon, so no longer do we need to stand and stare into heaven.

The Apostle Paul in Romans 8:18 advises us to disregard *"suffering"* in comparison to *"the glory that will be revealed in us"*. Let me draw on a passage from Proverbs 10:28 to close: *"The expectation of the wicked will fail, but the hope of the upright provides joy"*. I won't say anything else.

Sis Vivean Pomell

May 2023
Theme: The Christian Hope
National Walking Month & Stroke Awareness Month
29th May - National Barbecue Week begins

THURSDAY 18th

There shall be no night there - Revelation 22:5

HEAVEN IS REAL - Reading: Revelation 22:1-6

A vision depicting the spiritual, heavenly dimension - with crystal clear rivers, the Lamb's throne, the life healing tree with twelve types of fruits. A place free from the curse and effects of sin. The centre of Power and Might. A place of worship by saints who behold Him face to face.

Heaven. There Christ's abode is illuminated from the presence of His glory, there *"the Lamb is the light"* (Revelation 21:23). He dwells in: *"unapproachable light"* (1 Timothy 6:16). He is the God of all lights, the light of the world, God of the day. Father of lights, in Him there is no darkness at all.

In this eternal land, time stands still; there are no clocks or watches. The moon and sun cease, no longer having a purpose. There's no measurement of time by sunrise nor sunset. No dividing of time into seconds, minutes, hours or the four seasons.

There's no night, only endless day where we never grow old. Perpetual light of an unclouded day. No lamps or artificial lights. The Lord shines on the faithful who have dominion with The Lamb. And there we'll be forever with The Lord, in the city where The Lamb is the light.

Sis Jx

May 2023
Theme: The Christian Hope
National Walking Month & Stroke Awareness Month
29th May - National Barbecue Week begins

165

FRIDAY 19th

I will come and get you, so that you will always be with me - St John 14:3 (NLT)

HE'S COMING BACK AGAIN - Reading: Revelation 22:16-21

I remember when my youngest daughter was a toddler, it was very hard for me to leave her at the nursery while I went to work. She would cry so much when I said goodbye that it tore at my heart. Sometimes the staff would try to distract her so that she did not see me leave.

Whenever I went to collect her after work, I wouldn't always call out her name straightaway, I would just stand and watch what she was doing. But no matter how engrossed she seemed to be, as soon as she turned and saw me, she would drop her paint brush or her drawing, and run towards me with the biggest smile on her face which said: *"Mummy has come back, I don't have to stay here"!* Sometimes she wouldn't even turn around to say farewell to her teachers and friends.

I feel like that about Christ's return. No matter what I'll be doing I will, without hesitation, be glad to drop it when the trumpet of God sounds, and I won't look back!

Sis H

May 2023
Theme: The Christian Hope
National Walking Month & Stroke Awareness Month
29th May - National Barbecue Week begins

166

SATURDAY 20th

God shall wipe away all tears for the former things are (gone) - Revelation 21:4

NO CAUSE, NO TEARS - Reading: Revelation 21:1-7

Tears are one of the international non-verbal languages understood in any part of the world to which we may go. They are more often an expression of sadness than of joy.

Do you remember the last time that you cried? What was the cause? It may have been because of physical or emotional pain, hearing some sad or bad news, a major disappointment, frustration, etc. Nobody cries for no reason, even if they cannot fully explain their tearful state.

I've heard my pastor say that, in heaven, God will not go around with a handkerchief wiping our eyes. He will simply remove the cause for tears, i.e., *"the former (sad, painful) things will have passed away" (Revelation 21:4).*

JEJ

May 2023
Theme: The Christian Hope
National Walking Month & Stroke Awareness Month
29th May - National Barbecue Week begins

167

SUNDAY 21st

Eye has not seen, nor ear heard...what God has prepared for us - 1 Cor. 2:9

GOD IS WORKING - Reading: 1 Corinthians 2:1-16

Many times, we cannot make sense of what is happening in our lives, or in the lives of our family.

We may try to process the situation by our own rational thoughts, but our human wisdom cannot fathom what God has prepared for us.

We can only trust Him by faith, and believe that He is working it out for good.

Rev. Dr. Una M. Davis

May 2023
Theme: The Christian Hope
National Walking Month & Stroke Awareness Month
29th May - National Barbecue Week begins

168

MONDAY 22nd

Then shall (we) also appear with Him in glory - Colossians 3:4

WORKING FOR THE CROWN – Reading: Colossians 3:1-16

1. Shall I be content with one star in my crown,
   When heaven's bright portals I see?
   The answer comes back—strive a cluster to win,
   And the way will be brighter for thee.

   Refrain:
   Working for the crown,
   Working for the crown,
   Working for the crown,
   We shall wear by and by

   2 When, Lord, must I work? shall I go in the heat,
   To white and to wide harvest fields,
   Where work is so great and the labourers so few,
   And the promise a bountiful yield? [Refrain]

   3 Yes, all kinds of work I will find in this field,
   My task then quite plain I can see,
   And now having found it I'll labour and wait,
   For wholly Thine, Lord, would I be. [Refrain]

   4 And how shall I get these rare gems for my crown?
   Must I wait till heaven I gain?
   Yes, yes, but toil here for the Master's renown,
   Day by day for the Lamb that was slain. [Refrain]

   Mrs H A Mabry

TUESDAY 23rd

They sent fifty men; they sought three days, but found him not - 2 Kings 2:17

DON'T LOOK FOR ME! - Reading: 2 Kings 2:1-18

The catching up of Elijah into heaven by a whirlwind, paints a clear picture of what The Rapture will be like, and things to consider as we await our change:

1. Elijah and Elisha both knew that Elijah would soon be taken away, but neither of them knew the date or time.

2. When Elijah was caught up, although expected, it was very sudden.

3. Although Elijah had a close relationship with Elisha, Elijah could not take Elisha with him. Elisha was left behind and wept for Elijah.

4. Elisha needed what Elijah had (the mantle) which was no longer required where Elijah had gone.

5. Finally, because this event was unprecedented, fifty men went to search for Elijah, in case after the whirlwind he had landed upon a mountain or been dropped into a valley, they could bring him back. They refused to listen to Elisha who told them that Elijah would never be found (2 Kings 2:16-17).

I wonder for how many days after The Rapture those left behind will search for us? What stories will be made up to explain the mass disappearance of saints from all over the globe? How many sniffer-dogs will be out trying to trace our scent from the clothes which we'll leave in our wardrobe?

But we won't have been dropped off somewhere on earth! Praise God, our bodies by the indwelling power of the Holy Ghost, will have defied gravity and been transported through the air to our heavenly home. Nobody from down here will be able to find us safely abiding up there!

JEJ

May 2023
Theme: The Christian Hope
National Walking Month & Stroke Awareness Month
29th May - National Barbecue Week begins

170

WEDNESDAY 24th

After a long time the lord...cometh and reckoneth with them - St Matthew 25:19

THE FINAL AUDIT - Reading: St Matthew 25:14-30

There are some people who have a very short concentration span, short attention span, short commitment span. They struggle to do anything for a long period of time.

Each of us has joined the Christian Journey at different stages; some have been travelling for what feels like ages and may be getting a bit weary. But don't worry, Jesus is still coming.

The day of Christ's return will be like having the auditors review your business accounts. They thoroughly check the ledgers and ask you to explain your accounting. They ask for evidence of approval for transactions in your accounts, and ensure that you have stringently followed the rules of your governing body.

Sometimes there are things you hope that they will not notice, questions you hope that they will not ask. But the accountant will not sign-off the company's accounts until they are satisfied that the 'books' are clean.

It's been a long time since Jesus ascended back to heaven, but He said that He will be back. We've had His Word with us to follow 'to-the-letter'. He will question why we did what we should not have done, and did not do what we should have done. A songwriter said: *"When at the judgment bar, I stand before my King, and He the book will open He cannot find a thing! Then will my heart be glad...".*

Check that at today's date, your life measures up to heaven's constitution which is God's Word.

JEJ

May 2023
Theme: The Christian Hope
National Walking Month & Stroke Awareness Month
29th May - National Barbecue Week begins

171

THURSDAY 25th

We shall be like Him; for we shall see Him as He is - 1 John 3:2

CHRIST RETURNETH - Reading: St Mark 13:35-37; 1 John 3:2

1. It may be at morn, when the day is awaking,
   When sunlight through darkness and shadow is breaking,
   That Jesus will come in the fullness of glory
   To receive from the world His own.

   Refrain:
   O Lord Jesus, how long, how long
   Ere we shout the glad song—
   Christ returneth! Hallelujah!
   Hallelujah! Amen.
   Hallelujah! Amen.

2. It may be at midday, it may be at twilight,
   It may be, perchance, that the blackness of midnight
   Will burst into light in the blaze of His glory,
   When Jesus receives "His own".

3. While hosts cry Hosanna, from heaven descending,
   With glorified saints and the angels attending,
   With grace on His brow, like a halo of glory,
   Will Jesus receive "His own".

4. Oh, joy! oh, delight! should we go without dying,
   No sickness, no sadness, no dread and no crying;
   Caught up through the clouds with our Lord into glory,
   When Jesus receives "His own".

   H L Turner

May 2023
Theme: The Christian Hope
National Walking Month & Stroke Awareness Month
29th May - National Barbecue Week begins

172

FRIDAY 26th

I John saw new Jerusalem, coming down from God out of heaven – Rev. 21:2

THAT CITY - Reading: Revelation: 21:1-8

It's worthy to note of his many writings, that John never directly referred to himself.

Yet he does this three times in Revelation, as though he's amazed, he's honoured, to behold such spectacular sights. A city descending from heaven. No ordinary city but a Spiritual Settlement; holy, righteous, a brilliantly pure city. Beautiful beyond description, yet expansively documented.

It replicates *"Mount Zion, the side of the north, the city of the great King" (Psalm 48:2)*. O, Jerusalem of Judah; the former purged and passed away. Although God had put His name there, signifying His character, yet was it not blameless. For Salem of peace had seen wars, degradation and destruction.

But it's been replaced by a renewed foundation of peace, *"whose builder and maker is God (Hebrews 11:10)"*. Inhabitants are dressed in robes of righteousness, and decked in true holiness. Where God's awesome presence lights up the city so gloriously that there is no night; the moon and the sun are redundant!

So must His Bride, the Church, be robed in white and ready for His appearing. Ready to dwell in that eternal habitation. Even so Lord Jesus, come quickly.

Sis Jx

May 2023
Theme: The Christian Hope
National Walking Month & Stroke Awareness Month
29th May - National Barbecue Week begins

173

SATURDAY 27th

We have...a house not made with hands, eternal in the heavens - 2 Cor. 5:1

WHOSE HOUSE ARE WE LEANING ON? - Reading: 2 Cor. 5:1-10 (NKJV)

Our bodies are our current living tabernacle that we have been blessed with by God – to give of our best to Him, and be worthy vessels of honour in which He would want to dwell.

Of course, we have to look after ourselves physically while we are alive, but when our bodies are no longer functioning as in the 'flush of youth', or when we cease to live on this earth, what then?

Will our spiritual lives have connected with God in such a way that He receives us into the heavenly mansion He has gone to prepare for us? While on earth we live in that HOPE of eternal life, so let's live the way He wants us to live – in, through and by His Spirit.

Let's lean on His understanding – the benefits will literally be out of this world!

Sis Elaine

May 2023
Theme: The Christian Hope
National Walking Month & Stroke Awareness Month
29th May - National Barbecue Week begins

174

*SUNDAY 28th

He that sat was to look upon like a jasper - Revelation 4:3

THE THRONE ROOM - Reading: Revelation 4:1-11

John, in the spirit, is caught up into heaven through an entrance by invitation from He whose authoritative, melodious voice invites him to *"Come…" (Revelation 4:1)*.

He enters God's throne room and is overwhelmed by splendid sceneries. John gazed on The One who sat upon the throne. John stared, but He is indescribable! Without the appropriate language, John uses similes: *"was like"*, to compare relatable objects to the sights he saw. Comparative of gems and precious stones. *"The figure on the throne looks like jasper" (Revelation 4:3)*. Jasper, an opaque mass in varieties of colours, such as red, yellow, brown, green, orange. He was also *"like sardine/sardius"*, a red glossy stone similar to a ruby. He is undefined but beautiful like colourful jewels.

The whole picture is framed by *"a vibrant emerald green arch like a rainbow"*. The sparkling radiant light, and fiery glow of these precious jewels, shone the brilliance of His glory and the awesomeness of God's divine presence. The Great I Am is inexpressible, His face outshines them all.

The *"open door" (Rev. 4:1)* which John saw could represent entry for the Rapture of the Church, when we shall be faultless to stand before The Throne.

Sis Jx

*Pentecost Sunday

*MONDAY 29th

(Bank Holiday)

Rejoice because your names are written in heaven - St Luke 10:20

YOUR NAME IS WRITTEN UP THERE! - Reading: St Luke 10:17-24

Have you ever done that, i.e., just had a time of thanksgiving, praise and worship because your name is written in heaven?

I know that we sometimes speak of dancing in golden shoes on heaven's streets when we get there, but there's nothing wrong with having a rehearsal down here! So many have heard the same gospel message that we've heard, yet they rejected it. Some have yet to hear it. But you and I have heard and accepted God's message, and our name is already written up there.

Even if you woke up in a bad mood this morning, or you've not had the best of days, here is a reason to rejoice: *Your name is written in heaven!*

Oh, hallelujah!

JEJ

*National Biscuit Day

May 2023
Theme: The Christian Hope
National Walking Month & Stroke Awareness Month
29th May - National Barbecue Week begins

176

TUESDAY 30th

Those whose names are in the book of life will be in the city – Rev. 21:27

A HEAVENLY HOPE - Reading: Col. 3:1-4; Revelation 21:21-27 (CEV)

One of my favourite Scripture verses is Colossians 3:1 which says: *"If ye then be risen with Christ, seek those things which are above".*

This is a wonderful lesson to learn, i.e., how important it is to seek those things which are above.

When going through difficult situations we may wonder why, but my troubles remind me not to just look on the things in this life. Especially at my age, and the times in which we are living, we should all be looking towards heavenly things. We have a better land with a new body in view.

Evangelist V Patrick

WEDNESDAY 31st

What I say unto you I say to all, Watch! - St Mark 13:37

WE MUST KEEP WATCH - Reading: St Mark 13:32-37

Jesus warns us in His Word that we must watch.

You might say, what am I watching for? We are to watch in anticipation for the Lord to return. The problem we have is not knowing the day nor the hour, but if it's any consolation, not even the angels are given any timeline. All we know is, that our Lord is going to return to earth again.

It's important for us ALL to watch and pray. We must always be in a state of readiness, watching and praying. We must remain vigilant, and on high alert and not allow ourselves to be complacent nor in a state of slumber. We must remain wide-awake, recognising the signs of the times, which are clearly visible everywhere. They signal that the Lord is soon to put in his appearance.

It won't be long now...so let's keep watch.

Evangelist Maureen Morris

SOME THINGS THAT I DIDN'T KNOW ABOUT WIDOWHOOD

I didn't know…

- that being the one left behind it would be like starting life all over again

- there is a lot of 'getting used to…', and 'drawing on all your mental and emotional reserves', just to keep going

- being surrounded by a community of people you can still feel very lonely and reluctant to engage

- it can sometimes only be a matter of time before your situation (understandably) appears to be erased from the memory of others, though it will never be erased from yours

- genuine love, support and encouragement sometimes comes from those from whom you least expect it, when you don't expect it

- 'moving on' becomes an everyday activity as you are only able to deal with each day and each situation as it comes. Anything more than 'today' is far too overwhelming

- I would get a feeling of sadness and loss every time I walked into my local church building, visit another church or attend a church event, because church was our whole life and still is mine

- the feeling of loss would be so strong at special family occasions, celebrations, holiday seasons, and making important decisions

- that when people are trying to use words of strength such as: *"We don't mourn as others mourn who don't have a hope"*, although I agree with them, I am thinking: *"Yes, but my feeling of loss is still real"*

Name withheld

May 2023
Theme: The Christian Hope
National Walking Month & Stroke Awareness Month
29th May - National Barbecue Week begins

June

Women of the Bible

*THURSDAY 1ˢᵗ

She answered, It is well - 2 Kings 4:26

THE KEY QUALITIES OF A GODLY WOMAN - Reading: 2 Kings 4:8-37

It is easy to turn to the 'Proverbs 31 Woman' to summarise the qualities of a godly woman.

However, the depth and richness of understanding can be found in numerous biblical women. It is through these women that the reality of being a godly woman comes to life. For example:

Mary: know how to ponder the words of God in your heart (St Luke 2:19)
Hannah: know to pray and pour out your soul before God (1Samuel 1:10, 13)
Esther: know how to fast (Esther 4:16)
Shunammite Woman: say, and believe, *"It is well'*, in your darkest moments (2 Kings 4:26)
Martha: know how and when to be hospitable (St Luke 10:40)
Mary: know when it's time to stop and focus on the Lord (St Luke 10:39)
Naomi: care for the wellbeing of others even when your life appears to be falling apart (Ruth 1:8-13)

I give God thanks for the many women in the Apostolic Faith that have been/are examples to me of how to be a godly woman.

Prayer: Lord, help us to continually develop and exhibit the qualities that represent you.

Lady Pam Lewin

*Say Something Nice Day

June 2023
Theme: Women of the Bible
National Osteoporosis Awareness Month
16 June is British Nutrition Foundation's Healthy Eating Week

182

*FRIDAY 2nd

Amram's wife was Jochebed, she bare Moses - Numbers 26:59

YOU SHALL LIVE AND NOT DIE - Reading: Exodus 2:1-10

Jochebed was a woman of extraordinary faith and received honour in Hebrews 11. Jochebed was a wife and mother of three children from the tribe of Levi. During her third pregnancy, she was faced with the possibility of her infant's homicide pronounced by Pharoah upon the birth of every Hebrew male.

Blessed with a healthy son, Jochebed looked in the face of her baby, and saw that he was not only beautiful but was born for divine purpose. Determined that her son would live and not die, she set out to preserve his life. Had she perhaps heard how God preserved the life of Isaac through the faithfulness of Abraham?

Her faith and courage kept her baby hidden for three months until this visionary woman created a plan to transport her baby to safety on the very Nile that was supposed to kill him. Her faith paid dividends as her child was placed under the care and protection of the executioner's daughter, and Jochebed was paid to nurse her own son until he was weaned.

Jochebed lived up to her name, i.e., 'Jehovah is her glory'. Her son, Moses, became one of the greatest leaders, and author of the Torah. Her son, Aaron, became Israel's first high priest, and her daughter was a gifted musician and worshipper.

"A woman who fears the LORD, she shall be praised" (Proverbs 31:30)!

LEL

*National Fish & Chips Day

June 2023
Theme: Women of the Bible
National Osteoporosis Awareness Month
16 June is British Nutrition Foundation's Healthy Eating Week   183

SATURDAY 3rd

Abigail was a woman of good understanding - 1 Samuel 25:3

ABIGAIL: A WISE WOMAN - Reading: 1 Samuel 25:1-44

Abigail is a lesser-known heroine in the Scriptures.

She was a humble woman, married to Nabal who was a scoundrel! Abigail combined her wisdom with her wealth before an appearing enemy, to plead for the safety of her husband's household.

She is described as beautiful and intelligent. Her conduct indicates a most appealing character and unwavering faith (ref Wikipedia).

Abigail persuaded David not to shed blood and prophesied that he would be the next King of Israel. Abigail intervened secretly and provided food for David and his men. Abigail was not in agreement or defensive of her husband's behaviour, but she acted secretly in his favour.

As Christian women, we have got to be loyal to our calling, faithful even to death for what we believe, and mediate for others who may need our intervention. Trust God to lead and guide our steps so that we don't act impulsively, but demonstrate careful, rational thinking. In critical situations, make critical but wise decisions to get the best outcome.

Express your beauty, not just externally, but also from within by being tactful in your approach in the most appealing and inoffensive manner. Be patient, humble and wait on the Lord.

Be an Abigail-example, a woman of good understanding.

Missionary M Fraser

June 2023
Theme: Women of the Bible
National Osteoporosis Awareness Month
16 June is British Nutrition Foundation's Healthy Eating Week   184

SUNDAY 4th

With long life will I satisfy him, and shew him my salvation - Psalm 91:16

90 YEARS OLD BY THE GRACE OF GOD! - Reading: Psalm 91:16

Greetings to you all in Jesus Name.

I can truly say that: *"I am here today because God kept me".* He kept me so I was able to see and celebrate my 90th birthday in 2022. I am giving Him all of the glory and praise. *"With long life will I satisfy him" (Psalm 91:16)*, and He has blessed me with long life.

All the glory and honour belong to God because He has been my keeper and protector.

I was so overwhelmed with all the love I received on my birthday. I am so blessed to have you all in my life. Thanks for the cards, gifts, phone calls, visits, and words of encouragement.

Thank you all for making my 90th birthday a memorable one, but most of all I thank God for making it possible.

Mother Victoria Nicely

June 2023
Theme: Women of the Bible
National Osteoporosis Awareness Month
16 June is British Nutrition Foundation's Healthy Eating Week   185

MONDAY 5th

Let God arise, let his enemies be scattered - Psalm 68:1

PRECIOUS TO ME - Reading: Psalm 68:1-19

Jesus has done so much for me; He is precious to me.

I remember being in my kitchen using the blender and my finger somehow got caught in the machine. Part of my finger was cut off and the force from the electricity threw me up to the ceiling and landed me on the kitchen floor. I went to the hospital and they managed to stitch my finger back together.

Years afterwards, I was very sick in the hospital, nobody knew what was wrong. One of the nurses looked at me and told me that I was going to die. I told her I am not going to die because God showed me that He is not ready for me yet.

I am now 91 years old and still strong. Thank you, Jesus!

Mother Agatha Wallace

June 2023
Theme: Women of the Bible
National Osteoporosis Awareness Month
16 June is British Nutrition Foundation's Healthy Eating Week

186

TUESDAY 6th

I commend unto you Phoebe, which is a servant of the church - Romans 16:1

PHOEBE: RADIANT FOR JESUS - Reading: Romans 16:1-2 (NKJV)

Paul spoke about this notable lady, Phoebe, in Romans 16:1. Her name means shining, radiant.

Paul sent a letter of commendation about Phoebe to the church in Rome. He asked them to receive her and stated how. They should receive her as a believer and as they would have received Jesus Christ had He come to the church in Rome. The church was to give her any support and help that she needed from them. Phoebe, like ourselves going into a strange city, would need orientation, guidance, comfort, friendship and fellowship. They were to receive her in a worthy manner as believers should receive one another into their hearts, churches, homes, and with love as people of God.

Paul describes Phoebe as our sister, meaning that Christians are family. Phoebe was equally a sister of the saints in Rome as she was of Paul. She was an active member and deaconess of the church in Cenchrea. We see in Romans 16:2 that Paul described her as a *"succourer"*, i.e., someone who gives help in times of need or distress, to many including himself.

Like Phoebe, we are to graciously be good examples, shine our light into the darkened world so *"others can see our good works and glorify our father which is in heaven" (St Matthew 5:16).*

Missionary M Fraser

June 2023
Theme: Women of the Bible
National Osteoporosis Awareness Month
16 June is British Nutrition Foundation's Healthy Eating Week

WEDNESDAY 7th

Mary Magdalene told the disciples that she had seen the Lord - St John 20:18

NO LONGER BOUND - Reading: St Luke 8:1-2; St John 20:1-18

Today's main Scripture focus is on a woman in the Bible whose name is not only mentioned, but cited several times. Her name is Mary, she was born in an ancient Jewish city not far from the Sea of Galilee called Magdala, hence why she is referred to as Mary Magdalene.

We know that before Jesus met her, she was possessed with seven devils (*St Luke 8:1-2)* but Jesus delivered her from them all. Having experienced such a transformation and healing in her mind, she had a deep reverence and love for the Lord. She was also the first person to whom Jesus appeared after His resurrection. What an honour! From being one of society's outcasts to being the first to see the risen Lord!

As you read this page, you may reflect upon a time where you too were possessed by unclean spirits. When you are reminded by others, or think about some of the things you used to do, you wish you could forget. The memory brings a feeling of shame.

Yes, it is good to remember where we're coming from, this should prevent us from feeling superior to those who are still where we once were *(1 Corinthians 6:9-11)*, but we should not allow our past to keep us bound by guilt for sins for which we are now forgiven. David writes in Psalm 103:12: *"As far as the east is from the west, so far has (the LORD) removed our transgressions from us".*

JEJ

June 2023
Theme: Women of the Bible
National Osteoporosis Awareness Month
16 June is British Nutrition Foundation's Healthy Eating Week   188

THURSDAY 8th

Who knows (if you are) come to the kingdom for a time as this? - Esther 4:14

WOMEN: THE INFLUENCE OF MEEKNESS - Reading: Esther 4:1-17

Across many cultures women are often known for our culinary skills. Many a child rejoices at mom's home cooking after a time away at study or work.

Some cultures use the term 'turning the hand' to anything, i.e., being able to apply skill, including that of the culinary kind. We see seas of women in our churches who have such creative flare that, so much of the Christian community is nurtured in the hands of these beautiful women, whose ideas and hard work serve so well.

But our focus on women today is not only how she knows to stir ingredients in a recipe, but how she also knows how to mix ideas, glances, words, deeds, for God's kingdom. The prayer of a mother, the gentle hand of a sister, an encouraging or stern word. Women.

What is always present in a godly woman is meekness. Let's make no mistake, women are powerful influencers. Therefore, a godly woman knowing the influence she possesses must house her character in meekness to know when, where and how to use that influence.

Our words have power, our decisions have effect, our sensibilities set atmospheres. We must exercise meekness to use and not abuse what comes to us naturally.

"Lord Jesus we are your daughters and servants. We trust that only your plans and desire for our lives will be fulfilled. We use our gifts, talents and influence under your almighty anointing and will for our lives. We will be pleasing to you and minister to others. In Jesus' name. Amen".

Joy Lear-Bernard

June 2023
Theme: Women of the Bible
National Osteoporosis Awareness Month
16 June is British Nutrition Foundation's Healthy Eating Week

FRIDAY 9th

They came into a harlot's house, named Rahab, and lodged there - Joshua 2:1

DESPITE OUR HISTORY - Reading: Joshua 2:1-24

In today's lesson we read of two spies who went to view Jericho to see how it could be conquered.

Upon entering the city, they stayed overnight at a house which many Christians would walk past quickly. It was the house of a harlot!

Although their reason for going in there was not to evangelise, one of the outcomes was that Rahab and her family were saved. Full credit to those two men who maintained their integrity whilst in a sinful place. Rahab saw God in them and, although she was a prostitute, was able to tell them in advance that: *"The LORD has given you the land" (Joshua 2:9).*

Sometimes God places our blessing in an unexpected place and because of that, we miss it! If God can speak to a prophet through a donkey *(Numbers 22:21-39)*, He certainly can give a prophetic Word through a harlot or any other instrument which He chooses.

If you or I had to write Hebrews 11, the chances are that we would not record Rahab's name in the Gallery of Faith (v31). But the author of Hebrews gives Rahab special recognition. He deliberately mentions that Rahab was a harlot, not because she remained a harlot, but to let us know that God saves harlots!

God makes room for those who are not accepted, the ones whom others will whisper about their former life when they see them coming. He says: *"Rahab - she's mine"*! And ladies, all of us are His despite our history!

JEJ

June 2023
Theme: Women of the Bible
National Osteoporosis Awareness Month
16 June is British Nutrition Foundation's Healthy Eating Week

SATURDAY 10th

(Hagar) called the name of the LORD, Thou God seest me - Genesis 16:13

GOD KEPT ME - Reading: Psalm 27:1-14

Let me tell you just a little bit of my testimony!

Growing turbulence proved so challenging and though it quelled for a time, conflict and tension would resurface. By 2011 there was a breaking point. The following season became a ten-year 'hour of temptation'- there was trouble on every level.

Spiritually dark days and darker nights became 'normal'. I entered an even darker wilderness of depression, of shame and sickness. *"This is it"!* I thought life was over. The taunts, guilt, accusations, fears, were like boisterous angry waves. The marriage had crashed, numbness set in. Nonplussed by threats, gossip, sin, and pain, I wanted to escape anywhere out of the country. I thought about emigrating to start over again.

"Where is your God now? The children are better off without you"! But God burst through my darkest time with His light! He picked me up, sending help through caring brethren who prayed, supported, and stood in the gap for me. He has brought me out of a horrible pit.

With the time he has reset for me, I purpose to serve God with all my heart. He is faithful, my exceeding great reward. I testify that there is none like the Lord Jesus. *"Cast your cares on Him for he cares for you" (1 Peter 5:7).* There are no gaps in his Agape love for us. What a God, what a Mighty God we serve!

Name withheld

June 2023
Theme: Women of the Bible
National Osteoporosis Awareness Month
16 June is British Nutrition Foundation's Healthy Eating Week

191

SUNDAY 11th

Who can find a virtuous woman? Her price is far above rubies - Proverbs 31:10

THE CHARACTER OF A GODLY WOMAN - Reading: Proverbs 31:10-31

Godly is defined by the Cambridge dictionary as conforming to the laws and wishes of God. Jesus, the only wise God, gives us His Word as a pattern for godly behaviour. Let us strive to be doers of the Word:

Guides: *"The aged women likewise, that they be in behaviour as becometh holiness, ...teachers of good things" (Titus 2:3)*

Obedient: *"As obedient children, not fashioning yourselves according to the former lusts in your ignorance" (I Peter 1:14)*

Dedicated: *"And there was one Anna, a prophetess...which departed not from the temple, but served God with fastings and prayers night and day" (St Luke 2:36-37)*

Loving: *"And now I beseech thee, lady, not as though I wrote a new commandment unto thee, but that which we had from the beginning, that we love one another." (2 John 1:5)*

Yes to God: *"And Mary said, behold I am the servant of the Lord; let it be to me according to your word. And the angel departed from her." (St Luke 1:38)*

Min. K Codner

June 2023
Theme: Women of the Bible
National Osteoporosis Awareness Month
16 June is British Nutrition Foundation's Healthy Eating Week

MONDAY 12th

Remember Lot's wife - St Luke 17:32

TAKE YOUR MIND WITH YOU - Reading: Genesis 19:1-38

This is one of the shortest verses in the Bible, a warning to remember Lot's wife.

We don't know her name and there isn't really that much commentary about her in the Scriptures. So, what do we need to remember?

Lot's wife was comfortable living in a sinful environment although it corrupted the thinking and subsequently the behaviour of her husband *(Genesis 19:5-8)*, and also her daughters *(v. 30-38)*, and no doubt her own. She was attached to the riches of Sodom and her possessions. Despite being warned to *"escape for your life"* and *"look not behind thee"* (v17), only her body left Sodom but her mind remained.

The caution to remember Lot's wife is positioned within a discourse between Jesus and His disciples concerning *"The day when the Son of man shall be revealed"* *(v30)*. This helps us to understand the warning to: *"remember"*. We're living now in times very similar to the days of Sodom and Gomorrah. Sin is at its peak, Christ is about to return for His Church, yet there are many Christians who are relaxed because they have not discerned the season and are comfortable on earth.

Now is the time to cut emotional ties and attachments with every possession and connection to this world which could cause you to miss The Rapture. *"Set your affections on things above…" (Colossians 3:2)* so that you are ready to leave!

JEJ

June 2023
Theme: Women of the Bible
National Osteoporosis Awareness Month
16 June is British Nutrition Foundation's Healthy Eating Week   193

TUESDAY 13th

How is it that you, ask a drink from me, a Samaritan woman? - St John 4:9

RENDEZVOUS IN SAMARIA - Reading: St John 4:1-42 (NKJV)

As in His teachings that we see through parables, Jesus took this appointed opportunity to meet with the Woman of Samaria.

This He did to demonstrate the love for those whom many assume unlovable. It was a rendezvous He had to keep. The Samaritans were mainly a mixed race of Israelite-Assyrian people, born through intermarriage between Israelites and Gentiles after the Assyrian captivity of the Northern Kingdom of Israel. Samaria was once the capital of the Northern Kingdom hence the name Samaritans was given.

'Pure' Jews classed Samaritans as low, 'bottom of the barrel', unclean. Samaritans had a different religious system, temple and Pentateuch from the Jews. We see references in the New Testament of how Samaritans were scorned by Jews.

However, Jesus uses this meeting to show how we must reach out and love those who society rejects. The Samaritan woman was very well aware of this history with the Jews, so is taken aback by Jesus' request to share the water she draws from the well, an interaction she knew was not commonplace between Jews and Samaritans. Little did she know that this man knew her history and was about to change her story!

We must allow the Holy Spirit to guide us to opportunities to show God's love, to present to the lost the Living Water (Jesus) that never runs dry. Let us pray for those days that we may have a rendezvous, just as Jesus had, to love and minister to those that others call *"common and unclean" (Acts 10:14-15).*

(Definition of Rendezvous: a meeting at an agreed time and place)

Hedy Edmund

June 2023
Theme: Women of the Bible
National Osteoporosis Awareness Month
16 June is British Nutrition Foundation's Healthy Eating Week

194

*WEDNESDAY 14th

The women said, blessed be the LORD, which hath not left thee…- Ruth 4:14

GENERATIONS WORKING TOGETHER - Reading: Ruth 4:14-17; Titus 2:1-15

I greet you in the most precious name of Jesus Christ.

Today I take great pleasure in writing these few lines as women working in unity. When the older and the younger women work together in this ministry, sometimes the older women can strengthen the younger women in prayer and fasting, and so likewise the younger women can also do for the older generation. Each one of us can encourage one another, we learn from each other.

In Titus 2:1, 3-5, 7 Paul says: *"But speak thou the things which become sound doctrine. That the aged women, likewise, that they be in behaviour as becometh holiness, not false accusers, not given to much wine, teachers of good things; that they may teach the young women to be sober, to love their husbands, to love their children. To be discreet, chaste, keepers at home, good, obedient to their own husbands, that the word of God be not blasphemed…in all things showing thyself a pattern of good works: in doctrine showing uncorruptness, gravity, sincerity".*

May God continue to keep and bless us in heavenly places.

Missionary Joycelin Griffiths

*World Blood Donor Day

June 2023
Theme: Women of the Bible
National Osteoporosis Awareness Month
16 June is British Nutrition Foundation's Healthy Eating Week   195

THURSDAY 15th

Rebekah loved Jacob - Genesis 25:28

PARENTAL PARTIALITY - Reading: Genesis 25:27-34

In Genesis we read of the relationship between Isaac, Rebekah and their two children.

Isaac and Rebekah were the parents of Esau and Jacob who were born fraternal twins. Isaac loved Esau, (the hunter) because he did eat of his venison, but Rebekah loved Jacob. When Rebekah was pregnant, God told her that there were: *"two nations in her womb, one people stronger than the other, the elder shall serve the younger" (Genesis 25:23)*. By this Rebekah may have understood that Jacob was going to be greater than Esau in the end.

However, the behaviour of both parents was wrong and biased. It is clear that the parents showed partiality, each to their favourite twin. Partial behaviour, even towards one's children, is unacceptable according to the Scriptures, e.g., Romans 2:11, James 2:1-4, Ephesians 6:9. Being partial brings division. It can also cause distrust and bitter rivalry, and result in a feeling of insecurity.

Every child is unique and special, and should be made to feel valued without being compared or measured against the achievements or abilities of a sibling. Openly preferring one child over their siblings can cause jealousy and family tension. It does not encourage a healthy relationship in the home, and can generate all kinds of problems in the long-term.

Mothers, let us carefully guard against favouritism.

Missionary M Fraser

June 2023
Theme: Women of the Bible
National Osteoporosis Awareness Month
16 June is British Nutrition Foundation's Healthy Eating Week   196

FRIDAY 16th

Absalom, son of David had a fair sister, named Tamar - 2 Samuel 13:1

BROKEN BUT BEAUTIFUL - Reading: 2 Samuel 13: 1-22

Tamar was the daughter of King David, sister of Absalom and the half-sister of Amnon.

She was young, kind, innocent and trusting of those whom she loved; there was no reason to be otherwise. In her innocence, she could never have anticipated the dreadful tragedy that would befall her when she went to the home of her brother, Amnon, to cook for him when he tricked their father into believing that he was sick and in need of care.

Amnon raped his sister and then, filled with hatred, had her thrown out of his house and bolted the door. Tamar was inconsolable. Absalom found her and asked if Amnon had been with her *(2 Samuel 13:20)*. Why would Absalom ask such a question? Had he seen some signs in Amnon's behaviour of his intentions?

Absalom told Tamar not to say anything about her ordeal. David heard about the crime committed but, although he was angry, we don't read that he did anything about it. You too may have had a similar experience to that of Tamar, or some form of domestic abuse or violence, and have been warned to keep it quiet. But being unable to talk about it is destroying you.

Tamar changed the clothes that she used to wear. After being violated she no longer dressed in the vibrant colours that the king's daughters who were virgins wore. But she was still a princess, a child of the king (and so are you)! She was still beautiful (and so are you)! She still had purpose and so do you!

JEJ

(Please see our Support Directory at the back of this book if you have been affected by today's reading)

June 2023
Theme: Women of the Bible
National Osteoporosis Awareness Month
16 June is British Nutrition Foundation's Healthy Eating Week   197

SATURDAY 17ᵗʰ

Jesus touched (the hand of Peter's mother-in-law) - St Matthew 8:14-15

HEALER, HEALER, HEALER! - Reading: St Matthew 8:1-15

I want to share this testimony regarding how much my precious Lord has done for me. My Lord has been my strength.

I was diagnosed with Multiple Sclerosis in my early 20s but I am still standing tall in my Lord's name. I am not on any medication; my Lord is my medication.

In early 2018, I was diagnosed with breast cancer. Amen, Amen, I am in remission; next year will be my 5-year mark.

As well as everything else, along came Fibromyalgia but I am fighting on with my Lord.

I migrated to live in Toronto and went blind in my left eye. Again, I give thanks I am healed!

One thing I know is that my Lord is my healer and deliverer. Do not worry, the blood of Jesus ALWAYS prevails!

Joyce M Baum

June 2023
Theme: Women of the Bible
National Osteoporosis Awareness Month
16 June is British Nutrition Foundation's Healthy Eating Week

198

*SUNDAY 18th

(The little maid) said: my master needs the prophet - 2 Kings 5:3 (NIV)

NAMELESS BUT NEEDED - Reading: 2 Kings 5:1-14

Whilst watching sports with my husband and sons, I will ask them who is the under-dog? Regardless of who is expected to lose, that's the team that I am going to support and want to win the game.

This is also a principle I have adopted in my life and ministry; I find myself drawn to those who are marginalised, left behind, the last and the lost. While it is not always the case, I find at times that we as women are the ones that are in these spaces. However, it takes a special kind of grace and strength to overcome and succeed when the light shines brighter on others than on you.

The Word of God is filled with the testimonies of those who society rejected, those who were at the bottom, seemingly without hope or direction, and yet Jesus finds them, heals them, empowers them, restores, and renews them.

Naaman was a man of wealth and military power, but the Bible said that he was a leper. His healing was activated by a young woman who would have been overlooked but only for her ability to serve as a maid. She was a young woman of great faith; she had confidence in the ability of Jehovah to make good on the promises that He had made.

I thank God for you, my dear sister. Wherever you are reading this, I thank God for you! I thank God for your faith, your strength; I thank God for your healing, your resilience to keep going when you feel like giving up. May the God of this young, nameless woman inspire us to speak even when no one might want to listen. Jesus Himself was the stone that the builders rejected, but He became the Chief Cornerstone.

First Lady Yolanda Edmund

*Father's Day UK

June 2023
Theme: Women of the Bible
National Osteoporosis Awareness Month
16 June is British Nutrition Foundation's Healthy Eating Week   199

MONDAY 19th

I remember the genuine faith of your mother Eunice - 2 Timothy 1:5 (CEV)

JESUS IS MY DELIVERER - Reading: 2 Timothy 1:1-5

Two years ago, I suddenly became unwell and would have died but God blocked it.

This sickness came upon me suddenly. I went to bed feeling well. I read my Bible, prayed and fell asleep. When I got up the following morning, I wasn't feeling myself. I developed severe diarrhoea which continued for a few days. It affected my appetite and I was unable to eat. As a result, I was tired and sleepy. I continued to take my blood pressure and warfarin tablets. I was getting weaker and weaker each day and I was unable to walk by myself, I was so weak and tired and just wanted to sleep.

My daughter noticed and contacted the rest of my children to make them aware of my condition. My children and grandchildren prayed for me. The ambulance came and the paramedics examined me; they confirmed that my temperature was 38.9. They planned to admit me into hospital but warned that the entire hospital was full of Covid-19. The family was concerned about this and the paramedics didn't force me to go to hospital but encouraged me to attend.

My condition deteriorated during the night and my daughter called the doctor the next day. He said that I should be admitted into hospital immediately. When I arrived at the hospital, they put me on a ward that was Covid-19 free! Bearing in mind that the paramedics had told us that the hospital was full of the virus, God had a ward for me that was free of Covid-19.

I was so severely ill that I wondered how I got to the hospital. They examined me and gave me a chest X-ray and the doctors told me that when they looked at my lungs it was 'Ground Glass Opacity' which means that's how sick I was, it showed up on my lungs. I was also anaemic and received a blood transfusion, and remained in hospital for a few days. I was finally discharged from hospital and, Saints of God, I am still on the land of the living, praising and worshipping my God.

St Mark 12:30 KJV says: *"And thou shalt love the Lord thy God with all thy heart, and with all thy soul, and with all thy mind, and with all thy strength: this is the first commandment".*

My daughter reminded me that, just before I went into the ambulance feeling very sick and helpless and ready to die, I'd said that I just needed to get to the hospital to get help and recover, and promised that I would return home in a few days, and had told the family not to worry. Brethren, I didn't remember saying those words. I know it

June 2023
Theme: Women of the Bible
National Osteoporosis Awareness Month
16 June is British Nutrition Foundation's Healthy Eating Week   200

was the Holy Ghost reassuring my children that God was in control from the time I got into the ambulance until I came back. Thank you, Jesus. Hallelujah!

I lost so much weight and still haven't regained what I lost. However, my doctor took me off the blood pressure and warfarin tablets permanently. I give God all the glory honour and praise. He healed my body and I am alive to give my testimony.

Through it all I have learned to trust in Jesus. *"He is my Shepherd I shall not want".* This is why my favourite Scripture is Psalm 23.

Mother Marian Bell

June 2023
Theme: Women of the Bible
National Osteoporosis Awareness Month
16 June is British Nutrition Foundation's Healthy Eating Week   201

TUESDAY 20th

Elijah said unto her, make me a little cake first - 1 Kings 17:13

THERE IS MORE – Reading: 1 Kings 17:8-16

Elijah was sent to Zarephath by God's instruction.

He was told that his hostess, a widow, would look after him. Yet when he got to the widow's house, and asked for bread and water, she told him that she only had a handful of meal remaining, and after eating whatever she could make from it, she and her son would die.

Has God ever spoken to you, and you know that it really was Him, but when you acted upon what He told you to do, you wondered: *"Was that really God? Did I hear right"?*

Elijah's faith had to be firm to rebuke any possible doubt arising, to ignore the widow's prognosis of imminent death, and to remember that God said: *"I have commanded a widow woman there to sustain you" (1 Kings 17:9)!* She didn't resist making Elijah a cake first because, before Elijah arrived, God had worked on the widow's heart, making her willing to sustain His servant. Even though the widow's container was now empty of flour, Elijah knew that there was more! Samuel was sent by God to the house of Jesse to anoint the next king of Israel. It looked like all of Jesse's sons were present, but by the Spirit, Samuel knew there must be more.

Sometimes do you pray: *"Lord, this can't be it, there's got to be more!"?*

When the facts seem to contradict a direct Word from the Lord, we keep walking by faith and not by sight…

JEJ

June 2023
Theme: Women of the Bible
National Osteoporosis Awareness Month
16 June is British Nutrition Foundation's Healthy Eating Week

WEDNESDAY 21st

(Jesus') mother said to the servants, do it - St John 2:5

WHATEVER HE TELLS YOU, DO IT - Reading: St John 2:1-12

You may know the chorus of this song: "*Yes Lord, yes Lord, from the bottom of my heart, to the depths of my soul. Yes Lord! Completely yes, my soul says yes*".

If only that was true all of the time!

God often speaks to us to do something, and we hesitate rather than moving into action. Of course, there are times when we need to seek confirmation and direction, but sometimes immediate action is required.

At a wedding in Cana there was an emergency, a crisis, they had run out of wine! Thank goodness that Jesus was there, and someone who knew that Jesus was no ordinary person was also there. Mary was able to confidently instruct the servants that whatsoever Jesus told them to do, they should do it without querying. Mary couldn't be more specific because she did not know how Jesus would fix it, she just knew that He would. To prevent the servants from coming back to her to question whatever the instruction turned out to be, Mary used a catch-all statement of: "*whatsoever*".

You may be wondering how God is going to solve a complex situation on your behalf. Don't be surprised, you may have to get involved, just like the servants had to fill six large jugs to the brim with ordinary water when what they needed was wine! You may wonder how will what God told you to do change anything. Do it and see!

JEJ

June 2023
Theme: Women of the Bible
National Osteoporosis Awareness Month
16 June is British Nutrition Foundation's Healthy Eating Week

THURSDAY 22nd

There was a certain woman named Lydia, a seller of purple - Acts 16:14

LYDIA: A DEVOUT CHRISTIAN WOMAN - Reading: Acts 16:11-15

Lydia, a woman whose name is derived from Greek origin and means beautiful, noble-one or a worshipper of God (Ref Wikipedia.org).

Lydia's career was a seller of purple, possibly textiles, which was a luxury item in the ancient Mediterranean. Purple is often associated with royalty, nobility and represents wisdom, dignity, grandeur, independence and peace: Ref:bourncreative.com.

Lydia from Thyatira, heard the good news of Salvation. Note: Thyatira is also mentioned in Revelation 2:18-29. God opened Lydia's heart, she showed a humble trusting spirit, became receptive of the gospel and was baptised along with her household. She is considered to be the first recorded convert to Christianity in Europe.

A generous, hospitable woman, Lydia is a great example for us to follow. We may not have a large house to accommodate many visitors but we can minister in so many different ways. There are always opportunities to make a difference in the lives of others.

Lydia is still remembered for her selfless contributions to early Christianity. Lydia opened her house to travelling missionaries like St Paul and his travelling companions. She's a good role model of evangelism to our families and others whom we know. We too have a duty to be committed supporters of the Church and serve others to help win them to Christ.

Missionary M Fraser

June 2023
Theme: Women of the Bible
National Osteoporosis Awareness Month
16 June is British Nutrition Foundation's Healthy Eating Week

204

FRIDAY 23rd

Miriam took a timbrel and all the women went out after her... - Exodus 15:20

THE POWERFUL MOVE OF A PROPHETESS - Reading: Exodus 15:1-27

The beginning of Miriam's instruction from God came not in her mere words, but also in the actions of her hands: *"And Miriam took a timbrel in her hand" (Exodus 15:20)* such was the clarity and obedience to God's Spirit that *"all the women went out after her"*. We need such power today.

There is something about prophecy that demands action. It requires those who believe what God has said to **do it**! The women worshipped too, and though no discussion was exchanged, the Bible says Miriam answered the women. How could she have answered when there is no conversation recorded?! Deep truly called to deep here. They were so locked into what God was doing that heaven spoke and they followed. Such is the elevation of God's Sovereignty over our mere humanity that His Spirit converses. Without words, without intellect, discussion or debate, the people of God employed boldness and obedience to move in the moment!

His command moves through His people with power. We are in an awesome time where God's will is being done so profoundly, that those of us who yearn to be used of Him must present our bodies, holy, acceptable to God so that His Spirit can use even our shadows to heal *(Acts 5:15)*.

Our music and timbrels must not just create noise, but a prophetic change! How seriously must we take our actions that they reflect God? When Miriam moved, she launched an army of worshippers.

Let's look for the victory in armies being raised for His kingdom, and truly desire that God use us!

Joy Lear-Bernard

June 2023
Theme: Women of the Bible
National Osteoporosis Awareness Month
16 June is British Nutrition Foundation's Healthy Eating Week

SATURDAY 24th

Deborah, a prophetess, she judged Israel - Judges 4:4

DEBORAH: EPITOMIZING WHAT SUCCESS LOOKS LIKE - Read: Judges 4 & 5

At the time of my writing this article, Serena Williams is playing her last game of professional competition tennis, as the greatest player of all time. The success that she has attained reaches far beyond her early ambitions as a tennis player.

Success often looks very different to the human imagination than to God who makes all things possible. Deborah's successes, in Judges chapters 4 and 5, are largely direct outcomes of her ability to concurrently trust God with every aspect of her life *(Judges 4:4)*.

Surely, in the age of the Hebrew judges during which Deborah was executing all of the above roles, the success of one area depended on how she managed the other areas. That is very much the case today. We are wives, mothers, women with vocations/careers, prophetesses, ministers, administrators, entrepreneurs, carers, and the list goes on! The pressure is on to be great at everything all the time. But one thing is clear: Deborah was unequivocal about her connection to and direction from God. This is what led to success in each area of her life, and to her multi-dimensional leadership model that is still so inspirational today:

1. Deborah served people in her community *(Judges 4:5)* – SERVANT LEADERSHIP

2. Deborah under prophetic anointing refused to assimilate into Barak's mode of thought and lack of action by giving clear direction *(Judges 4:6-14)* – AUDACIOUS LEADERSHIP

3. Under Deborah's leadership she ensures that God gets the glory every time *(Judges 5:3)* – HUMBLE LEADERSHIP

The question is:
1. Are you trusting God with every area of what you've been called to do or to be?

2. Are you serving?

3. Are you audacious when God directs you?

4. Are you humble?

If your answer is yes to the above questions, you are a modern-day Deborah. Stay focused and practice your Victory Song.

Sister Latoya Foster
June 2023
Theme: Women of the Bible
National Osteoporosis Awareness Month
16 June is British Nutrition Foundation's Healthy Eating Week

SUNDAY 25th

And (Rachel) said, the LORD shall add to me another son - Genesis 30:24

SPEAK OVER YOURSELF - Reading: Genesis 30: 1-24

Rachel was the younger sister of Leah and favourite wife of Jacob.

Rachel was barren for many years after marrying Jacob. We feel her sorrowful anguish of her condition in Genesis 30:1 where she exclaims to Jacob: *"Give me children, or else I die"!*

Sometimes we vent our frustrations to the wrong person. We complain to someone who cannot help or change things for us, they are as helpless as we are. Really, the passion of Rachel's feelings would have been better directed to Almighty God.

When she cried unto God, in time: *"God remembered Rachel, and hearkened to her and opened her womb" (v22)*. After Rachel received what she thought she would never have, she prophesied to herself: *"The LORD shall add to me another son" (v24)*.

From time-to-time we long for someone to 'speak a Word into our life', but there are moments when by faith we need to speak over ourselves and declare what shall be! Rachel's self-prophecy did not come to pass until years later. Benjamin was many years younger than Joseph but those prophetic words remained in orbit until they materialised:

"Lord, please don't let this be a one-off blessing. Please bless me like that again!"

JEJ

June 2023
Theme: Women of the Bible
National Osteoporosis Awareness Month
16 June is British Nutrition Foundation's Healthy Eating Week   207

MONDAY 26th

Vashti, the queen, made a feast for the women in the royal house - Esther 1:9

WOMEN AT THE KING'S TABLE - Reading: Esther 1:1-22

Throughout Scripture, the beautiful tapestry of women who served God was given to undergird us as women of God today.

Women; God's incredible creation, a reflective part of His nature. Still today the mandate for women of God to reflect Him remains essential.

The king in Esther 1 planned an extravagant feast yet his wife Vashti, knowing his heart, had her own agenda and maintained a feast of her own.

If we truly desire to be women of God, our timing, our feastings (teachings) will not be with contrary motivation. We cannot be both Esther who was purged and perfected by her process, and Vashti who no longer delighted in presenting herself to the king.

We also have a sobering and weighty responsibility that when we gather as women, we do not alter God's decree, nor set another throne, but stand in the anointing of God. There is a threat against women to stand in God's divine truth because Scripture has shown what true Women of God can accomplish in Christ when we are sold out for Him.

We are indeed beautified with this Gospel of Salvation. Let's be aware that every conversation, phone call, platform and opportunity to nurture the hearts of others towards Jesus, is an invitation to His holy table.

We are not afraid for our own agendas to dissolve; we are called to deeper and anointed for greater. We are called to be the Esthers who are fearless in pursuit of saving a nation and bringing them to the King's table.

Joy Lear-Bernard

June 2023
Theme: Women of the Bible
National Osteoporosis Awareness Month
16 June is British Nutrition Foundation's Healthy Eating Week

TUESDAY 27th

As Peter knocked, a damsel came to hearken named Rhoda - Acts 12:13

RHODA'S UNWAVERING FAITH - Reading: Acts 12:1-19

Peter has been mentioned several times in Scripture, but Rhoda only once.

To put context to today's focus verse we need to look briefly at what had happened to Peter. Peter was imprisoned by Herod Agrippa I after the execution of James, son of Zebedee, with a view to have him killed also. Peter was asleep between two soldiers and bound with chains. However, Peter was relaxed enough to have fallen asleep despite his pending death sentence.

An angel came and led Peter out of the prison. Miraculously, nobody saw or heard the escape. Meanwhile, many brethren were at the house of Mary, John Mark's mother, praying and beseeching God to release Peter from prison. During the service, as his first stop after rescue, Peter went to Mary's house and knocked on the door of the gate. Rhoda (her name means Rose), a servant girl, went to answer.

Rhoda was so excited when she heard Peter's voice outside that she ran and told the others that Peter was at the door. With all that excitement, Rhoda forgot to open the door! Ironically, none of those who had just been praying for Peter believed Rhoda's report; they said that she was mad! When Rhoda insisted it was Peter, they then said it was his angel *(Acts 12:13-16)*.

Though they did not believe her, Rhoda held her conviction that she was speaking the truth, she knew Peter's voice. Likewise, when we are sure that something is right, or that God has spoken to us, we should not let anyone sway our belief. We should not be intimidated by ridicule. Rhoda was told that she was mad, quite a belittling statement, possibly because of her young age or her servant status.

We may face a similar predicament but let us show faith in our prayers that God will answer, like Rhoda's own prayer was answered for Peter.

Missionary M. Fraser

June 2023
Theme: Women of the Bible
National Osteoporosis Awareness Month
16 June is British Nutrition Foundation's Healthy Eating Week   209

WEDNESDAY 28th

O Lord, my daughter is grievously vexed with a devil - St Matthew 15:22

A CRY FOR HELP - Reading: St Matthew 15:21-28

A woman, not known by name, known as a sinner, and a descendant from Canaan.

She knew that she didn't have the rights and privileges afforded to God's chosen people. In desperation she cried unto Jesus, reverencing him as Lord. She first asked for mercy *(St Matthew 15:22),* believing she did not deserve forgiveness for sins.

She must have heard about what Jesus had done for others, and believed that only He had the power to heal her daughter: *"Faith comes by hearing and hearing by the word of God" (Romans 10:17).*

In a state of distress, she cried with such desperation that the disciples begged Jesus to send her away *(St Matthew 15:23).* How many times are people silenced when they cry desperately to God so that it doesn't draw unwanted attention, or disrupt agendas?

Jesus listened attentively, allowing the woman to seek His help, and as her faith increased, she worshipped Him, saying: *"Lord, help me" (Matthew 15:25).* Her persistence was faith in action, showing faith by works *(James 2:18).* She didn't give up, knowing only Jesus could help her.

How desperate are you to have God deal with your grievous situation? When we cry out to God, we will get His full attention and be strengthened *(Psalm 138:3).* Jesus said the woman had great faith, and her daughter was made whole that same hour.

Tell God what you need, increase your faith and God will deal with your grievous situation. Be persistent like the Canaanite woman. Whatever you need, seek God until you get it *(St Luke 11:5-13).* Whilst seeking, give Jesus what He deserves - worship!

Rachel Lewin

June 2023
Theme: Women of the Bible
National Osteoporosis Awareness Month
16 June is British Nutrition Foundation's Healthy Eating Week   210

THURSDAY 29th

And Adam called his wife's name Eve - Genesis 3:20

LIFE - Reading: Genesis 2:18-25; 3:20

Eve is often thought of in relation to her contribution to the fall of humankind into sin, but she is more than her mistakes and failures.

Eve was the embodiment of God's vision of a perfect woman; complete, holy, and pure. She was a seamstress *(Genesis 3:7)*, she supported and helped her husband to look after the garden of Eden. Eve was the first woman to be called 'wife', and the only woman in the Scriptures literally given to a man by God to be his companion and counterpart.

Adam named his wife Eve meaning *"life"* which spoke prophetically of her purpose and destiny *(Genesis 3:20)*. In Eve was life; she was the mother of us all and through the seed of the woman, victory over spiritual death was conquered through Jesus Christ. Just as Eve was created from the wounded side of Adam, so The Church was birthed from Jesus' wounded side *(St John 19:33-37)*.

Just like Eve, you are more than any mistake or failures, there is life in you. God's plans and thoughts towards you are that you live peacefully, have hope in your future and fulfil your purpose *(Jeremiah 29:11; St John 10:10)*. He has not given up on you, Jesus came that you might have life!

LEL

June 2023
Theme: Women of the Bible
National Osteoporosis Awareness Month
16 June is British Nutrition Foundation's Healthy Eating Week   211

*FRIDAY 30th

Greet Priscilla and Aquila my helpers in Christ Jesus - Romans 16:3

HELPERS IN THE MINISTRY - Reading: Acts 18:24-26; Romans 16:3-5

Priscilla and Aquila were a married couple, they are mentioned more than once in the New Testament.

They were tent makers and friends of Paul the apostle who was also a tent maker. They met Paul in Corinth having left Rome due to the expulsion of Jews from Italy by the emperor, Claudius. Aquila was a Jew.

God knows how to relocate us for His purpose and His glory. It may be by expulsion or rejection. God may turn our comfortable nest upside down to get us out. But whatever the method, it propels us to where God wants us to be next.

As well as being extremely hospitable in accommodating Paul and holding church services in their home, one of the highlights of Priscilla's and Aqulia's joint ministry was their expounding the Word of God in greater depth to Apollos. He was an excellent Bible scholar but knew only about John's baptism. Priscilla and her husband patiently walked Apollos, and others, through the Scriptures to bring doctrinal enlightenment, and build and grow their faith.

Everybody will not have the fame or anointing of Paul, but each 'Paul' needs helpers to work with them to nurture the seeds sown of the gospel of Jesus Christ, and to help them to grow. Is that person you?

JEJ

National Cream Tea Day

June 2023
Theme: Women of the Bible
National Osteoporosis Awareness Month
16 June is British Nutrition Foundation's Healthy Eating Week

212

OSTEOPOROSIS

The word osteoporosis literally means "porous bones". Osteoporosis is a condition that weakens bones; it is reasonable to describe the condition as 'thinning' of the bones, making them fragile and more likely to fracture (break).

Although losing bone is a normal part of ageing, some people lose bone much faster than normal. This can lead to osteoporosis and an increased risk of broken bones. Risk factors include:

• the menopause

• taking high-dose steroid tablets for more than 3 months

• long-term use of some medicines that can affect bone strength or hormone levels, such as anti-oestrogen tablets that are sometimes used after breast cancer

• Some medical conditions such as rheumatoid arthritis, SLE, thyroid problems, coeliac disease

• a family history of osteoporosis – particularly a hip fracture in a parent

• having or having had an eating disorder such as anorexia or bulimia

• having a low BMI - being underweight

• not exercising regularly

• heavy drinking and smoking

A diagnosis of osteoporosis is often only made when a fall or sudden impact causes a bone to fracture. The most common injuries in people with osteoporosis occur in the wrist, hip and spinal bones (vertebrae). However, breaks can also happen in other bones, such as in the arm or pelvis. Sometimes a cough or sneeze can cause a broken rib or the partial collapse of one of the vertebrae.

If your doctor suspects you have osteoporosis, they can work out your future risk of breaking a bone using a special risk calculator. You may also be referred for a bone density scan (Dexa scan).

Osteoporosis can be treated with bone strengthening medicines. However, there are steps you can take to improve your bone health and reduce your chances of developing osteoporosis. These include:

• taking regular exercise to keep your bones as strong as possible

• healthy eating – including foods rich in calcium and vitamin D.

• taking a daily vitamin D supplement - discuss with your GP.

June 2023
Theme: Women of the Bible
National Osteoporosis Awareness Month
16 June is British Nutrition Foundation's Healthy Eating Week   213

• making lifestyle changes – such as giving up smoking and reducing your alcohol consumption

If you're diagnosed with osteoporosis, there are steps you can take to reduce your chances of a fall, such as removing hazards from your home and having regular sight and hearing tests.

The Royal Osteoporosis Society is the UK's national charity for osteoporosis. It has detailed information on osteoporosis prevention and treatment and a free telephone helpline.

Submitted by: Dr Carol S. Ighofose GP, Author
BSC (Hons); MBChB; MRCGP

June 2023
Theme: Women of the Bible
National Osteoporosis Awareness Month
16 June is British Nutrition Foundation's Healthy Eating Week   214

July

Back to Basics

SATURDAY 1st

Only Jesus has the power to save! His name is the only one...- Acts 4:12 (CEV)

JESUS WAITED FOR ME - Reading: Acts 4:1-22

When I was five years old my mother left me and my siblings in Jamaica with our grandmother, and came to England to join with her husband to make a better life for us. Our grandmother took good care of us and made sure that we went to Sunday school and Sunday night service each week. It was a New Testament Church of God.

I left school at sixteen years old and moved to live and work in Kingston. After some years, I had my first son and went back to live with my grandmother. I would still visit the church but was not a Christian.

One day I met a lady who invited me to come to her church which was Emmanuel Apostolic Pentecostal Church. I went with her that night, and listened to the teaching and preaching very carefully. I was so overjoyed and happy with what I had heard.

After the service, the pastor, Bishop Clovis Muschette, came and greeted me and asked whether I would like to be saved. I told him that I was living with a young man and would have to think about it, but I carried on going to church.

After two years I got married and then decided to get saved. I got baptised in the name of the Lord Jesus, and was filled with the Holy Ghost six months later. I really enjoyed the church and serving the Lord, walking in the Spirit.

Missionary Joycelin Griffiths

SUNDAY 2nd

Love your enemies, pray for those who mistreat you - St Matthew 5:44 (CEV)

A HUGE CHALLENGE: LOVE YOUR ENEMIES! - Reading: St Luke 6:27-36

Jesus rejected the teaching of those who said one should hate one's enemy *(St Matthew 5:43)*.

To love your enemy is to be able, from your heart, to put aside any wrongs that they have done to you, and love them as you love yourself. I think that this might be one of the most difficult Scriptures.

Love is the fulfilling, i.e., complete obedience, of the law *(Romans 13:10)*. Jesus not only taught but put into action the same when He was crucified: *"Father, forgive them; for they know not what they do" (St Luke 23:34)*. Stephen prayed for his enemies whilst they stoned him to death *(Acts 7:60)*. In spite of the pain that our enemies cause us, without retaliation, we must still love them, and pray for them too!

Women, let me share a personal experience! A family member and I were falsely accused; an allegation was made against us by a church sister and the police became involved. Before the real scenario unfolded, I dreamt of what was going to happen; I felt the same turmoil and anguish in the dream as it was when the dream came to pass.

I questioned God, maybe somewhat impertinent you may think, but I asked God how He could expect me to love someone who has caused such injury to me and my family. Did He really expect me to forgive them, pray for them, and do good to them when they caused me to suffer such an atrocity and cruelty? It was so hard even to pray. But strength came from God, out of whose mouth came those same words written in St Matthew 5:44.

Eventually, my accuser confessed that they had been lying, but refused to go to the police. However, after a long wait for the investigation to be completed, we were exonerated. Thank you, Jesus!

Sometime after all of this, I was able to open my door to that same person for a much-needed cup of tea and biscuits. I saw them struggling, staggering and falling on the street, and I took them to the doctor and waited with them until their family arrived. I visited them throughout their sickness. I offered them comfort and reassurance, and prayed for them in their distress.

I am telling you that living-out St Matthew 5:44 is intensely hard. It can only be achieved by the grace of God assisting, with obedience to God's Word, and by practicing holy habits.

Missionary M Fraser

July 2023
Back to Basics
10 – 18 July: National Doughnut Week (The Children's Trust
- supporting children with brain injury)

MONDAY 3rd

Sanctify them through thy Word: thy Word is truth - St John 17:17

THE WORD MANIFESTED IN ME - Reading: St John 17:1-26

The Word of God is a manifestation of the mind and will of God.

"In the beginning was the word, and the word was with God, and the word was God" (St John 1:1).

The Word of God is in written form (from the Logos), and in spoken form (Rhema word). The Lord communicates to us through His Holy Scriptures and through anointed, inspired preachers and teachers.

St John 17:1-26 is known as the 'High Priestly Prayer'. Verse 17 expresses the need for sanctification through the Word of God. The Word is a cleansing agent: *"Now ye are clean through the word which I have spoken unto you" (St John 15:3).* God speaks to us through His words to cleanse and purify us. The Lord has set us apart for His purpose. There has to be a transformation of character, but if we don't believe His words, which are *"truth"*, we can't be sanctified through them. No change will take place, and God's purpose will not be fulfilled in our lives.

"The Word of God is powerful, effective and penetrative. It is a discerner of the thoughts and intents of the heart" (Hebrews 4:12).

Question: What do we therefore have to do with the Word of God?

Answer: Read it, study it, meditate on it, memorize it, believe it, apply it and share it!

Min. Genevieve Dinnall

July 2023
Back to Basics
10 – 18 July: National Doughnut Week (The Children's Trust
- supporting children with brain injury)

218

TUESDAY 4th

Out of their belly shall flow rivers of living water - St John 7:38

THE WELL WITHIN - Reading: St John 7:32-53

I visited Bethel Gibson Road church a long time ago to get two of my babies blessed. In those days the church building was not as large as it is now, they were only on what is now the rostrum.

When I arrived, I had a peep inside before going in. It was just the choir in there getting ready to begin. I felt such a conviction when I saw them, even before one word had been spoken.

That day, Bishop Dunn preached an anointed sermon from Acts 2:38, followed by an Altar Call. I don't know what happened, but I suddenly had a pain in my belly that I had never felt before, and I started not just to cry but to bawl. I bawled so much that the only thing left was for me to speak in tongues, but I did not.

I was taken to where the baptism pool was, and someone asked me if I'd like to be baptised. I said no because I was living with the father of my children, and was not married to him. Bishop Dunn came over and asked if my boyfriend would come to service in the evening. I said that I didn't know but would ask him.

After the day's service, some of the Church Sisters asked me if I knew what I did today. I guessed they were referring to me bawling. I asked my partner to come with me to church that night and he agreed. Bishop spoke with us and offered to help get us married. We got married on a Saturday and both got baptised the next day.

But I received the Holy Ghost before I got baptised; it was on a Tuesday night. I was sitting next to a young lady and thought that I saw one of the deacons beckoning to me to come forward for prayer. I went to the altar only to realise that the deacon had been signalling to the lady beside me, he was not calling me. However, Jesus was calling me because I received the Holy Ghost that night. There was an evangelist visiting from Jamaica. She prayed with me and shortly after, as I was coming through with the Holy Ghost, Bishop Dunn came and stood nearby.

I started to speak in tongues but Bishop felt that I was copying his tongues. He said: *"That's mine!"*. I carried on reaching out for God until I got 'my own' tongues. I heard when Bishop shouted out: *"YES!"*. I carried on speaking in tongues and saw a vision of a bright light and a large green field. In the field there was a man dancing and speaking heaven's language. I felt so drunk with the anointing of the Holy Ghost that I had to be carried home. It was an experience that I will never forget!

July 2023
Back to Basics
10 – 18 July: National Doughnut Week (The Children's Trust
 - supporting children with brain injury)

I always say that you must get to know Jesus for yourself to stay firm and keep the anointing going. Keep in contact with God, keep your mind stayed on Him.

Mother Eulalee Evans

WEDNESDAY 5th

Divided tongues, as of fire... sat upon each of them - Acts 2:3 (NKJV)

PENTECOSTAL FIRE! - Reading: Acts 2:1-13

I had been raised going to church in Jamaica. Back home, I used to attend an Anglican church, before I started to go to a Church of God with my family. I always used to love to go to church although I was not saved. We had to walk far to get there. The joy of the Lord made me want to go but I never got baptised.

I got saved in England. I heard teaching and preaching that you must be baptised in the name of Jesus Christ, be filled with the Holy Spirit and live holy, and if you didn't do these things, you wouldn't go to heaven. They talked about hell. I didn't want to get burned, I wanted to go to heaven. One day I attended a church programme. Whilst I was there, Mother Modest (mother of Pastor Webster Modest) said to me: *"Mrs Pinnock, would you like to get baptised?".* I told her: *"Yes".* O! My husband was so upset when he heard afterwards that I got baptised!

I got baptised in January and got filled in the same month, there was no hesitation. Someone said to me that they were going to get filled first, but I said to them that I did not know what God would do.

We went to church; it had a small room. Boy! When you heard the fire come! Oh! Fire man! The night when I received the Holy Ghost, a sister was leading testimony service. I was sitting about the third row from the front and I felt like a fire flashed past me! I went to grab on to one of the chairs, but the chair didn't have the power to hold me; I even burst the back of the nice dress that I was wearing! In that place, if you didn't get filled, you would never get filled! It was so wonderful.

Here I am, giving God the glory. I'm still alive to give God thanks for keeping me.

Mother Alma Pinnock *(aged 93 years old)*

July 2023
Back to Basics
10 – 18 July: National Doughnut Week (The Children's Trust
- supporting children with brain injury)

221

THURSDAY 6th

You shall receive the gift of the Holy Ghost - Acts 2:38-39

BACK TO BASICS - Reading: Acts 2:36-39

"Then Peter said unto them, Repent, and be baptised every one of you in the name of Jesus Christ for the remission of sins, and ye shall receive the gift of the Holy Ghost. For the promise is unto you, and to your children, and to all that are afar off, even as many as the Lord our God shall call" (Acts 2:38-39)

Pentecost is a Jewish feast day held 50 days after Passover, where Israel celebrates the first fruits of the wheat harvest. Jewish tradition states that the feast marked the day when the law was given to Israel by Moses on Mount Sinai. Before Jesus ascended back to heaven, He commanded His disciples to wait for the promised baptism of the Holy Ghost. Believers of the New Birth in two parts are promised the gift of the Holy Spirit.

After the saturation of the Holy Ghost, Peter stood up and preached Jesus Christ and Him crucified. After hearing the message, immediately the crowd responded: *"What shall we do?" (Acts 2:37).*

The Holy Ghost, working through Peter, informed the crowd of the first gospel word, i.e., *"Repent"*, which is not a feeling of being sorry but it is a 180-degree-turn in change of mind and direction. It is a genuine feeling of brokenness. The word *"Repent"* gives every hearer hope; you can turn to Jesus you don't have to continue in sin.

Baptism in the name of Jesus Christ signals to the world that you are buried with Him in death, nailing your past, present, and future sins to the cross. Believers rise to walk in a new life in Christ Jesus. The work of sanctification begins, setting the believer apart from sin.

Today, the promise of the remission of sins and the gift of the Holy Ghost, is for anyone who the Father draws to Him. Everyone who repents and believes, demonstrating active faith, and obedience by baptism, God promises the gift of the Holy Ghost.

Missionary Audrey Simpson

July 2023
Back to Basics
10 – 18 July: National Doughnut Week (The Children's Trust
- supporting children with brain injury)

222

*FRIDAY 7th

He who believes and is baptised will be saved - St Mark 16:16 (NKJV)

A NEW BEGINNING FROM DARKNESS INTO LIGHT - Reading: Mark 16:15-18

Bless the LORD, O my soul and all that is within me…

I have overcome many challenges in my life but thank God, while I was a sinner, God was shielding me for the time when He would call me into His fold.

My calling began in 1987; I heard a voice whisper in my spirit: *"There's more to life than this".* I replied: *"What?".* *"What about your spiritual life?"* came the reply. Over the following weeks I pondered in my heart what I had heard, and became very quiet. Others noticed my quietness and questioned me. A few months went by and the menopause became a new word in my vocabulary. I was in a managerial position and the menopause was not kind! Arthritis set in my left knee and collar bone.

I moved into an apartment where it was time for just God and me. This was a season of repentance and decision-making. It was a time of tears. I asked God to choose a church for me. He made a way for me by bringing into my life a family member who I had never met before, I had only heard of her. She was a member of the Apostolic Faith. I phoned her, and with tears in my eyes, said that I would come to church with her.

In May 1989, I walked into the church knowing that I was ready for baptism and to accept Christ as my personal saviour. There was an upcoming Convocation and I felt an inside pulling to attend a prayer service one Saturday. There I received the infilling of the Holy Spirit. Hallelujah! On the Sunday I was baptised in the name of the Lord Jesus.

I am blessed and loved. There's no other place that I would rather be than in the house of the Lord. My aim is to keep on praying and fasting for the souls of those who do not yet know Christ. As the Lord directed my pathway to Him, may He do the same for others.

Freedom from sin is sweeter as the days go by.

Sister Norma Greene

*World Chocolate Day

SATURDAY 8th

Pray for me that none of these things come upon me - Acts 8:24

DISCERNMENT AND CONFESSION - Reading: Acts 8:5-25

In today's lesson we read of Simon the Sorcerer who, in the midst of a revival in Samaria, sought to buy the gift of the Holy Ghost. Clearly, although Simon had been baptised, it was not with a changed heart.

Peter, still fully charged from the day of Pentecost, and the episode with Ananias and Sapphira, was able through the Spirit to discern and deal with Simon appropriately.

The gift of discernment is not usually one of the more popular gifts. By that I mean, if God has blessed you with that gift, you will often be avoided and have very few friends, if any.

Whilst all Spirit-filled believers have a level of discernment, there is a specific gift of Discerning of Spirits *(1 Corinthians 12:10)* and Word of Knowledge *(v8)*. Just as we all have a level of mercy, and a level of faith, still there is a Gift of Mercy *(Romans 12:6-8)* and a Gift of Faith *(1 Cor. 12:9)*.

Discernment has no favouritism or partiality. It is never based upon gossip and hearsay. It is God who reveals what is hidden to the naked eye. The revelation cannot be denied, even if it is never acknowledged as being true.

Whilst we could criticise Simon for his selfish motives, I would at least admire him for readily admitting that he was guilty as charged. He knew that only God could have read his heart which prompted him to say: *"Pray for me" (Acts 8:24)*. Unlike Achan who knew that he had hidden the Babylonian garment in his tent, then feigned innocence until finally, he confessed: *"I have sinned against the LORD" (Joshua 7:20)*.

When we are confronted with our sin our response should simply be: *"I have sinned against the LORD"*. James 5:16 says: *"Confess your faults one to another, and pray one for another, that you may be healed"*.

JEJ

July 2023
Back to Basics
10 – 18 July: National Doughnut Week (The Children's Trust
- supporting children with brain injury)

224

SUNDAY 9th

The Holy Ghost fell on all them which heard the Word - Acts 10:44

PRECIOUS MEMORIES - Reading: Acts 10:34-48

I am one of fourteen children; seven brothers and six sisters.

We used to attend Mount Beulah church in Green Hill, Saint Ann, Jamaica. The pastor there was Elder Walker. I was attending the church from a young age, not really to get saved, but because it was our custom to go and I enjoyed it. One Sunday night, at the age of 19 years old, I went to service as usual. I did not think that I was ready to give my heart to God but God was ready for me.

The power of God was so rich in the service. I went to the altar for prayer and was filled with the Holy Ghost! I remember that I had only one pair of shoes which I called my 'church shoes' because I only wore them to church. When the Lord had finished dealing with me at the altar that day, the poor shoes bottom had gone! I had to find a way to tie up the shoes so that I could walk home. I was baptised in the name of the Lord Jesus the following Sunday.

I joined the young people's choir and afterwards the adult's choir. Sister Etta Barnes, plus my cousin and I, loved to go to night services. We would walk a mile from our home to the church, we held hands as we walked and talked together. We did the same to attend very early morning prayer services. We loved going to church and serving the Lord. We were faithful.

Our pastor, Pastor Walker, was very strict. He was the only person in our district at the time who had a car. If we were ever anywhere doing anything which he might think was wrong, when we heard his car coming, we would hide! There were times when brethren were disciplined for wrongdoing and put on the 'back bench' for a period of time. They still had to attend the services although they were not allowed to do anything.

One of my sisters sent for me in 1962 to come to Birmingham, England. When I came to Gibson Road church it was just like Mount Beulah in Green Hill. Because of that, I didn't miss Jamaica as much as I could have done. It felt like home-from-home because the standard of holiness, the principles, and the worship, all of those were very high.

I joined the Gibson Road young people's choir. On Friday nights we would have choir practice. Elder Jones was the choir director. The power of God would fall during those rehearsals and sometimes choir members had to be carried home still under the anointing of the Holy Ghost. We travelled around the country to minister in song; Elder York, Elder Taylor, Elder Nicely, and many more. We used to travel in the church van and worship on our way there and back. The power of God used to be so strong as we worshipped in the van that I don't know how the van did not turn over! These are some of my precious memories.

I was local women's president for six years and national women's president for two years. I used to go with others and minister at a Nursing Home but we had to stop due to the Covid-19 pandemic. Some of us now do online prayer with the shut-ins each week.

I encourage you as women reading this book, let Jesus hold your hand. It is not us holding on to Him because our hands will get weak and tired, but He will never let us go. He is our strength. I have failed Him at times but thank God for grace and mercy.

Evangelist Mother Dorcas Campbell

MONDAY 10th

From a child thou hast known the Holy Scriptures - 2 Timothy 3:15

DIVINE ENCOUNTER AT SIX - Reading: 1 Samuel 3:1-10; 2 Timothy 3:14-15

I was born in Lewisham, London, and grew up in Bibleway church, Lewisham, where my parents were members.

I don't remember much about the Sunday day services, but the evening services were a highlight for my sister and I. We loved seeing brethren rejoicing in the Spirit, and then trying to replay what we had seen the following day. I didn't understand what I saw but for me it was a pleasure to observe.

My father was sent to start and pastor a new work in East Dulwich. We moved to East Dulwich and, to begin with, held the church services in our home. As the congregation grew, it became necessary to find an alternative place of worship. God provided a place for us to rent not far from our home, and we continued there.

One Sunday morning I became ill, I couldn't keep down anything that I ate but I still wanted to go to church. I pleaded with my mother however, she could not be persuaded, and I had to stay at home with her. In my mind I wondered what I could do in order to be able to go to church for evening service. I then remembered that I had heard my mother pray, and I would often stand outside her door and listen to her. It was then that, as a six-year-old, I decided that I was going to pray and ask God to heal me so that I could go to church that evening. I prayed and went to sleep.

I awoke later when my father and siblings had returned from church. I was given my dinner and ate it without being sick afterwards! As a six-year-old I was terrified, although pleased. Terrified because for the first time, I recognised for myself that there was 'something up there'. I didn't know to say what it was, just 'something'. I then acknowledged in my six-year-old way, that God is real. My environment changed from that day forward. I was only six, but knew that God is real.

A while after, we had our London District Watch Night service. I hadn't planned to get baptised, but during the service I felt that I wanted baptism. By now, I was seven years old. My mother was hesitant to my getting baptised because it was felt that, at such a young age, a child has no understanding of what they are asking for. Nonetheless, after discussing my request with my father, they both agreed, and gave their consent for me to be baptised.

I started to seek for the Holy Ghost at every possible opportunity. I was so sad when I tarried and got up without being filled. What made me more determined was on one occasion, I overheard someone saying to my mother that I, and some other children who were seeking for the Holy Ghost, would not receive it because we were too young.

About a year later, at our London District Convocation, I decided that I was going to receive the Holy Ghost and not just get it, but be the first to get it. So said, so done; I received the Holy Ghost! The joy, the joy, the joy! The joy was indescribable insomuch that, although I was such a shy, quiet child who wouldn't talk much to anybody, I would now talk to everybody! It was so out of character that my mother thought something was wrong with me. But nothing was wrong, it was just the Joy of the Lord.

Evangelist Deveen Smith

TUESDAY 11th

They ... began to speak with other tongues...- Acts 2:4

JUST BELIEVE! - Reading: Acts 2:1-13

At eight years old I didn't know much about anything, except dinosaurs, Sonic the Hedgehog, and Manchester United. I also *loved* church; and although I didn't understand everything, I knew that I wanted to be a part of it.

At Youth Congress that year, I was captivated by the words of a preacher: *"If you want the Holy Ghost, all you have to do is believe".* That night in my room I prayed, *"Dear Jesus. I believe you. Tomorrow night I will go to the altar and receive the Holy Ghost. Amen".*

The following night, in the heaviness of God's presence, I became lost in worship and began to speak in tongues; but this frightened me, and I was conscious of the people watching. Tenderly, the preacher said: *"You are almost there. Don't lose focus".*

The following week at my local assembly, I began to worship and was transported to a dark place except for a blinding light shining through the gap of a slightly opened door. I was eventually brought-to by rapturous shouting and embraces. I had received the Holy Ghost **with power**.

I couldn't sleep that night; I was still worshipping, dancing, and speaking the new language. Still not knowing much about anything, I had no idea just how my life had been completely changed forever.

Beulah McKenzie

July 2023
Back to Basics
10 – 18 July: National Doughnut Week (The Children's Trust
- supporting children with brain injury)

229

WEDNESDAY 12th

The Lord...sent me that thou may... be filled with the Holy Ghost - Acts 9:17

HOW I GOT SAVED - Reading: Acts 9:1-19

I was brought up by godly parents and lived a Christian life until I came to England to start my Nurse Training.

Now, like The Prodigal Son, I was in a *"far country"* where I could do what I liked without being monitored or recognised. There is a saying that: *"When the cat is away the mice will play"*. I started to go with my colleagues to parties, and dinner and dance! But there came a time when 'Conscience' spoke and I was no longer satisfied with my lifestyle.

I came into contact with an Apostolic community midwife who always invited me to church. However, one night I had a dream that she and I met at a church and had a conversation. The very next day I had a call from her. She told me that the Lord woke her up three times during the night and spoke to her about me, and the last time she responded: *"Yes Lord"*.

She told me exactly what I dreamt! I was amazed and convinced that it was the work of the Lord, so decided to visit the church the next Sunday. From that day I was in regular attendance to church and Bible study. Convicted by the Word, I accepted Jesus as my personal Saviour, and was baptised in the name of Jesus Christ at Bethel, 2 Gibson Road, Birmingham.

Now desperate for the Holy Spirt, I went to a Retreat. As soon as someone laid their hands on me, something happened! Thanks be to God I was blessed with the gift of the Holy Spirit, and began to speak in tongues.

Oh, the joy that filled my soul! What a day that was! And today, by God's grace assisting me, I am living a rapture-ready life. Hallelujah!

Mother Fay Derby

July 2023
Back to Basics
10 – 18 July: National Doughnut Week (The Children's Trust
- supporting children with brain injury)

230

THURSDAY 13th

And all that believed were together, and had all things common - Acts 2:44

A MOTHER'S PRAYER - Reading: Acts 2:40-47

I was a member of a New Testament Church of God in Jamaica. My husband came over to the UK in 1959, but I remained in Jamaica for another five years to take care of my mother.

My husband started to attend a church in Trowbridge one year before I came over. When I joined him in England, I went with him to a service and heard Minister Gerald Edmund preaching. Afterwards, Minister Edmund came to our home to have a talk, and asked if I wanted to get saved. I told him that I had already been baptised back home. When he heard that I was not baptised as outlined in Acts 2:38, Minister Edmund explained to me about the Oneness of God. I believed what he said and asked for baptism in the name of the Lord Jesus. God continued to give me revelations and teachings to further enlighten my understanding.

Although someone passed me as receiving the Holy Ghost, I felt that something was missing – something was wrong. I couldn't feel anything moving within me. It was strange, I was quiet with no anointing. One night I dreamt that I was in a river and I was sinking. A hand reached down and picked me up, and put me on a mountain. I was soaking wet. I woke up from the dream feeling frightened.

Our church had a week of fasting. In those days we did not have our own church building so, after work, we would go from house to house to have prayer services for the week. On the second day of the fasting, at home I had been reading Psalm 42:1: *"As the hart panteth after the water brook, so panteth my soul after thee O God".* When I went to the service at my sister-in-law's house that evening, it was the same Scripture that was read.

I went down on my knees to pray and was carried away in the Spirit. No one laid hands on me, I just started to speak with tongues and couldn't stop. God really worked on me. After the service I felt as though I was floating, like I was in another world. I knew that I had at last received the Holy Ghost.

After I got filled, Satan started to work on my children. Sometimes I would have to go to court with them for their wrongdoings, sometimes I felt ashamed. Every New Year we had a week's fasting for the Church. In 1980, I decided to do a week of fasting for the Church and another week for my children, even though I didn't really feel I had the faith that they would all be saved.

But one-by-one, they all got saved. I just had to wait patiently on the Lord. I can encourage any mother not to give up on your children. Hold on. There were times when I couldn't pray, I could only call: *"Jesus!"*, but my cry was heard in heaven.

When I look now and see what God has done through my children in the ministry of the church, in different parts of the world, I have to give God thanks. I don't have to cry for my children any more, only tears of joy.

I encourage all of us to live in peace and love. Jesus is coming soon.

Mother Alice Lewin *(aged 99 years old)*

July 2023
Back to Basics
10 – 18 July: National Doughnut Week (The Children's Trust
- supporting children with brain injury)

232

FRIDAY 14th

See, here is water; what does hinder me to be baptised? - Acts 8:36

GOD CALLED ME IN THE LAUNDERETTE! - Reading: Acts 8:26-40

In 1967 I accepted the Lord as my personal Saviour.

In those days we would go to launderettes with our items for washing. One Saturday, while I was in the launderette, two church brothers were evangelising and they encouraged me with the Word of God. My heart was ready to receive God's Word.

Suddenly I was anxious for Sunday to come so that I could go to church. From there onwards I kept on attending, and told my husband that I was going to be baptised. My husband encouraged me, although at the time he himself was not a Christian! He told me that once I start, I should not stop!

By God's grace I am still here today worshipping God and I encourage you to keep holding on.

Missionary Louise Moore

SATURDAY 15th

They heard them speak with tongues, and magnify God - Acts 10:46

I LOVE JESUS BEST OF ALL - Reading: Romans 8:18-26

I remember the day when the Lord first touched my heart.

I had been attending the Shiloh Apostolic church as a Sunday school girl, my pastor was Bishop Thomas Germain. One Sunday I went to the altar for prayer and Bishop Germain pulled a chair over to where I was and started to counsel me to give my life to Jesus.

He asked me if I would like to be baptised and I said yes. I started to cry and was still crying when I got home, and didn't understand why I couldn't stop. I tried to think of lots of happy things but that didn't make any difference, I cried for days. The week before my baptism was the longest week. Bishop Germain was also excited, he said: *"On Sunday, I'm going to bury you!"*.

I recall on my baptism day seeing the saints standing on either side of the river singing and praising God. The water from the river came up to my neck before I was immersed in the name of the Lord Jesus. I was 14 years old and received the Holy Ghost one year later.

At the age of 15, my pastor appointed me to teach the Junior Sunday school class. Church was so rich and sweet in those days. My church used to hold fasting service every Monday, and sometimes I would slip away from school to go to fasting. Some of my school peers would tell my teacher and the next day, she would call me to the front and say: *"Hazel, I heard that you were not at school yesterday because you went to **fasting!**"* She would really emphasise on *"**fasting"*** and all of the children would laugh at me but it didn't matter to me. I would still slip away to fasting services from time-to-time.

When worship was at its peak, sinners used to stand in the church courtyard listening. Sometimes the Holy Ghost would anoint somebody to go and get them from outside and bring them to the altar. One of the most powerful preachers in our church, Deacon Reggie, he came to Christ like that. He was a smoker and was outside. His sister, under the anointing, went and pulled him in and the Holy Ghost worked on him at the altar. His pockets were emptied of the cigarettes which he was carrying – he never went back to smoking again.

I also remember Brother Briscoe. He used to wear a white suit to church most Sundays, but it was always red by the time he went home after rolling on the floor because of the power of the Spirit. He would have to walk through the town centre in his red suit that had been white! We were Holy Rollers back then.

When my mother came to England to prepare to send for me, she left me with brethren from the church. Unfortunately, they backslid and did not want me to go to church anymore either, but I kept on going. One Sunday night they locked me out of the house, and I had to go home with the church mothers who had walked me home.

I have come a long way, and been through many sufferings, but I know that God is with me.

Pastor Hazel Jacobs

*SUNDAY 16th

Except you be born of the water and the Spirit, you cannot enter... St John 3:5

DON'T TRY TO FIT IN TO THIS WORLD - Reading: St John 3:1-7

Oh, how the world has changed!

However, Jesus' words remain valid in this modern age. You must be born again - through water baptism and receiving the Holy Spirit - to enter the kingdom of God.

This is the New Birth, a spiritual birth that brings you back to life from being dead in trespasses and sin *(Ephesians 2:1)*. Trespasses and sin define the age we live in - no long list of its characteristics is needed! The 'new birth' makes it possible for us to become citizens of a spiritual kingdom where Jesus himself reigns as King *(St John 3:5)*.

A citizen of God's kingdom has the power to live a righteous life free from sin, and isn't concerned about their 'authentic truth' but the truth that comes from God. Of course, there may be conflicts because of how this world wants us to live, but it takes humility and a submitted will to ensure nothing jeopardises that citizenship.

Being transformed by thinking a different way, utilising the power of the Holy Spirit, is the only way to remain a citizen of God's kingdom *(Romans 12:2)*. Life in God's kingdom is far more profitable than trying to live in this one.

Name withheld

*World Ice Cream Day & National Cherry Day

July 2023
Back to Basics
10 – 18 July: National Doughnut Week (The Children's Trust
- supporting children with brain injury)

236

MONDAY 17th

They were baptised in the name of the Lord Jesus - Acts 19:5

A TRAGIC DEATH BROUGHT LIFE - Reading: Acts 19:1-7

I was born and raised in Jamaica. My biological father died when I was six years old. I had not much understanding of loss but I cried with my mother.

When I was about 13 years old, my family suffered a bereavement when my soon-to-be brother-in-law died tragically in a horrific accident on his way from work. The grief was immense because he was one of the most kind and beautiful people in my life. He cared for my mother when he lived with us and was there as a big brother for the children, including me. My sister had moved to Canada, and the wedding was planned.

After his death, his mother came down to see the family. She was walking from room to room holding her belly and repeatedly cried: *"His soul, his soul"*. I had no idea what that meant at the time, but I knew that I was totally devastated and scared. I noticed it sounded as if it was a prayer. I used to listen to a Christian radio broadcast called 'Back to the Bible'. I wrote to them and asked for prayer for my brother-in-law's soul, his and my family.

They wrote back to me and said that they will pray for comfort for the families, but the prayer would not be of any benefit to my brother as he had already died; they said that his chance had passed. They quoted: *"There is no repentance in the grave and no pardon given to the dead"*. When I read that letter, I was even more devastated and could not explain my grief and anguish. I mourned for a long time.

When I was about 16 years old, some church people from a Shiloh Apostolic Church came to our district to have weekly Open Air Evangelistic Services in the shop precinct. They sang: *"Why do you wait dear brother and why do you tarry so long? Your Saviour is waiting to bless you, and give you a place in his sanctified throng Why not, why not, why not come to Jesus now, why not why not, why not come to Jesus now"*.

They sang: *"Have you any room for Jesus, He who bore your load of sin? As he knocks and asks admission, Sinner will you let him in? Room for Jesus King of Glory, let Him by His words obey. Swing your heart's door widely open Bid him enter while you may"*.

They sang: *"I've wandered far away from God, now I'm coming home…"*.

July 2023
Back to Basics
10 – 18 July: National Doughnut Week (The Children's Trust
 - supporting children with brain injury)

They preached: *"For God so loved the world that He gave His only begotten Son, that whosoever believeth in Him should not perish but have everlasting life" (St John 3:16).* They preached, *"He that believeth and is baptised shall be saved, he that believeth not shall be dammed" (St Mark 16:16).* They also preached from Acts 2:38-39.

Those songs and more were sung consecutively over the weeks, and Scriptures quoted equally over the weeks. They preached about heaven where you will be safe with God, and hell where the soul will be separated from God forever.

My heart felt remorse and sorrow for my sins. Here the soul was mentioned again. I wanted to go to heaven when I died, and my soul not to be separated from God in eternal hell. I remembered my brother-in-law and the words in my letter from Back to the Bible Broadcast. I decided to go to the altar and ask for prayer.

They prayed for all who came. Then they spoke about baptism and wanted to take us to the Mother Church in another district to be baptised. The Elder arranged a trip in his minibus. One lady decided that she wanted to get baptised, the rest only wanted to see the baptism.

On our way going up a hill near the church, the minibus gears failed. The bus rolled back down the hill and turned over with its full load. No one, including a pregnant lady, was hurt, except a gentleman who jumped out of the van. God protected us!

Then hearing the people in the minibus crying and asking for their baptism, I knew that's what I also wanted to do. I felt the Lord had called me and was offering me a place with his sanctified throng. I was remorseful and felt sorry for my sins.

I was still a child, and my mom did not agree for me to be baptised. She did not believe that I had enough understanding of what baptism was about. However, the people at the church advised her not to be responsible for my soul if I wanted baptism. I was baptised in the name of the Lord Jesus; I was happy and blessed. I felt new.

Then one day I went to a fasting service at one of the sister-churches in another district. I closed my eyes and felt I was gone far away. I saw Jesus on the cross, His hands and feet were bleeding. His forehead was bleeding from the crown of thorns on His head. A light as bright as the sun surrounded him. I looked up and started to walk towards him. I felt someone touch me and I came back to myself; I realised that I was still at the fasting service.

I was convicted in my heart that Jesus is real for I saw Him there hanging on the cross, just as it said in the Scriptures. I have never regretted accepting Jesus as my personal Saviour.

Missionary M Fraser

TUESDAY 18th

I am the LORD, and there is none else, there is no God beside me - Isaiah 45:5

PROPHECY: ALL EYES ON ME - Reading: Isaiah 45:1-25

Let's consider Isaiah 45's prophecy, that to Cyrus declaring God's authority.

Imagine the modern-day sensation of such a powerful message upon this great King and leader. *"God is going to make every crooked place straight in your life, give you treasures and reveal hidden things to you, breaking bars of iron and gates of bronze".*

Imagine the rapturous applause, the victory, all eyes upon the recipient and teller. How great must Cyrus have appeared. Now, let's grasp some things, simple and yet profound, about God's intention for His prophetic voice in our nation:

- That we will know the God who we have not known (v4)
- That enemies will know that *"I am God"* and have NO equal (v6)
- That my people will recognise my power (v8)
- That we will not dare to strive against His holiness (v9)
- To humble us to understand that he is Maker and orchestrator over our lives, and not us (v 9-10)
- That we will begin to humbly ask Him for His plans (v12)
- That we will witness to others so they will say *"Surely He is God"* (v15)
- To consecrate us and call us to repentance (v20)

Our gracious God allows us victory so that we will be turned back to Him. Let us make the wonders of God more than a sensation. The bigger picture is that, when God puts all eyes on us for a moment, it is with intention for all eyes to be on Him for eternity!

Joy Lear-Bernard

WEDNESDAY 19th

Repent ye: for the kingdom of heaven is at hand - St Matthew 3:2

REPENTANCE - Reading: St Matthew 3:1-12

The Greek word for repent is Metanda meaning to have a change of mind, and to have a genuine sorrow towards God for sins committed *(2 Corinthians 7:9-10)*.

God needs to see works of repentance, where we turn from our evil ways *(Jonah 3:10)* and return to God *(1 Kings 8:47-48)*. Repentance is a gift from God *(Acts 5:31)*, enabling us to see differently, eschewing evil.

The kingdom of heaven speaks of the past, present and future *(St Luke 12:32; 13:28, 17:21)*, and within this Scripture the message is futuristic, speaking of a time when all humankind will see God as Lord of all.

The completion of God's redemptive plan is yet to come, but is imminent. It will be a time of separation, when the saints of God will dwell in the new heaven and new earth, but the children of disobedience shall be cast out into outer darkness *(St Matthew 13:24-30; 2 Peter 3:13)*.

I beseech you to repent before it's too late.

Rachel Lewin

THURSDAY 20th

If I don't go the Helper (Comforter) will not come - St John 16:7 (AMP)

I HAVE TO GO BUT IT'S TO YOUR ADVANTAGE! - Reading: St John 16:1-16

Sometimes we may feel that we are alone, that God's not there or even hearing our prayers. But Jesus told the disciples I have to go, but it's to your advantage.

He had to go so that He could send His Spirit unto us: *"And we know that He abideth in us by the Spirit He has given us"* (1 John 3:24). It is God's Spirit who comforts us and teaches us in all things *(St John 14:16,26)*. When we are lost for words to pray in our weakness, it is the Spirit who intercedes on our behalf with groanings which cannot be expressed in words *(Romans 8:26)*.

It is His Spirit within us who enables us to overcome all things, because: *"Greater is He that is in us than He that is in the world"* (1 John 4:4). My sister, whatever you are going through know that you have overcome, because God's Spirit within you is greater than your circumstances.

Just believe His Word, our God cannot lie!

Name withheld

FRIDAY 21st

The Comforter... shall teach you all things - St John 14:25-26

THE HOLY GHOST - JESUS' PRESENCE - Reading: St John 14:25-31

Jesus was on the threshold of returning to heaven, so assured His disciples of His presence continuing with them in the form of the Holy Ghost. The first time that the Comforter, i.e., Paraklétos, Helper who walks alongside us, is mentioned is in St. John 14:16. We note evidence of this promise being fulfilled in Acts 2:1-4.

The Holy Spirit is a gift, it imitates, and is, the nature and character of Jesus shown in His Word. The natural work of Jesus, i.e., teaching and guiding His disciples as a Rabbi had come to an end. The continuation of teaching and guidance would now be accomplished by the promised Helper, the Holy Spirit. The Holy Spirit enables the words of Jesus to be brought back to remembrance.

Today, Spirit-filled believers are continuing the work which Christ and His disciples did, as we too were commissioned *(St Matthew 28:19-20)*.

Jesus also left His peace, which was a common thing to say in Jewish culture, i.e., *"Shalom" (St Luke7:50).* When Jesus said *"Peace",* it was not an empty word, it meant something powerful. We are thankful that Jesus left His disciples, and us today, the power of the Holy Ghost and His peace.

Missionary Audrey Simpson

SATURDAY 22nd

It is written, Be ye holy; for I am holy - 1 Peter 1:16

ENJOY BEING HOLY - Reading: Hebrews 12:14; 1 Peter 1:1-16

The word 'holiness' can bring different thoughts to mind and, for some, a misconception of its true meaning may cause a feeling that for them holiness is hard or unachievable.

To be holy is to meet God's standard, to satisfy His requirements in every way. Holiness is a lifestyle; it is not an on/off behaviour. It is totally attainable for every Spirit-filled believer provided that we allow the indwelling spirit of God to work and conform us to His image.

It is not unreasonable that a Holy God should want a Holy People to serve Him, neither would He ask us to do something which is impossible. Holiness should not be considered to be a chore or an ordeal, it should be a delight! We should take pleasure in the thought of becoming like Jesus.

Holiness is progressive. The closer that we get to Christ, and the more that we learn about Him, the easier it is to be like Him. When we spend quality time with Jesus, His attitude 'rubs off' on us. Holiness is always in fashion, it's not something seasonal or to be associated with the distant past. Holiness is the beauty of God.

God wants us to reflect Him accurately to others, so be the 'Jesus' whom people will see today. Make sure that you represent Him well, and enjoy the experience!

JEJ

SUNDAY 23rd

SUNDAY 23rd

The Holy Ghost came on them, and they spake with tongues - Acts 19:6

MY SPIRITUAL CONVICTION TO CONVERSION - Reading: Acts 19:1-7

I was about 15 years of age living in Kingston, Jamaica.

I was singing this song: *"Come into my heart Lord Jesus".* Something happened and I made the declaration that I would have to go to the country to get saved.

God heard me that day and circumstances sent me to the country with my siblings. A Shiloh Apostolic Church was next door to my grandparents' house. My aunt was ministering to her sister about God, but the Word came into my heart, and I made a vow that I would give my life to the Lord. My Granduncle was the pastor of the church but would not baptise me; I gathered that he did not think I would continue in the faith when I went back to Kingston!

I was finally baptised on 4th August 1951 and filled with the Holy Ghost in February 1955. Praise God! Through many dangers and trials, I am here today because God kept me.

As the Apostle Paul said: *"Having therefore obtained help of God, I continue unto this day" (Acts 26:22).* I am now 82 years old; God be praised.

Evangelist Cherry Smith

*MONDAY 24th

If anyone is in Christ, the new creation has come - 2 Corinthians 5:17 (NIV)

EXCHANGING OLD FOR NEW - Reading: 2 Corinthians 5:11-21

We cannot be in Christ and remain in our old state; we exchange from our old nature to being a new creature in Christ by baptism in His name and being filled with the Holy Ghost.

The purpose of baptism in water in the name of Jesus Christ is for the remission of our sins *(Acts 2:38)*. Baptism in Jesus' name is proof that the believer has taken on His name, and the filling of the Holy Ghost gives us our identity in Christ. An example would be when a woman gets married. She exchanges her maiden name and takes on her husband's name, and with that comes a different role and responsibility. She no longer lives a single life; she is now identified by her husband's name not her old name (maiden name).

When we are in Christ, an exchange has to take place. We exchange from weakness to strength, from darkness to light. There can be no exchange without giving up sin, and being filled with the Holy Ghost, which results in being a new creature in Christ.

"So long, bye-bye" to the former life, everything now becomes new in Christ. Our old life has been buried… *"even so we also walk in newness of life" (Romans 6:4).*

Min. Genevieve Dinnall

*International Self Care Day & Cousins Day

TUESDAY 25th

See, here is water; what doth hinder me to be baptised? - Acts 8:36

LIKE LIGHTNING IT WENT THROUGH ME! - Reading: Acts 8:26-40

I used to visit a Baptist church sometimes whilst living in Jamaica, but I knew that there was nothing there for me. I carried on visiting a Baptist church occasionally after moving to England, but still knew that it was not the right church for me.

I knew that the Lord was speaking to me, and wanted me to serve Him, but I did not take heed. I knew that if I became a Christian there would be certain things which I was doing I would no longer be able to do. I used to smoke and drink and I would have to give up those things, and more.

One day, a friend of mine asked me if I was still smoking. I told him yes, but said that I wanted to give it up. Not long after that, I went to work and did not buy any cigarettes. My colleagues asked me at break-time if I was going to the Smoking Room. I said: *"No, I am going to the Rest Room instead"*.

After about a week of not having any cigarettes, one of my friends said to me: *"It looks like you mean it!"*. I had really given up smoking and drinking.

One night when I went to bed, I suddenly started to cry and didn't even know why I was crying, and I couldn't stop. Then I fell asleep and had a dream that I was travelling but did not know where I was going.

Along the way, I could hear singing; the sound seemed to be coming from the top of a hill. I said to myself: *"Where is this singing coming from? It sounds good to me"*. In the dream I climbed to the top of the hill and there I saw a church. I sat down at the back and the minister pointed at me and said: *"I'm calling you; yes, you! There is room for you!"*. Then they started to sing: *"Follow, follow, I would follow Jesus, anywhere, everywhere, I would follow on. Follow, follow, I would follow Jesus, anywhere He leads me I would follow on"*.

When I woke up, I started to cry again and could not stop the tears.

I had another vision and in the vision a woman asked me why I was crying. She said that she had something to tell me, and it was about fasting and prayer. I fasted for a whole week after that, although I was not yet a Christian.

I had visited the church in Camberwell a few times. Some of the brethren came to have a prayer service at my home. When they came, they started to sing. Whilst they were singing, I felt something hit me and I dropped to the floor! I did not know what had happened to me. I felt something going through me, a bit like pins and needles, and then I wondered if I was dead! But then I jumped up. After I jumped up, I heard a voice, it must have been God, say: *"You need to go back down there, I'm not finished with you yet"*. I fell to the floor again and started to say: *"Hallelujah, hallelujah"*. I rolled under the dining table and back. I felt my tongue was getting loose and I started to speak with other tongues. It was wonderful! I was not yet baptised.

I was baptised in the name of Jesus Christ by Bishop Simmonds at Wimbledon church. I will never forget that day.

Mother Agatha Wallace *(aged 91 years old)*

*WEDNESDAY 26th

Now if any man hath not the Spirit of Christ, he is none of His - Romans 8:9

WHY WE NEED THE HOLY GHOST - Reading: Romans 8:1-17

The gift of the Holy Ghost is our 'adoption certificate' which is our proof that we are sons of God. The Holy Ghost authorises us to claim and receive the blessings and inheritance that are stipulated for every son *(Galatians 3: 29)*.

Incumbent upon us as Sons of God, is the need to walk circumspectly, i.e., *"soberly and godly in this present world" (Titus 2:12)*. In order to accomplish this, we have to be led by the Spirit.

This relationship is a deeply intertwined one, and the Bible makes it explicitly clear that one cannot exist without the other, i.e., to be a Son, you have to have the Holy Spirit, and without the infilling and resultant leading of the Spirit, one is simply not a Son *(Romans 8:14)*.

Children carry the DNA of their parents so if we have Christ dwelling on the inside, we will show forth His characteristics and bear the fruit of the Spirit.

Min. K. Codner

*Aunts & Uncles Day

THURSDAY 27th

Therefore we are buried with him by baptism into death - Romans 6:4

NEW LIFE IN CHRIST - Reading: Romans 6:1-14

The day that I went down into the baptism pool, is as clear to me today, as it was then. I approached the pool, under the weight of my sins, fears and anxieties, but Jesus Christ washed away every guilty stain.

The Scripture says that by being baptized into Jesus Christ, our old, sinful life is dead and buried. We are resurrected to new life in Christ.

To walk in *"newness of life" (Romans 6:4)*, we completely abandon our old sinful ways: *"Old things are passed away; behold, all things are become new" (2 Corinthians 5:17)*. We do not live this life in our own strength. We live by faith in the Son of God *(Galatians 2:20)*. Our affection is focused upon things above, instead of earthly things, which have no lasting value *(Colossians 3:2)*.

My Sister, be anxious for nothing. Our God has given us everything that we need for a dynamic spiritual life and godliness *(2 Peter 1:3 AMP)*. Continue to walk in God's Word, and embrace every God-given opportunity with both hands.

Name withheld

FRIDAY 28th

By their fruits ye shall know them - St Matthew 7:20

FRUITS NOT FOLIAGE - Reading: St Matthew 7:15-20

Have you ever considered the task Adam had in tending to the garden?

Imagine when the first seed fell from an apple tree how, over time with diligence, he had to decipher that the next tree that flourished had in fact come from that first apple tree seed God had created. Time and diligence showed him that it grew to be just like God's first tree; it was a natural occurrence. He watched closely and determined what it really was.

Fruits and their authenticity take time to identify. If one satisfies oneself with the identity of a tree just by its pretty flowers and foliage, we haven't truly understood the importance of that seed and its season.

The potency of the seed contains everything that made the first apple tree what it was. Growth produces offspring that behaves just like it! We all too often identify one another by our gifts but fail to truly seek out character that looks like God.

Our gifts are FOR God and His Church, our fruits are LIKE God. Beyond the flowers and foliage there must be FRUIT. Our maturity is not reflected by the foliage of our gifts, but by the degree of time spent with God which results in us looking like Him. So important was character that Jesus cursed the fig tree that looked mature but had not the fruits it should have portrayed.

Let's daily soak up the nutrients of His Word allowing the reign of His Spirit. Let's focus much on watering our mind with God's Truth and submitting to the soil of His Word.

Indeed, it is by our fruits, not our foliage, that others shall know us.

Joy Lear-Bernard

SATURDAY 29th

God was manifest in the flesh - 1 Timothy 3:16

THE MYSTERY OF GODLINESS - Reading: 1 Timothy 3:1-16

Paul's letter to Timothy *(1 Timothy 3:16)* has a sense of urgency; it was sent ahead in case his journey was delayed.

This was Paul's stance concerning 'conduct' and 'doctrine' in the house of God. Emphasis is added: *"...which is the church of the living God, the pillar and ground of the truth" (1 Timothy 3:15).* He cared about the correct operation, growth and mindset of the Church.

Being pillar and ground - the Church still upholds basic truth. At a time when influential false teachers were rife, even in the Assembly. One of the great foundational truths that came under attack was: *"the mystery of godliness".* This mystery is His incarnation! Mary's baby in the womb was called *"Emmanuel; that is, God with us" (St Matthew 1:23),* and when she finally brought forth her firstborn son, Joseph obediently named Him Jesus *(St Matthew 1:25).* God was manifest in the flesh!

"And without controversy great is the mystery of godliness: God was manifest in the flesh, justified in the Spirit, seen of angels, preached unto the Gentiles, believed on in the world, received up into glory" (1 Timothy 3:16).

According to Apostle Paul, this basic truth is without controversy or debate. It is not for strife or simply admiration, but to be believed and received. Jesus Christ and all who He is; is the foundation that has been laid *(1 Corinthians 3:11).* He is the Truth which must settle in the minds of the believers in Christ, even in modern times.

A *'Back to Basics'* approach always helps with our self-reflections - to check our spiritual roots - if we are still rooted and grounded in Christ, in belief and lifestyle or someone else's. We can re-examine the value and credence we loosely or dearly hold, and take another grip.

Such opportunity gives the blessed assurance that we are not sold a 'lie', a 'mix' or a 'twist', and our destination is still intact and on track: *"conformity to the image of Christ" (Romans 8:29).*

Pastor Josephine Lewis

*SUNDAY 30th

I will put my laws into their hearts, and in their minds - Hebrews 10:16

THIS IS THE COVENANT - Reading: Hebrews 10:1-18

God initiates agreement with man.

He has always kept His Word and upheld covenants throughout generations. His promises of old have been fulfilled. Today we are beneficiaries. His promise is sure, no matter how long it takes. His track record, impeccable.

Since man was unable to serve and obey faithfully by regulations, God orchestrated for man the capacity to worship from a position of love and intimacy, instead of legislative. Prophets foretold God's plan to put His Spirit within the human frame; Jeremiah 31:31-34 reveals His promise to change past rituals to true worship.

Joel 2:28 states an *"outpouring of His Spirit upon all flesh"*, to empower humankind with ability to do God's will. Hence, *"treasure in earthen vessels" (2 Corinthians 4:7)*, so He can manifest in and through us. The Holy Ghost, the enabler for weak and fragile mortals to operate by His Spirit. Sanctifier, reprover, comforter, revealer and teacher, is Jesus on the inside.

That same Spirit which moved upon the face of the waters in Genesis 1:2, the same power that rose Jesus Christ from the dead *(Romans 8:11)*, God's divine promise fulfilled in AD33 *(Acts 2:1-4)*, still continues today.

Sis Jx

*International Day of Friendship

*MONDAY 31ˢᵗ

You were sealed with that Holy Spirit of promise - Ephesians 1:13-14

SEARCHING FOR SOMETHING? - Reading: Ephesians 1:3-14

Truth is what it is – the Gospel of our Salvation. Jesus Christ is our good news because He hath purchased salvation for us with His own blood in His death, burial and resurrection. He has paid it all in full *(1 Corinthians 15:1-4)*.

Every religion is searching for something that will grant forgiveness of sins and hope beyond death, i.e., eternal life. Good works, self-punishment, rituals, fasting etc, attest to this fact. Yet there is no guaranteed hope at the end; religion by nature is aimlessly searching for God. But God, manifested in flesh, came on earth to humankind: *"God was in Christ reconciling the world unto Himself"* (2 Corinthians 5:19).

Those who are confident in your self-effort for salvation, look what Jesus Christ did for you! Put your trust **in Him** and be saved by His grace: *"Whosoever believeth on Him… hath everlasting life"* (St John 3:16).

The saved are: *"Sealed with the Holy Spirit of promise which is the earnest, or down payment, of our inheritance"* (Ephesians 1:14); also: *"An incorruptible, undefiled body"* (1 Peter 1:4) inherited at Christ's second appearing in the air, when He receives the saved unto Himself.

Isn't this the authentic Salvation you are truly searching and longing for?

Pastor Josephine Lewis

*National Avocado Day

BAD BREATH

Bad breath, otherwise known as halitosis, is quite common. It can make us feel embarrassed and affect our social, work and family lives. There are multiple causes and it can be treated.

Causes include:

- Eating strong-smelling foods e.g., onions, garlic, certain spices and herbs
- Problems with your teeth and gums such as gum disease, dental decay and dental infections
- Medical reasons, e.g., certain stomach conditions, tonsilitis, acid reflux, dry mouth, smoking.

There are simple things you can do to treat bad breath:

- Brush twice daily with fluoride toothpaste to prevent dental decay and gum disease
- Use fluoride mouthwash at a different time to brushing your teeth. This will help to prevent dental decay and freshen the mouth. Choose an alcohol-free option.
- Clean between your teeth with dental floss or interdental brushes at least once a day. This will remove any trapped food that can lead to bad breath and dental problems
- Attend regular check-ups at your dentist
- After eating strong smelling foods or drinks, use sugar-free chewing gum or mints
- If you wear dentures, keep them clean and remove them every night

See your dentist for help if:

- you have tried to solve bad breath yourself but things are not improving after a few weeks
- you have painful, bleeding or swollen gums
- if you have toothache
- if you have wobbly teeth
- if you have problems with your dentures

Dr Nadine Miller BDS MFDS RCS Ed

Reference:

www.nhs.uk/conditions/bad-breath

August

The Mind

TUESDAY 1st

God has not given us the spirit of fear - 2 Timothy 1:7

SAY NO TO THE SPIRIT OF FEAR - Reading: 2 Timothy 1:1-18

Timothy, smothering his fear amidst the hostile reality of the afflictions that come with preaching the gospel of Jesus Christ. Forsake or partake? That was and still is the question. Paul was already a fully-fledged partaker which fear's-wind must have known, and thus whispered and sniggered at the new young leader: *"You are on trial next"!*

This spirit of fear is not of God; it cripples and produces cowardice toward the Lord's work, e.g., shrinking back at the thought of life-threatening consequences, from the displeasure of authorities, although yes, these challenges can be highly frightening.

Paul's undergirding letter to brace his protégé, came at a time when he needed it most. You have got this Timothy! *"For God hath not given us the spirit of fear"* (2 Timothy 1:7) to make us cowardice.

Fear not! We too are empowered! Stir that power; be unashamed of the testimony of our Lord. Stir up what God hath given us: the fear-busting gift of the spirit of: *"power; of love and of a sound mind"*.

Pastor Josephine Lewis

WEDNESDAY 2nd

You will keep him in perfect peace, whose mind is stayed on thee - Isaiah 26:3

THE MIND - Reading: Isaiah 26:1-8

The mind is a set of faculties responsible for mental phenomena. These faculties include thought, imagination, memory, will and sensation. The importance of the health of the mind, or mental health, has been widely publicised by organisations like the World Health Organisation (WHO), MIND and the NHS.

Mental health is defined as 'a state of emotional and psychological wellbeing in which an individual is able to use his or her cognitive and emotional capabilities, function in society, and meet the ordinary demands of everyday life' (Merriam-Webster Dictionary). The WHO believes that mental wellbeing is an integral part of overall health.

God's desire is for us to have a healthy mind. God is aware that as humans our minds can be negatively affected by circumstances that happen in our life, or the environment we live in. God's Word promises peace of mind if our focus, trust, and commitment is in Him *(Isaiah 26:3)* Paul encourages us that the peace of God shall protect our mind, and that we should occupy our thoughts with things that are truthful, honest, clean, lovely (friendly towards others) and reputable *(Philippians 4:7-8)*.

When life's challenges arise, put them before God in prayer and His peace will reassure and guard your heart and mind *(Philippians 4:6)*.

LEL

THURSDAY 3rd

Whatsoever a man soweth, that shall he also reap - Galatians 6:7

BE MINDFUL OF WHAT YOU SOW - Reading: Galatians 6:1-10

In the last three years the world has changed beyond our imagination, and ushered in major transformation and challenges.

In times like this, we seek to find God's will through prayer, worship, meditation, the Scriptures and listening to His voice for direction in every area of our life.

A good farmer does not worry about the weather. He plants his seeds, takes great care to till his soil, and is confident that the seed will produce.

Our thoughts are the seeds which we plant. Our success, health, wealth and all of our relationships are fruits of the seeds we plant. If we want an abundant harvest and healthy fruits, we must carefully tend the soil. Get rid of the weeds of doubt, fear and negativity. Plant every thought with care of prayer, praise, worship, faith and the Word.

Today I am planting a mindful of goodness.

ASD

FRIDAY 4th

The peace of God surpasses all understanding...Philippians 4:7 (NKJV)

STAY CALM - Reading: St Matthew 14:23-33

There's a saying: *"It's easier said than done".*

Depending on what you're going through right now, you may wonder how the Word can say: *"Don't be worried"* or: *"Don't be anxious" (Philippians 4:6).* How on earth is that possible in the midst of what is happening?

The truth is that worry changes nothing. Worry keeps us in the past with what has already occurred, and can give a distorted vision of the future because our mind is clouded with a series of possibilities that may never materialise. Worry is an enemy of peace!

JM Scriven said: *"O what peace we often forfeit, O what needless pain we bear. All because we do not carry, everything to God in prayer" (What a Friend We Have in Jesus).*

Our cause for worry may be because we are afraid that God's preferred outcome will not be what we want. So rather than trusting His sound judgment, which includes purpose, we fret. Or perhaps we have limited God's ability in our mind, and don't think that He is capable of turning things around on our behalf.

It makes God sad to see His children anxious and stressed-out as though we have a Father who fails.

If the cares of life are getting you down, allow the peace of God to envelop you, to control the way that you think and feel. That's the only way to stay calm.

JEJ

SATURDAY 5th

Be ye transformed by the renewing of your mind - Romans 12:2

IT'S ALL IN THE MIND - Reading: Romans 12:1-2

I am someone who has battled with depression for years. To understand why, you would have to know what happened to me as a toddler. But that's for another time.

The mind really plays tricks with you, it is a constant battle; it tells you things that are not true! The mind may tell you that you are useless, unlovable, that nobody wants to hear what you have to say, and these lies can lead to self-loathing, and the list goes on.

God's Word tells you something completely different. When you were fashioned together in your mother's womb, God looked on you and said: *"It is good"*. God knows and loves you despite all of your failings. He is ever mindful of you.

How do I know this, you might ask? The Holy Bible tells us the truth of who we are, and how God loves us. As you read the Bible you discover that Jesus, who died for humankind, went to Calvary. Another name for Calvary is Golgotha which means *"The place of a skull"*. Nothing is ever random with God. I believe that through Golgotha He was showing us that our mind is the place where all our battles are fought.

Don't listen to the lies of the enemy anymore. Stand upon the Word of God and confess what He says about you. You can only have your mind transformed by reading and applying God's Word to your life. His Word gives us freedom in Christ.

Marie Chisnall

SUNDAY 6th

My sheep hear my voice, and I know them, and they follow me - St John 10:27

KNOWING THE VOICE OF GOD - Reading: St John 10:22-42

My late Pastor Bishop Dunn used to say don't be quick to say 'God said'. Rather say, 'something said to me'. It's a learning process.

Samuel didn't recognise that it was God calling him at first *(1 Samuel 3:8-10)*. Perhaps that's why we need the wisdom of those who are spiritually mature to help discern the call of God on our lives, and impart godly council.

It can be a feeling of: "… Oh … was that you Lord Jesus?". It can be a subtle dawning; a sweet and gentle cooing of the Holy Spirit *(1 Kings 19:12)*: *"And after the earthquake a fire; but the LORD was not in the fire: and after the fire a still small voice"*.

I don't always initially know that it's God speaking. Relationships require a commitment to first engage, then build trust and ultimately a recognition of the presence of who it is you are communicating with. Once trust has been established through regular, intentional communication, a bond is formed. This becomes the basis upon which future dialogue is launched.

Finally, there is just a peace and confidence in knowing my Heavenly Father.

Missionary Susan Higgins

MONDAY 7th

Be renewed in the spirit of your mind - Ephesians 4:23

YOU CANNOT HAVE IT BOTH WAYS - Reading: Ephesians 4:17-32

There are several schools of thought about the power of the mind in shaping our destiny.

One writer argues that the mind has two main parts: the conscious and the subconscious. Moses wrote to the children of Israel these words from Deuteronomy 11: 18: *"Fix these words of mine in your hearts and minds; tie them as symbols on your hands and bind them on your foreheads".* In other words, God's words should be the focus of our meditation day and night *(Psalm 1:2).*

Beloved, the mind is a very powerful force that can shape our eventual destiny. Remember that Paul wrote in *Romans 7:21*: *"When I want to do good, evil is right there with me".* Does this mean that the unconscious part of the mind, if not filtered, can lead us away? Romans 8 reminds us that if we live in the flesh, we will do the things of the flesh and the converse is true of living in the Spirit.

Finally, to the women of a Great God, speak life over every aspect and facet of your life and allow that 'creative word' that was breathed by God into you, to shape your thinking (thoughts), which will influence your behaviour, which in turn will become habitual, which then will propel you towards your God-given destiny, knowing that we have the mind of God in us.

Sister Vivean Pomell

TUESDAY 8th

Let my words and meditation be acceptable in thy sight - Psalm 19:14

THE POWER OF WORDS - Reading: Psalm 19:14; James 3:1-12

Words are powerful. They are capable of making or breaking, building up or tearing down.

James tells us: *"Even so the tongue is a little member, and boasteth great things. Behold, how great a matter a little fire kindleth" (James 3:5).* An unbridled tongue is dangerous!

In Proverbs 15:2 we read: *"The tongue of the wise useth knowledge aright; but the mouth of fools poureth out foolishness".* Our words are birthed in our hearts. If you look at St Luke 6:45, Jesus says: *"A good man out of the good treasure of his heart bringeth forth that which is good; and an evil man out of the evil treasure of his heart bringeth forth that which is evil; for out of the abundance of the heart his mouth speaketh".*

We often use Psalm 19:14 as a benediction or word of blessing at the end of a service. It should serve as a reminder to us to be on our guard: *"Set a watch, O LORD, before my mouth; keep the door of my lips" (Psalm 141:3).* We cannot do this of ourselves, only by the spirit of God.

Next time that we say Psalm 19:14 as our benediction, may we ponder and do what we say.

Beverley V. Galloway

WEDNESDAY 9th

I know the plans that I have for you declares the LORD - Jeremiah 29:11 (ISV)

MY MOTHER ABANDONED ME - Reading: Psalm 27:6-10; Jeremiah 29:11

I recall my grandmother often shouting at me in disappointment: *"Your mother left you on me since you were 18 months old, and I cannot afford to look after you!".*

My grandma was a domestic helper. My grandfather, who loved me very much, was a farmer who went out before daybreak and returned at night. They had twelve children; my mother was their second child.

I was subjected to every kind of abuse from my uncles and aunties, as they believed I did not belong in their home. I was told that I was never going to amount to anything because I was worthless.

Someone reminded me the other day how much I used to cry as a child. They told me jokingly that they never heard anyone else cry as much as I did. We lived on a hill and my crying could be heard for miles! I was not liked very much. I used to steal food as I was always hungry. I got a lot of beatings.

My grandmother could not afford to send me to school but I was determined to go, even if it meant going without lunch. I occasionally went to school and when I did, I went without shoes, books, or a proper uniform. Sometimes I would pick an orange from the tree and take it to school for my lunch, and at times my grandfather would give me a little money which could only buy a drink.

My mother never let anyone know that I was her child. I remember seeing my mother and admiring her for being so beautifully dressed with long flowing hair. I thought that she was so pretty and I was so ugly. I thought that's why she did not want anything to do with me. One day she visited my grandma's house with a male guest and I was ushered to the back of the house, out of sight, because I was so dirty and unkempt. She did not want her guest to know that I was her child. That guest later became my sister's father.

I left school at 15 years old, then went to work as a live-in helper. I was determined to be 'somebody'. Therefore, the money that I earned I used to go to an evening class.

I met my husband and came to England where I got the opportunity to study Maths and English. Studying was very hard and I had to repeat every year for four years until I passed. I would not give up and saw every failure as a step closer to a pass.

I worked at a care home, then in a hospital as a nursing assistant. One day my manager at the hospital called me into her office and told me that the government was advertising a job where I would be able to study Adult Nursing for two years, instead of three, because of my hospital experience. Also, my university fees would be paid by the government including a full salary. I prayed and applied for the post and God answered my prayers.

I went to nursing school and was awarded by the university 'most outstanding' and received an award by Health Education England. I was then asked by the university to assist in writing a program for future nursing students. I later went back for further study at the university where I achieved BSc (Hons) First-class Honours in Adult Nursing.

Studying at university-level was very challenging but I fought for my degree with prayer and supplication. I was never afraid to ask for prayers, no matter how small the test I had to take, and I never stayed home from church because of a university assignment. I always put God first.

God had a purpose for my life. My mother abandoned me, and my guardians saw no good in me, but the LORD took me up! God knew me, yet He loved me.

Name withheld

THURSDAY 10th

Wherefore gird up the loins of your mind, be sober - 1 Peter 1:13

READY FOR ACTION - Reading: 1 Peter 1:13-25

The biblical expression to *"gird up the loins"* signified that the person was ready for action or service.

When anyone in ancient Jewish times was ready to work, they would put a loincloth around their waist; then tuck in their robe so that their legs would not be hindered. This is the meaning of *"girded up his loins" (1 Kings 18:46)*. On the other hand, to loose the girdle, meant the person was either lazy or resting (Isaiah 5:27).

To gird up the loins of your mind means to prepare for strenuous mental activity, and warns of the necessity to guard your mind *(Proverbs 4:23)*.

To be sober minded is to ensure that we are not intoxicated or influenced by any spirit other than the Holy Spirit of God. The Holy Spirit will guard our hearts and minds as we run this race of salvation, and set our hope completely on the grace to be brought to us at the revelation of Jesus Christ.

Just as people in biblical times would gather up their long robes and tie them around their waists so they could move quickly and freely, we need to do whatever it takes to focus our thoughts on those things that allow us to serve God without hindrance and completely *(Hebrews 12:1)*.

Minister Sylvia Dean

FRIDAY 11th

The god of this world has blinded the minds of unbelievers - 2 Corinthians 4:4

THE GOD OF THIS WORLD - Reading: 2 Corinthians 4:1-7

According to Romans 1:16: *"…the gospel is the power of God unto salvation, to every one that believeth".*

The gospel of Christ has power to save, changing lives for those who believe. Compare Romans 1:16 with: *"…the god of this world has blinded…".* Satan does this by controlling world systems. He blocks and influences the minds and hearts of individuals with distractions, using lusts of the flesh, eyes and pride of life, obstructing the light of the glorious gospel from penetrating the mind.

Closed minds cannot see or perceive truth so it may appear like the gospel is hid, covered, or out of reach to some. But if our gospel be hid, really our gospel is not hidden to them that believe. Indeed, the gospel of salvation is free universally, and available to all.

It is powerful and effective, and actually not concealed otherwise none would receive salvation. Therefore, unbelievers make a wilful decision to choose Satan's vices, refusing to accept the gospel, choosing worldly pleasures, carnal things over spiritual.

A choice for what is seen above the unseen. Anyone who responds to God's drawing, and hears the gospel, can be saved because: *"Entrance of the Word of God gives light" (Psalm 119:130).*

Sis Jx

SATURDAY 12th

How precious are thy thoughts unto me, O God! - Psalm 139:17

THE SAFE PLACE OF HIS THOUGHTS - Reading: Psalm 139:1-18

David is in awe of how deeply God formed and knew us.

It surpasses our ability to truly comprehend and, as a true worshipper, David held an awe for the nearness of the magnificence of God to him as a human. David helps us to consider how intricately we are formed even before we are in our mother's womb. This consideration is very deep. That we are a result of His thoughts is not the only wonder that struck David, but that we are perpetually in the thoughts of God is an amazing truth. Being in God's thoughts keeps us in a place of eternal safety.

What wings of the morning have we taken? What is the bed of hell we find ourselves in? God's thoughts are on you and I, and there we find Him waiting – wherever we go, watching and speaking to our hearts.

I think that there is no more convicting image of our reflection of God our Father than a parent gazing over their sleeping babe, or watching their child's faltering feeble steps as if they were their own. God is our more than able Father, strong and unfailing. His love and attention for us is because of His Sovereignty.

There is no safer place for you and I than in the thoughts of God.

Joy Lear-Bernard

SUNDAY 13th

Let this mind be in you, which was also in Christ Jesus - Philippians 2:5

MIRROR THE MIND OF CHRIST - Reading: Philippians 2:1-11

As I pondered on this verse, I thought of the Serpent's subtleness and how he deceived Eve by attacking her mind.

Satan is still messing with people's minds today. He presents lies, false imageries, low self-esteem, and self-destructive notions of *"I can't"* or *"I am not good enough"*. When Satan attacks the mind, he relegates us to a helpless position, where we cannot achieve our potential in Christ.

However, having a godly mind means we should mirror Jesus' way of thinking. Jesus accepted He was the Son of God. His way of thinking meant He knew His identity and He lived accordingly. His way of thinking meant He desired to always please His father. He was obedient and lived the life that fulfilled His potential as Son and Saviour.

We are called to live a fulfilled life without self-doubt and anxiety. By mirroring the mind of Christ, we will accept our identity as children of God with authority over Satan and we will not limit ourselves, rather, we will walk in faith and liberty.

J Henry

MONDAY 14th

Do not think of yourself more highly than you should - Romans 12:3

GOD'S GRACE IS OUR ENABLER - Reading: Romans 12:1-5

God's great mercy and grace for us should change the way we live daily as Christians.

We often elevate ourselves and view ourselves better than others. We can make judgments about others by our own distorted standard. Apostle Paul tells us that we must not think of ourselves more highly than we ought to think.

Jesus was a servant-leader. He put aside His glory to serve sinners, to even wash their feet. He died upon the cross to save every kind of sinner, e.g., fornicators, idolaters, drunkards and revilers, and Paul reminds us: *"such were some of you" (1 Corinthians 6:11)!* Jesus never once said: *"Look at all those losers!"*. No, He showed compassion, despite his divine deity.

We must not boast of any works that we have done. Lucifer lifted up himself, iniquity was found in him when he said: *"I will be like the Most High" (Isaiah 14:12-14)*. Pride was the iniquity.

Paul did not say that we should put ourselves down as ugly, worthless, terrible or even unimportant. But instead, think truthfully of ourselves so that we can trust God to make us what He wants us to be.

Let's remind ourselves that: *"God resisteth the proud but gives grace to the humble" (1 Peter 5:5)*.

Missionary M. Fraser

TUESDAY 15ᵗʰ

I had fainted unless I had believed to see the goodness...Psalm 27:13

FAINT NOT! - Reading: Psalm 27:13; Isaiah 40:28-31

It is through this division of the Psalms that we are reminded to have full confidence in God, knowing that He will see us through difficult and turbulent times.

If we don't believe, lose hope and have no faith in God, we will indeed faint. But: *"He giveth power to the faint and to them that have no might He increaseth strength (Isaiah 40:29).*

As a song writer said: *"All my life you have been faithful, all my life you have been so good"*. So, there is no doubt that without help from God we are weak and will come short in our own strength.

Always try to have a positive outlook in life, and in all that you do put God first. You will see the goodness of the LORD for He is faithful and just to deliver you. Believe and you will receive!

Name withheld

WEDNESDAY 16th

Casting all your cares upon Him; for He careth for you - 1 Peter 5:7

GOD CARES - Reading: 1 Peter 5:1-11

God cares about the afflictions of every one of His children; this truth is emphasised throughout His Word.

Throughout my life I have been a beneficiary of God's continuous care and love, even when I didn't know God or understand Him. I have come to know Christ better through my trials, troubles, and afflictions. I am a firm believer that God cares and because of this, we can cast all our burdens upon Him. Hallelujah!

All our fears, anxieties and concerns must be decisively given to God. Why? Because we trust Him. Psalm 37:5 says: *"Commit thy way unto the LORD, trust also in Him and He shall bring it to pass"*. We must learn to first give all our ways unto the Lord. This includes our personal lives, family, work, spouse, children, work, interests, sports, leisure; absolutely everything we are about to do put into God's able hands.

Trust is important too. To trust means to have a firm belief in or confidence in someone. That someone for me is God. He is almighty, omnipotent, omnipresent, omniscient, all by Himself.

God cares for us so cast all your troubles, worries and anxieties upon Him. He is more than able to bring us through.

Sis E Miller

THURSDAY 17th

Kept by the power of God through faith unto salvation - 1 Peter 1:5

A WORD OF ENCOURAGEMENT - Reading: 1 Peter 1:2-12

Life is not always easy, there are so many ups and downs.

We never know from one day to the next what life will throw at us. But trusting in God, and taking Him at His Word, will never disappoint us. If you listen to the news, it's all doom and gloom, but God's Word is uplifting.

We have a living 'Hope', that means every day our hope in Him is alive because our Saviour, Jesus Christ, lives. He has given us an inheritance that is there for all eternity.

We are kept by the power of Almighty God every day. Let us continue to put our hope in Him because He cannot fail.

Marie Chisnall

FRIDAY 18th

Jesus, have mercy on me...and Jesus stood still...- St Mark 10:47-49

RELEASE TO GET RELIEF - Reading: St Mark 10:46-52

Have you ever had something that you wanted to say, but did not say it, because you thought that it would not be important to anyone else but you?

It is good that Bartimaeus continued to call out to Jesus even when many from the great number of people with Him ordered Bartimaeus to be quiet. His desperate tone and persistence caught Jesus' attention to the extent that St Mark records Jesus stopped walking, stood still and commanded Bartimaeus to be called.

I do believe that there is a cry which captures God's attention. It says: *"Father, I stretch my hands to Thee, no other help I know" (C Wesley).*

Jesus sent a message to Bartimaeus: *"Be of good comfort, rise; He (Jesus) calleth for thee"*. Jesus did not have to call Bartimaeus twice; He knew that Jesus might never pass his way again!

The invitation from Jesus meant: *"Come closer, let's talk. Your cry really touched me. I couldn't carry on walking! Tell me what is bothering you; what would you like me to do for you?"*. Although Bartimaeus had been begging, he did not ask Jesus for money. And although Jesus knew that Bartimaeus was blind, He did not assume that Bartimaeus wanted to see. Instead, Jesus gave Bartimaeus the opportunity of relief by release, i.e., He encouraged Bartimaeus to talk to Him.

We too can obtain relief by release that comes when we enter into God's presence. No wonder F Crosby said: *"Let me at Thy throne of mercy, find a sweet relief..."*. There, like Bartimaeus we can tell God about our blindness, like Hannah we can tell Him about our barrenness. Those slowly bleeding to death find virtue and new life, and every Prodigal Son can be forgiven and restored.

Were there no other blind men or beggars that Jesus passed by on that day? I'm sure that there were. But the pitch of Bartimaeus' cry penetrated not just the ears but the heart of Jesus Christ. He had to stop!

He who feels it knows it! Release to get relief!

JEJ

SATURDAY 19th

We are troubled on every side, yet not distressed - 2 Corinthians 4:8

THE STRENGTH OF THE FENCE - Reading: 2 Corinthians 4:1-18

In the UK we now experience severe storms with strong winds and torrential rain on a scale not previously known.

As a result, many people have had their homes flooded and suffered damage to personal possessions beyond repair. After one such storm, I saw that many garden fences had been ripped apart but, somehow, our fence was still standing. Someone said to me: *"See how strong that the wind was!"*, but I said: *"See how strong the fence was!"*.

Sometimes we are warned that a storm is coming and can prepare, but at other times its arrival, and severity, takes us by surprise. It is during these tempestuous ravaging seasons that we identify the strength of our personal spiritual infrastructure. We will then know the real strength of our faith, of every testimony given, every *"Amen!"* we've shouted, every sermon spoken and every song which we've sung.

So if we can see, and feel, that our spiritual strength has been weakened by a series of back-to-back trials, back-to-back temptations, back-to-back sicknesses, back-to-back appointments, may I suggest that we take some urgent time out to reinforce our 'fence' before the next storm hits. Note - there isn't always a long gap in between storms. Also note that with no fence we have no defence!

We know that we're at the brink of a spiritual collapse when we have no time to study and digest the Word, no time to fast and pray, no quality time alone in the presence of God. It is true that an empty bag cannot stand up; we are on countdown to fall.

But when we have done all to stand (Ephesians 6:13), and our fence is intact, we can say as Paul the apostle said: *"We are troubled on every side, yet not distressed; we are perplexed, but not in despair, persecuted but not forsaken, cast down but not destroyed"* (2 Corinthians 4:8).

I learned simply by looking out of a window that it's not really about the strength of the storm, it's the strength of the fence!

JEJ

SUNDAY 20ᵗʰ

Thou shalt love the Lord thy God with all thy heart, soul, mind - St Mark 12:30

ARE YOU 100% COMMITTED? - Reading: St Mark 12:28-34

God requires 100% commitment from us. 99% will not do. He requires us to submit totally, completely and wholly. That's 100%.

The Heart is our passion, our affection - that is, our inward man. As with the soul and mind, the heart is not seen. When our flesh lies rotting in our grave, the inward man lives on. God requires us to love Him 100% with our inward man.

The Soul is our will, our intellect, and our emotions. The part of us that says: *"I want!", "I think!", "I feel!".*

When our minds are renewed by daily reading and submitting to the Word of God, we realise that what we want isn't important, what we think isn't important, and what we feel isn't important. The only thing that is really important, is for us to be submitted and aligned to the Will of God. That is when God will change what we want, what we think, and what we feel, and make us a new creation in Him.

That is true Strength: a renewed mind and a renewed spirit leads to a renewed attitude that is 100% submitted to God.

Min. Jo Earle

MONDAY 21st

Out of the heart of men proceed evil thoughts - St Mark 7:21

CLEAN CUPS THAT HOLD OUR THOUGHTS - Reading: St Mark 7:1-23

Traditions of men had such a grip on the Pharisees that they confused it for holiness, judging the disciples for not washing utensils and their hands.

Taking what we can control allows us to feign purity by rituals, ignoring the spots on our heart.

God cannot be contained or adapted to our habits. Neither does He allow us to present simple ritual to redeem ourselves. He only looks at the heart. The shed blood of Jesus by brutal execution, this alone cleanses us, and it is at our surrendered heart that He looks to see if we're clean.

The disciples had to be taught what defiles us, i.e., the things that start on the inside. An evil thought, murder, blasphemy, pride, foolishness, fornication. Observe this! Actions like murder, blasphemy, fornication, are physical acts of the body. We can easily see how these acts defile a person. Yet they're described among such things as pride and evil thoughts! God sees the nurture of an evil thought just as an act of murder done in the body. The thought determines the behaviour, and that thought defiles us even when we do the traditional things happily observed by others.

The plea for us to wash our thoughts thoroughly like cups, and cleanse our heart as we do our hands before eating, is to help us remain undefiled! It is how God judges us before we perform a ritual or uphold a tradition. With humility let us ask God: *"Please show me Lord, how clean are my thoughts?"*.

Joy Lear-Bernard

TUESDAY 22nd

If there is anything worthy of praise, think about that - Philippians 4:8 (AMP)

A THOUGHT DIARY - Reading: Philippians 4:1-9

If you've ever suffered with digestive problems, it's likely that you were asked to keep a Food Diary for a period of time to identify the food(s) to which you are intolerant. It can be cumbersome keeping a strict log of what you eat and drink, but it's necessary.

How about keeping a Thought Diary? Paul the Apostle makes a number of references to the mind in his writings, probably the most familiar being Philippians 2:5: *"Let this mind be in you which was also in Christ Jesus"*. What we allow to stay in our mind determines how we see and treat people, and also ourselves.

We have hundreds of thoughts daily which I'll call 'mind traffic', and we need a filter to control what we keep or let go. For instance, lots of good things can happen to us in a day, yet we lament for ages over one thing that went wrong. Twenty brethren give us a hearty handshake after service, but we go home feeling upset about one person who (we think) ignored us. You passed your exam with a B instead of an A, and you tell yourself that you have failed.

As with road traffic, from time-to-time there is congestion, nothing is moving, a lane is closed. That maybe you today, i.e., not moving, stagnant, stuck, because your mind needs a filter lane. You won't go higher than your thinking!

Will you do a Thought Diary with me for the next seven days? Honestly record your thoughts and whether they should be kept or cancelled. What you think about most will tell you a lot about who you are: *"As we think in our heart so are we" (Proverbs 23:7)*.

JEJ

*WEDNESDAY 23rd

My thoughts are not your thoughts, neither are your ways mine - Isaiah 55:8

HIGHER WAYS AND HIGHER THOUGHTS - Reading: Isaiah 55:1-13

God's way is unique in relation to man's way.

We can only see things one-dimensionally, consequently we make judgements without knowing all the facts. However, we serve a God who is omniscient therefore He knows the end from the beginning and sees things from an all-knowing perspective. Therefore, His plans for us and solutions to our problems are perfect.

Yet, too often we try to second-guess God and venture to predict or anticipate what He is doing, or even try to dictate to Him what we think He ought to be doing. But He reminds us in every area of our lives, that as the heavens are higher than the earth so His thoughts and ways are higher than ours.

Let us in humility rest in the knowledge that He knows best, and that His plans and purposes are perfect. Although sometimes our hopes are disappointed, our plans may fail and our expectations may be frustrated, God has a higher purpose to which He is working. As His children, we are a part of His eternal plan.

Let us never forget that His thoughts and plans and ways and works are all working together for good – to those that are the called according to His purpose.

Minister Sylvia Dean

*Sponge Cake Day

THURSDAY 24th

Your labour is not in vain in the Lord - 1 Corinthians 15:58

YOUR WORK IS NOT WASTED - Reading: 1 Corinthians 15:51-58

Discouragement is a destructive weapon consistently used by Satan upon the people of God, because it has such a high success rate! Its purpose is to immobilise us from completing our assignment(s), and it repeatedly works where Satan's other devices fail.

The feeling of: *"What's the point?"* or *"Why should I bother?"* is common especially when kind words and offers of support are not forthcoming.

However, the ISV of our focus verse from 1 Corinthians 15:58 says it this way: *"Therefore…be steadfast, unmoveable, always excelling in the work of the Lord, because you know that the work that you do for the Lord isn't wasted".*

Remind yourself who you're working for and who will give you your reward. Rather than giving up, endeavour to excel even more. Ask God for new vision, strength and ability to achieve as much as you can for Him in the days that The Church has remaining on earth.

Rise above every obstacle and each obstruction! *"Your labour, i.e., trouble and toil, is **not** in vain"* (1 Corinthians 15:58).

JEJ

FRIDAY 25th

Bring into captivity all thoughts to the obedience of Christ -2 Corinthians 10:5

LET GOD ARISE - Reading: 2 Corinthians 10:1-18

God is the head of our lives; we are but His children who follow and do His will.

Ephesians 6:11 tells us to put on the whole armour of God. We, as the people chosen of God, are followers of His Word. We look to Him to instruct us daily of His requirements. We do not follow vanity; we exalt God and not ourselves. We speak as He gives us utterance to do, we follow His commands and not that given to us by the world.

We need to submit our minds to God as our minds can lead us to be captives of this life. As God's children we must walk in obedience to His ways. We walk by faith and aim only to please Him. We are no longer under the law of man but under grace in Christ Jesus.

We have been rescued from certain death and everlasting damnation. God be praised for His saving grace and mercy towards His children.

Name withheld

SATURDAY 26th

Don't be troubled: ye believe in God, believe also in me – St John 14:1

BELIEVE & BELIEVE - Reading: St John 14:1; 1 Peter 1:1-9

Imagine…it's the night before Passover; thousands of pilgrims are in Jerusalem in preparation for the yearly feast/s of Jehovah. The presence of Jesus in the city is stirring anticipation and social unrest.

Behind the scenes, the angels of heaven are on critical alert, watching events unfold. Everything hangs in the balance for the battle of humankind's redemption. Uncertainty has stretched out from palace to local shelters. From breaking news to fake news, trouble is indiscriminate and rampant.

While lambs are prepared to be slaughtered for Passover, the Lamb of God has the Last Supper with his disciples, explaining all things to take place concerning Him. In the midst of their anxieties, Jesus speaks words of hope to His troubled brethren (St John14:1).

Note the double meaning "***Believe***" is highlighted twice in St John 14:1: *"Ye believe …",* this was connected with the current situation, i.e., the disciples were troubled. But they needed to recognise God in the midst of the trouble, they were therefore encouraged: *"believe also in me".*

In these times we are not to allow our peace to be disrupted by crisis. Though hard trials press us, we are to be courageous; our faith is more precious than gold that perishes (1 Peter 1:7). We are to have confidence in the knowledge that Jesus knows absolutely everything we will encounter and will provide a way of escape (1 Corinthians 10:13).

There is a process and purpose for the press. Sisters, let us who believe continue to believe in Christ Jesus.

Charm

SUNDAY 27ᵗʰ

Lean not unto your own understanding - Proverbs 3:5

I CAN'T DO IT WITHOUT YOU LORD - Reading: Proverbs 3:1-12

It can be interesting and sometimes amusing to watch a would-be-independent young child trying to do something by themselves which they just can't manage. Then, when as an adult you try and intervene to help, their indignant protest is often: *"I can do it!"*.

At times, we exhibit a similar independent attitude towards God. By this I mean that we don't always invite Him to be part of our decision-making or plans. We don't always pray and wait for His response. Sometimes we bring God into the discussion only when things have gone terribly wrong. If we remember that Jesus said in St John 15:5: *"without me, you can do nothing"*, we will save ourselves from a lot of stress and even save lots of money!

Let's not operate as though we don't need God - He knows the end from the beginning. So, ask Him whether to go or to stay, to say yes or to say no. We can use David as an example of someone wise enough to seek God before action: *"Shall I pursue after this troop? Shall I overtake them?" (1 Samuel 30:8)* and: *"Shall I go up to the Philistines? Will you deliver them into my hands?" (2 Samuel 5:19)*.

Acknowledge God's presence and respect His counsel, for: *"Except the LORD build the house, they labour in vain that build it: except the LORD keep the city, the watchman waketh, but in vain" (Psalm 127:1)*.

JEJ

MONDAY 28th

(Bank Holiday)

Look at the birds of the air. Are you not more valuable? - St Matthew 6:26 (NIV)

SING, SOAR, RELY - Reading: St Matthew 6:25-34

There is probably no better illustration than the birds for trusting God for all things. The birds sing, soar and rely on the goodness of God, every day.

Birds don't fret or worry about anything! Even as the seasons change, they remain carefree and are totally dependent on God to provide. In the rain, snow, sunshine or hail, birds know that He does not change because of their circumstances!

Trust God for everything, He is our Jehovah Jireh. He will not let you down. Psalm 33:3 says: *"Sing unto Him a new song"*. **Sing!**

Isaiah 40:31 says: *"But they that wait upon the Lord shall renew their strength; they shall mount up with wings as eagles…"*. **Soar!**

Proverbs 3:5 says: *"Trust in the Lord with all thine heart; and lean not unto thine own understanding"*. **Rely!**

Beverley V. Galloway

TUESDAY 29th

Mephibosheth shall eat bread always at my table - 2 Samuel 9:10

LEAVE LODEBAR! - Reading: 2 Samuel 9:1-13

Mephibosheth, son of Jonathan, grandson of King Saul, had been living in Lodebar from a young age. He was brought there crippled after being dropped by his nurse when he was five years old.

Lodebar means: *"no pasture"*, or *"land of nothing"*. It was a place of no word or communication. However, Mephibosheth may have considered Lodebar an ideal place to hide since it was not unusual for family members of a previous monarchy to be taken as Prisoners of War, or killed when a new King succeeded the throne.

You may be going through a lengthy unproductive, dry season, possibly because your mind is in the wrong location, i.e., in a type of Lodebar. There your thoughts are only negative: you feel like nobody likes or loves you, you feel that you're not good at anything, you feel that you're finished and are not beautiful.

The longer that you stay in Lodebar, the longer you will consider yourself to be worthless. See that although Mephibosheth was called out of Lodebar to King David's palace, after initial greetings and David doing his best to make Mephibosheth feel at ease, even with a promise of restoration of his father's land, Mephibosheth's response is that he is *"a dead dog" (2 Samuel 9:8)*. He totally missed David's message of Hope.

Affected by being in a thirsty environment for years, surrounded by no greenery, no life, no future, resulted in what I'll call 'Dead Dog Syndrome', further exacerbated by everybody else who lived in Lodebar. Certainly they would have had the same unhealthy mindset as Mephibosheth in order to stay there. What a place to live!

God has sent today's Word to fetch somebody who has become resident in Lodebar, either by choice or circumstance. He's saying: *"You've got to move!"*. You may need to drop some of your 'friends' and change your phone number! Also, take the limit not just off God, but yourself.

Not every move is a change of physical location. Quite often we just need a change of mind.

JEJ

WEDNESDAY 30th

We have the mind of Christ - 1 Corinthians 2:16

LET THIS MIND BE IN YOU - Reading: 1 Corinthians 2:1-16

"Let the Holy Ghost come in…let the Holy Ghost come in… make the consecration, trust in God and then …let the Holy Ghost come in" (R F Reynolds).

The operative word here is…**let (allow)**. Philippians 2:5 exhorts us to: *"**Let** this mind be in you, which was also in Christ Jesus":*

Beloved ones, the Lord will never force His dear presence upon us. Every wife had to first accept a proposal of marriage before becoming a Bride. So it is with us who choose to become followers of Jesus Christ. When we fully and completely accept Him, and let Christ access all areas of our mind, body, soul and **especially our spirits,** it is then that we develop a deep spiritual relationship with the Saviour. We can then also discern through the Spirit the will of Almighty God for our lives.

1 Corinthians 2:14-15 says: *"But the natural man receiveth not the things of the Spirit of God: for they are foolishness unto him: neither can he know them, because they are spiritually discerned. But he that is spiritual judgeth all things, yet he himself is judged of no man".*

So we have it, God the Creator of all things loves us and desires relationship with His creation so that we can know what does and does not please Him. How amazing is our God?

I love the simplicity of Almighty God and pray that as we **let** God into the minutest detail of our thoughts, we will through Christ's indwelling Holy Spirit within us, know the mind of Christ.

Missionary Susan Higgins

THURSDAY 31st

Friends sharpen the minds of each other - Proverbs 27:17 (CEV)

FRIENDS - Reading: Proverbs 18:8-24

We sometimes use the word 'friend' very loosely because we have a lengthy contacts list. But within those phone numbers, perhaps only a few are genuine friends.

A true friend may not be someone who you see or hear from regularly but you know that, when needed, they will be there for you. You don't worry about the time of day when you have to call; time is not a problem in friendship, and there are no 'airs-and-graces'.

Friends can offer stimulating conversation, stretch your imagination, and cause you to see things from a different point of view. They are a trusted confidante. A good friend will also tell you the truth.

Friendships sometimes have a stronger bond than familial relationships. We see an example of this with Jonathan and David. The Bible says that: *"Jonathan loved David as his own soul" (1 Samuel 18:3)*. We note also that Jonathan's loyalty was stronger towards David than for his father, Saul (1 Samuel 19).

The writer of Proverbs 18:24 says: *"There is a friend which stays closer than a brother"*. I know that many of us sing this as: *"Closer than a brother Jesus is to me, He's my dearest friend…"*, all true, but this verse, in its literal context, is not referring to Jesus being our best friend or closer than a brother! A statement is being made, i.e., friends can be closer than family.

It is an honour to be considered as someone's friend. See that Jesus elevated the status of His relationship with His disciples when He said: *"No longer do I call you servants…but I have called you friends" (St John 15:15 NKJV)*.

Thank God for good friends.

JEJ

BREASTFEEDING

What is Breastfeeding?

Breastfeeding, or nursing, is the process by which human breast milk is fed to a child. Breast milk may be from the breast or may be expressed by hand or pumped and fed to the infant. The World Health Organisation (WHO) recommends that breastfeeding begin within the first hour of a baby's life and continue as often and as much as the baby wants. Health organisations, including the WHO, recommend breastfeeding exclusively for six months. This means that no other foods or drinks, other than vitamin D, are typically given.

Common Breastfeeding problems

Sore or cracked nipples

This is very common in the first week of breastfeeding and is usually because the baby is not latching on (positioned or attached) properly. Mothers are advised to speak to their midwife, health visitor or breastfeeding specialist as soon as possible – breastfeeding should not be painful!

Milk supply

Generally, the more the baby feeds, the more breast milk is produced. However, there are a few things that can affect the milk supply:

- Feeding by the clock
- Topping-up with Formula feeds
- Dummies
- Being apart from the baby

Mastitis

Mastitis makes the breast tissue inflamed and painful. Mothers might notice a lump around the sore area, sometimes the inflammation turns into an infection. Mastitis can make mothers feel achy and run down, with flu-like symptoms or a fever.

Tongue-tie

Tongue-tie can make it harder for babies to breastfeed. It's when the strip of tissue, called the "frenulum" (attaching the tongue to the floor of the mouth) is shorter than normal. Tongue-tie can prevent the baby from latching on properly – which can then lead to sore or cracked nipples.

The Benefits of Breastfeeding

Breastfeeding can help to reduce the baby's risk of:

- Infections, with fewer visits to the hospital as a result
- Diarrhoea and vomiting
- Sudden infant death syndrome

- Obesity
- Cardiovascular disease in adulthood
- Relationship building – breastfeeding supports the mother – baby relationship and the mental health of both baby and mother

Benefits of Breastfeeding for the mother

Lowers the risk of

- Breast cancer
- Ovarian cancer
- Osteoporosis
- Cardiovascular disease
- Obesity

Is Breast Best?

The phrase 'breast is best' does not imply that parents who feed their babies formula are not doing their best; it's simply stating that in regards to the health benefits, breast milk is the best nutrition available for a baby's overall health. However, we must consider that not everyone is able to breastfeed or even wants to breastfeed.

Get Help

Many parents find breastfeeding a rewarding, empowering experience. But establishing breastfeeding can be challenging at times. There are many places where you can get help and support:

- **Association of Breastfeeding Mothers** have a group of trained volunteers who support breastfeeding mothers and their families. You can call them on 08444 122 949 https://abm.me.uk/
- **The Breastfeeding Network** have a helpline, online chat service, and information and support for families who are breastfeeding. You can call them on 0300 100 0212 https://www.breastfeedingnetwork.org.uk/
- **La Leche League** have a helpline service, and trained breastfeeding counsellors who can provide local and face-to-face support. You can call them on 0845 120 2918 https://www.laleche.org.uk/
- **The Lactation Consultants of Great Britain** website have a search function to help you find a lactation consultant in your area https://lcgb.org/

Sister Shereen Bryan, BSc (Hons) RM

September

Grace & Mercy

FRIDAY 1st

God is rich in mercy - Ephesians 2:4

BUT GOD! - Reading: Ephesians 2:1-10

As an unbeliever I was estranged from my kind, compassionate Heavenly Father.

I was a picture of hopelessness, controlled by the arch enemy, Satan; exuberantly indulging the flesh whilst aimlessly and inevitably sleeping my way into God's wrath.

"But God…". Two attributes of God meant that my pitiful state of being was cancelled and my life became a contrast to what it was before:

1. His MERCY (Greek ELEOS) – undeserved kindness, permanently atoned for my sins, ensuring I was not given the penalty I deserved
2. His LOVE (Greek AGAPE) – unconditional love embraced and protected me

Because of His mercy and His love I, a rebellious, unworthy sinner became the recipient of His redemption.

The natural response to me would have been separation from God and sure death. However, though Satan and sin demanded justice, God's mercy said, *"No"*. Moreover, Jesus Christ's unconditional love meant He was willing to pay the ultimate price for me, and guess what? He did! He gave his life for me on the cross of Calvary and He would have done it, even if I was the only sinner requiring redemption.

Now I am alive, purposeful and free. God, and He only, makes all the difference!

Missionary Carol Ighofose

SATURDAY 2nd

This thy brother was dead and is alive again - St Luke 15:32

GOD DIDN'T GIVE UP ON ME - Reading: St Luke 15:11-32

I am now a grandmother.

I did not know that I would still be alive today. My parents were very strict. They loved me but not in a way of showing outward affection. I grew up in church and got romantically involved with a young man, from a similar spiritual background, and became pregnant.

I still remember the day when the test showed as positive. I went cold and numb with shock and fear. I knew that the shame of my being unmarried and pregnant would cut the hearts of my parents who were in leadership ministry, as were the parents of the father of my child.

I went around in a daze. I thought of taking the life of my child, and even my own, to avoid having to face my parents and the church brethren. But I could not abort my baby, I knew that it would be wrong to take the baby's life to cover up my sin.

The father of my child felt that I should have taken precautions to avoid getting pregnant. I felt so alone. We told our parents. They were angry and hurt, and said that we must get married.

We got married but the marriage didn't work because we got married for the wrong reasons. My husband also felt that I'd trapped him into marriage because of the high status of his family. It was the Word of God in my heart that drew me out of the pit of depression after we separated.

God's love made me feel like I was worth something and could start all over again. When nothing else could help, God's love lifted me.

Name withheld

*SUNDAY 3rd

I will sing of the mercies of the LORD forever - Psalm 89:1

THE WAY AND THE WAY MAKER - Reading: Psalm 89:1-16

When my children were very young, I had a job which was far from where we lived. I would sometimes see a lady from another church at the bus stop early in the mornings. We would talk about life in general.

One morning I mentioned to her that I needed another job nearer to home as I didn't like working so far away and my children were at school. She looked at me and said: *"Jesus is not only The Way, He's also The Way Maker"*.

Some months later, I went to the Job Centre to see what was available within my skillset. There was nothing. There was a vacancy on the board; it was for a role working for the government, but I did not have the qualifications to apply. Nonetheless, for some reason I submitted my application and was granted an interview.

I sat in the interview room waiting for the manager to come and commence questions and give me a test. But when he walked in, after saying hello and introducing himself, he simply said: *"When can you start?".* I wondered if I had heard right but told him when I could begin. He then took me upstairs and introduced me to the team with whom I would be working, then took me downstairs again and said goodbye.

I left the building and stood outside for a while, questioning myself whether this was a dream! A job-offer for a position for which I was not qualified, without a test or interview, in walking distance from home? Then I remembered the lady at the bus stop who told me: *"Jesus is not only The Way, He's also The Way Maker"!*

I worked happily in that position for over ten years.

Pastor Hazel Jacobs

*Read a Book Day

MONDAY 4th

The lord of that servant was moved... and forgave him - St Matthew 18:27

HOW MUCH I OWE - Reading: St Matthew 18:21-35

In today's Scripture lesson we read of two servants who both had outstanding debts which neither could repay.

One of them owed a huge amount, ten thousand talents, which is the equivalent of millions of pounds or whatever your local currency is today. How generous it was of his lord to cancel the debt!

However, that same servant was owed a very small amount in comparison, and although he'd had his entire debt written off, he *"took (the one who owed him) by the throat, saying, Pay me what you owe" (v28).*

This does indeed make for alarming reading! We wonder how could someone who had been forgiven of so much, be so callous towards another person in the same position from which he had just been delivered.

The truth is, we are like the unjust servant when we choose not to 'write off' the unkind and trivial things which people have done to us. God has forgiven us for every transgression we've committed, and we expect him to forgive us next time too!

Is there somebody whom you, as it were, 'have by the throat' over something insignificant when contrasted against what God has cancelled for you? Since Jesus has released you, it's time that you let your debtor go also. See that because of the servant's merciless unforgiving behaviour, the debt previously written off by his lord was written back to his account. He therefore reverted to owing ten thousand talents!

We have to forgive to stay forgiven.

JEJ

WEDNESDAY 6th

By the grace of God, I am what I am - 1 Corinthians 15:10

LOOK WHAT GRACE DID! - Reading: 1 Corinthians 15:1-11

"But by the grace of God. I am what I am: and his grace which was bestowed upon me was not in vain; but I laboured more abundantly than they all: yet not I, but the grace of God which was with me" (1 Corinthians 15:10).

Paul called the attention of the Corinthian brethren, and our attention today, to the good news of Salvation: The death, burial, and resurrection of Jesus Christ according to Scripture. The atoning work on the cross paid the price for sin and the empty tomb was the receipt.

Jesus foretold that he would be three days and three nights in the grave (St Matthew 12:40). This was proof that Jesus was dead because only dead people are buried. The declaration of His death was made at the cross when His body was taken down for burial. Although no one witnessed when Jesus' body became a glorified body, many individuals and groups of people witnessed His resurrected body, evidence of His conquest over death. Paul also testifies that he too had seen Jesus after the resurrection.

In today's focus Scripture, Paul is reflecting on his Damascus Road experience, where his ego was killed. Unlike the twelve apostles who spent three years at the side of Jesus, Paul did not have this privileged experience featured on his résumé. Nevertheless, he was called to be an Apostle by the grace of God.

In humility, as he reflected upon his past, Paul confessed that he was not worthy of such a calling. He recalled persecuting the Church of God, killing, imprisoning and inflicting suffering on Christians before his conversion (Acts 8:3; 9:1-2).

It was the Grace and Mercy of God that saved and changed Paul, and still transforms believers today. Therefore, by God's grace (his unmerited favour) we are encouraged not to allow our past to determine our future.

Missionary Audrey Simpson

THURSDAY 7th

God can do exceeding abundantly above all that we ask or think… Eph. 3:20

GOD'S POWER IS IN YOU WHEREVER YOU GO - Reading: Ephesians 3:14-21

Wow! I was at the hairdressers today, and should have been out of there by 1pm but finished much later.

That's because a client who has a mental illness lost consciousness whilst under the hairdryer. We thought that she was dead as there was no sign of life, only a floppy body. The staff shook her, slapped her face, slapped her back, but no reaction was forthcoming, just a totally lifeless body. They called the ambulance and took the rollers out of her hair whilst waiting for it to arrive.

(*What transpired later is that the lady didn't eat this morning, is on medication but didn't take it, had a stomach problem, she is stressed from two adult daughters who were in care but are now living with her and are causing her problems.*)

My hairdresser and another woman were speaking in tongues and praying and calling out to God for help. I didn't speak in tongues but was trying to process what was happening, asking God what had happened. I asked my hairdresser: *"Has she got a pulse?"*. My hairdresser said in a panic that she didn't know what a pulse is. I asked again: *"Does she have a pulse?"*. She was still panicking and said she didn't know. I asked the question a third time, believing God, and said out loud: *"God is in control!"*. Immediately, the unconscious woman regained consciousness; she came around as though nothing had happened!

God is always in control and He gets the glory!

Name withheld

FRIDAY 8th

I will dwell in the house of the LORD for ever - Psalm 23:6

KEEP YOUR SEAT - Reading: Psalm 23:6; Romans 8:35-39

There are some things which every believer needs to know, and to say to ourselves, in order to keep on going when tough times come.

The Christian pathway can be very lonesome, just like driving down a quiet road in the night which has many twists and turns and bends. When life takes you on these kinds of journeys, it is comforting to know that Goodness and Mercy are right behind, pursuing and chasing after us. Their gaze is fixed upon us as we lose things and loved-ones through misfortune, death, and other circumstances. Goodness and Mercy, products of God's lovingkindness, have been assigned to stay with us, to surround us, all the days of our life.

I used to hear the senior saints encourage brethren to: *"Keep your seat in Zion!"*. Psalm 23:6 validates that counsel, for to dwell in the house of the LORD translates as: *"Sit down in the house of the LORD"*.

So I say to you, Dear Reader, keep your seat in God's house. Sit down, sit still, live there for the rest of your days.

Adapted from: From Me to You 90 Days in the Psalms by Jackie Jacobs

Woman, where are your accusers? Go, and sin no more - St John 8:10-11

A SURPRISE VERDICT - Reading: St John 8:1-11

We read of this nameless woman who was brought to Jesus by the scribes and Pharisees, having been caught in the *"very act"* of committing adultery.

Their indignation was evident, they were ready to stone her in accordance with the law of Moses (Leviticus 20:10). The good thing was that, before performing her execution, they brought her to Jesus to test Him, i.e., would He agree or disagree with what Moses had written?

Although their reasons for bringing her to Jesus were wrong, they actually did this woman a favour! Jesus did not contradict the law of Moses - He did not tell them not to stone the woman. In fact, He invited anyone in the crowd who had no sins, to start the stoning! O, the wisdom of God! It didn't take very long for it to be just Jesus and this woman left alone for a one-to-one. Thank God for those times alone with Him, even if it's for a confession.

With compassion Jesus looked at this woman and saw someone who did not know her worth, hence she allowed herself to be used by the man who is missing from this account. Perhaps their affair was a substitute for true love and gave a false boost to her self-esteem. Jesus saw someone who could do so much better, she needed not to accept second-best by being 'the other woman'. A songwriter wrote: *"When God dips His pen of love in my heart, He writes my soul a letter He wants me to know, His spirit all divine fills this sinful soul of mine, when God dips His love in my heart".*

This woman was brought to Jesus in disgrace, and to be disgraced, but instead received God's Amazing Grace!

JEJ

*International Beauty Day

*SUNDAY 10ᵗʰ

Grace be with you, mercy, and peace - 2 John 1:3

ORDER MY STEPS - Reading: Psalm 37:23-25; 119:132-134; 2 John 1:1-6

I met a lady when her children were babies. I worked for her as a babysitter and at times maintained the family's estate. She had married into a wealthy family and enjoyed the many benefits afforded by their riches.

The family loved and cared for me, and supported me through a lot of my difficult times. They often voiced that, although they had employed a lot of people over the years, they had never met anyone as loyal, honest, trustworthy, and kind as they found me to be. The lady said that she admired how joyful I was and wondered how, even when I was going through challenging times, she could still hear me singing and praying whilst doing my chores. She said that she enjoyed it very much and I should keep it up!

Unfortunately, the lady's marriage broke down. It was hard on her because the majority of her affluence was due to her husband's earned and inherited wealth. I remained friends with her and did what I could at this critical point of her life.

The divorce was very unpleasant with a total lack of respect shown to her by her husband. She was on the verge of losing her children, her comfortable lifestyle and everything to which she had become accustomed. As a result, her mental health started to decline. There were days when she did not get out of bed at all, however I would still go to the house and do my chores. As usual, while I was doing my tasks, I would sing praises and pray out loud to God. It was a very big house with her bedroom on the 3rd floor so I thought that she could not hear me.

I stood in the gap as an intercessor for her family. I asked God to remember the kindness that she had showed to me as His servant. The divorce was very expensive, long and hard and was destroying her mentally and financially but I kept praying for God to have mercy on her.

Thank God, she survived the divorce and the judge awarded her well. She later spoke to me and said: *"You are the reason why I am here. I wanted to kill myself but each time I thought about it, on that same day you would come into my house singing and making a lot of noise"!* I explained to her that it was God who had delivered her.

I want to encourage someone to pray without ceasing and not to let anyone rob your joy. Your joy can save a life!

Name withheld

*World Suicide Prevention Day
September 2023
Theme: Grace & Mercy
Awareness month for: Alopecia, Childhood Cancer, Gynaecological Cancer

MONDAY 11th

We have all received one gracious blessing after another - St John 1:16 (NLT)

BLESSINGS OVERFLOWING - Reading: St John 1:1-18

*"*M*any are the blessings that you give unto me, blessings overflowing like a mighty sea!"*

How well the writer of this chorus captures the essence of today's focus Scripture verse. Blessings received, whether we consider them to be great or small, we should thank God for them all.

Did you know that each day you receive blessings that you don't notice? Think about that! There hasn't been a day since you were born that you have not been blessed; even disappointments are often blessings in disguise. We owe God some thanks for what we classed as a setback when in fact it was a gracious blessing.

God would be pleased if we would stop complaining and instead reflect upon His kindness, His goodness, His provision, His care.

Meditate upon the blessings that we sing are: *"overflowing like a mighty sea"*. The favours which, although undeserved, God has lined-up in advance for us so that we keep on receiving one gracious blessing followed by another one; *"grace in place of grace already given" (St John 1:18 NIV)!*

JEJ

TUESDAY 12th

Have mercy upon me, O God - Psalm 51:1

MERCY REWROTE MY LIFE - Reading: Psalm 130:1-8

Like David, countless unending souls have been and continue to be the recipients of the *"lovingkindness"* of Almighty God.

When I read this passage, I notice that as David reflects upon the *"lovingkindness"* of God, he does not separate the two words. That's because they are inseparable in the context of our loving, forgiving, kind and gentle, delivering Saviour. No wonder a songwriter penned: *"Hallelujah what a thought, Jesus' full salvation brought, victory"*!

Just like the writer to the Hebrews encouraged, I believe that David was inspired to: *"...come boldly unto the throne of grace, that (he could) obtain mercy, and find grace to help in time of need" (Hebrew 4:16).*

Even so, we must take care how we build! Romans 6:1-2 says: *"What shall we say then? Shall we continue in sin, that grace may abound? God forbid. How shall we, that are dead to sin, live any longer therein?".*

I close by sharing some 'sound doctrine' once shared with me: **Salvation is free, but it is not carefree.** And to borrow from Reverend Mother Dr Davis: *"Continue to walk in victory Saints"*!

Peace be.

Missionary Susan Higgins

WEDNESDAY 13th

Gracious is the LORD, and righteous; yes, our God is merciful - Psalm 116:5

MEDITATIONS ON PSALM 116:5 - Reading: Psalm 116:1-19

The psalmist David, summarises why he loves the LORD, explaining how God heard his voice and his supplication.

God showed up for him and delivered his soul. David could testify that his prayer was answered by God, and he proclaims the graciousness of God in the fifth verse.

The grace of God is truly amazing, untainted, unspoiled and perfect. David declared his confidence with praise to God for answered prayer. The Lord is righteous in character; all his ways, thoughts and actions are perfection on every level. We can draw from a catalogue of personal experiences, deliverances, and also say: *"Yes, our God is merciful"* and gracious, towards us. He pities us as children needing direction and protection.

We must declare the mercy of God to a dying world! A Nimrod Society seeks to fix humankind's deterioration, labelling it as the 'Human Condition'. World Leaders convene in summit meetings across the nations to address the crisis, ignorant that they are a marionette in the devil's hand. Only the death of Jesus Christ on the cross, and the blood of Jesus Christ - antidote for sin, is supernaturally powerful to redeem.

We humbly call upon our merciful God and Saviour.

Gracious is the LORD.

Sis Charm

THURSDAY 14th

They that trust in the LORD shall be as mount Zion - Psalm 125:1

BACK TO LIFE - Reading: Psalm 125:1-5

Over, fifty years ago, when giving birth to my second daughter, Sylvia, the devil attempted to take my life. I was given the wrong injection to which I reacted really badly and I was taken into an area, basically, to die!

Bound to die, but by the mercies of God I was resurrected from the cruel hands of death. I was sure, and felt I needed to accept death at that time. I thought I was going to die and so lay there waiting; I was ready to die. I was not really understanding what was happening and I could hear something like the clink of a casket.

Then I heard my husband praying and it brought me back to my senses. He was reminding God of the prayer we had prayed as we had arrived at the hospital. He had heard a voice say: *"Well don't just sit there! PRAY!"*. I could hear him telling the Lord: *"What the doctors cannot do, God can do!"*.

As I heard my husband praying, a voice also came to me saying: *"What are you going to do? Think about your husband. Think about your children"*. My husband said that shortly after he had started praying, he heard me say: *"Thank you, Jesus!"*, and he told me he saw my countenance change and the weight of death left the room. I felt the heaviness and the blackness that I had on me, that was depressing my whole body, lift, and it moved. I was able to be discharged shortly afterwards and left hospital with my new daughter.

God has continued to keep me and delivered me through so much over the years. All praise to Jesus.

Mother Icilda Hall

FRIDAY 15th

But grow in grace, and in the knowledge of our Lord - 2 Peter 3:18

GROW IN GRACE - Reading: 2 Peter 3:1-18

Peter's mission before he departed from this life was to admonish the saints, to help build and encourage them to pursue spiritual growth to get deeper in God, and to mature in faith and Christian living. He also encouraged them to be certain of their calling and election. He thought he'd be negligent if he didn't remind them of these things.

The concept of growing in grace is intriguing. Usually, we view grace in a limited context. God gives us a measure of faith, and individuals can build or add to their faith. Similarly, anyone can access saving grace, the gift of salvation. Growing in grace is advancing in favour, or goodwill. Grace is unmerited favour, undeserved benefits or high honour, gifts that only God bestows upon us. Recipients exercise grace with gratitude, thankfulness and appreciation.

We can excel in undeserved favour by living His will. Increase also by demonstrating diligence, faithfulness, steadfastness and having intimacy with Him. Develop a deeper spiritual walk (2 Corinthians 8:7).

Even so God grants more grace, enabling us to sustain a spiritual stance. He adds grace in humility (James 4:6), and has enriched us with grace to know Him personally and doctrinally. He deserves all honour and adoration.

Sis Jx

SATURDAY 16th

Shall we continue in sin, that grace may abound? God forbid - Romans 6:1-2

DEAD TO SIN - Reading: Romans 6:1-14

To understand and answer the question Paul is asking above, we must first review a few chapters before where Paul opens the topic of Justification.

This speaks of a court room scene where Jesus is in the dock and, though guiltless of sin, takes the penalty for our sins, i.e., death on the cross to shed His blood for sins. The result of this is His righteousness being placed on, or credited to, our account. This declaration was made in the completed work on the cross, to reconcile humankind back to Himself: *"Therefore, being justified by faith we have peace with God, though our Lord Jesus Christ" (Romans 5:1).*

If we carefully review Romans 5, it will help us to understand that Romans 6:1-2 is dealing with the internal work of Sanctification. God works on us from the inside out. Jeremiah 18:1-6 captures God's Grace beautifully. Jeremiah was sent to the Potter's House to observe the work of the potter. At no stage did the potter discard the clay (us).

Christ draws us to Himself with our many issues that need His tender loving care, for: *"Where sin aboundeth, more grace abounds" (Romans 5:20).*

As believers in Christ, we are free to be obedient to the will of God because He has released us from the power of sin. This is why we sing: *"I am free, no longer bound, no more chains holding me".*

Believers are not permitted to do what is right in our own eyes. Dead to sin means it is extinct. We must always remember that God's Grace was not extended to us to encourage sin.

Missionary Audrey Simpson

*SUNDAY 17th

His mercy endureth forever - Psalm 136:1

GOD IS MERCIFUL - Readings: Psalm 103:8; Psalm 136:1-26

God is truly good to His people; He is not speedy in punishing us for our mistakes if we confess our sins to Him.

He is merciful and tender-hearted towards us. I know that God has bowels of mercy towards me. He is the best Father that I could have. Thank God that He does not keep a scorecard of my foolishness or else I would have been cut off long ago, and I'd never be able to enter into the Kingdom of God.

Thank God that His mercy is free, there's no money needed for purchase. God's mercy to me was communicated through the sacrifice of Jesus Christ when He came to give His life as a ransom for all who would believe.

I am so glad that Jesus found me, that He heard my cry. He has wrapped me in His loving arms and nurtures me each day, clothing me in His righteousness.

I will lift up my God and praise Him continuously for His goodness and grace towards me.

Name withheld

*Wife Appreciation Day

MONDAY 18th

He restoreth my soul - Psalm 23:3

ONGOING RESTORATION - Reading: Psalm 23:1-6

Years ago, I bought a small clay pot.

It was simple in design but to me it was beautiful. Unfortunately, one day it broke; it split down the middle. I almost threw it away but afterwards thought: 'Why not mend it?'.

The repair process conveyed so many messages to me:

- Although sometimes we are broken by life-events, it does not mean that we are finished
- In order to make the pieces into a pot, I had to apply some pressure whilst steadily holding both sides together with my hands
- After the pressing and sealing, I had to put the pot aside just for a little while for the glue to dry before I could use it
- The breakage and reset left a faint mark which indicated where the original break had been but, despite the scar, the pot was definitely useable

You may be wondering whether God can or will ever use you again as in former days because you broke. You may have decided that because of your circumstance you will have to live the rest of your life being less than God had intended, e.g., as a servant instead of a son (St Luke 15:19).

It is true that at times our experiences leave us with a limp or mark as a reminder of what has taken place (Genesis 32:24-25, 31). But give thanks unto the LORD for He is good: for His mercy endureth forever (Psalm 136:1). God did not throw us away on account of our being broken! He did not replace us with another vessel. He kept us to work on us.

If you feel like you have been broken by a previous or your present test, don't worry. Even during such seasons: *"Yet His blessings fall on me, sweeter than all..."*. If you're in the process of being reset, although you're feeling sore from the pressing and squeezing, it is God holding you and your pieces together with His hands for restoration.

He restoreth (keeps on restoring) my soul since surely after one trouble ends, there will always come another! Thank God for ongoing restoration.

JEJ

September 2023
Theme: Grace & Mercy
Awareness month for: Alopecia, Childhood Cancer, Gynaecological Cancer

TUESDAY 19th

Love mercy - Micah 6:8

GOD'S GRACE & MERCY - Reading: Micah 6:1-8

"He hath shewed thee, O man, what is good; and what doth the Lord require of thee, but to do justly, and to love mercy, and to walk humbly with thy God?"(Micah 6:8)

Thank God for His grace. God bestows His grace upon us when He grants us His unmerited favour: He also gives us goodness and blessings, none of which we deserve. Still at the same time, He holds back punishments from us, all of which we utterly deserve: that is His unmerited mercy.

Grace and Mercy control access in our lives, i.e., God's grace opens doors so that we can step into the next place to access blessings we **don't** deserve, yet God says, *"Yes!"*.

Our God is so great that, in addition, His mercy keeps other doors tightly shut so that we cannot walk through, i.e., protecting us from challenging, even dangerous situations that we **do** deserve, yet God says, *"No!"*.

Thank you, LORD, for your Grace and Mercy towards me, my family and my community, today and every day: *"Surely goodness and mercy shall follow me all the days of my life: and I will dwell in the house of the Lord for ever" (Psalm 23:6)*. Amen.

Min. Jo Earle

WEDNESDAY 20th

My grace is sufficient for thee - 2 Corinthians 12:9

I'VE GOT THE ANSWER - Reading: 2 Corinthians 12:1-10

Paul in 2 Corinthians 12:9 shares the Lord's answer to his prayer request: *"And he said unto me, **my grace is sufficient for thee: for my strength is made perfect in weakness"**.*

Paul's response: *"Most gladly therefore will I rather glory in my infirmities, that the power of Christ may rest upon me".*

In 2 Corinthians 12:8 (KJV), Paul uses the word *"besought"* which is para-kaleo in Greek. Para means by the side or alongside, and kaleo means to call; to call to one's side. We may earnestly pray, beseech, beg, calling out to the Lord to answer our prayers to remove the buffeters. However, what will we do with the answer?

Paul embraced the Lord's answer, and experienced transformation in his perception and attitude towards 'bothersome people'. He found joy in the ability of God's grace and overcoming power working within him and was satisfied.

The promise of God's grace is no light matter; He gives satisfactorily to help our weaknesses to make us strong. His strength, dunamis power, is a constant release of sufficient power within us to overcome and live successfully in this world amongst those who are troublesome.

People may not want to change but we can!

Pastor Josephine Lewis

THURSDAY 21st

Be ye therefore merciful, as your Father also is merciful - St Luke 6:36

BE COMPASSIONATE - Reading: St Luke 6:27-36

Mercy can be defined as compassion or pity.

It is not an entitlement, neither is it something which we deserve. We all love to receive mercy, but are not always gracious giving it in return. For example, the bus which you need has just driven past and you're still quite a distance from the bus stop. In their mirror, the bus driver sees you running with your shopping bags so waits for you to get on. How thankful you are!

Then next week, you are on a bus. The bus stands still at a bus stop for longer than you feel it should. That's because a woman with two small children is running to catch the bus. You've forgotten about your experience of mercy last week, and start to tap your heels impatiently, and look at your watch in agitation before calling out to the driver: *"Hurry up! I'm late for lunch with my girlfriends!".*

Mercy is not selfish.

Always remember that one day you will need someone to be merciful to you again, so: *"Do unto others as you would like them to do unto you" (St Matthew 7:12).*

JEJ

FRIDAY 22nd

For he that is mighty has done to me great things - St Luke 1:49

MY SILENT CRY WAS HEARD - Reading: Psalm 130:1-8

I am here to testify that Jesus is a deliverer, a way maker, a present help in times of trouble, and that there is power in the name of JESUS.

On 3 March 2022, I went to the hospital for a biopsy. The doctors found two large tissues, one in my nostril and the another in my throat. They also discovered a lesion on the back of my tongue. They suspected it could be cancer. That morning I was seen by doctors and nurses who came and carried out all of the necessary checks which included my blood pressure; the reading was normal.

I then asked the doctor how long the next procedure would take, to which he replied, 30 minutes.

On my way to theatre the only Scripture that came to me was Psalm 23:4: *"Yea, though I walk through the valley of the shadow of death I will fear no evil...".* It was like someone was saying it in my hearing, and when I heard those words, I said: *"Thank you Jesus"!*

Whilst in the theatre, the consultant anaesthetist said that I should think of a happy moment; the only thing that came to my mind is when I went Texas to visit my family in December and how amazing it was.

I do not know what time I woke up in recovery but I was soaking wet, I was bloody, weak, and voiceless. They took me to ward and each time I heard my name it was the nurse waking me up to have my blood pressure checked, and I went off to sleep. Two ENT (ears, nose and throat) doctors came twice to check on me, but I was too weak to keep my eyes open so I fell asleep. They came back the third time and woke me up, one doctor said: *"Mrs Blackwood we have to keep you in, you've lost a lot blood as your blood pressure was 209 in theatre which caused heavy bleeding. It has now elevated to 220 and you are heavily sedated",* I went back off to sleep.

The next time I woke up, it was due to heart palpitations. My heart was beating so fast, I felt it in my back. When I looked on my clothes, I could see the vibrations under the hospital gown. The nurse was two meters away from my bed and I could not call for help because I had lost my voice. I cried out on the inside for God to please send help! God heard my cry and suddenly the nurse turned around and looked at me. She ran over and yelled: *"I need an ECG machine now!".* The trainee nurses and other nursing staff started running in order to try to find one.

I laid there and all I could do was call on the name of JESUS on the inside. How many of you know that the name of JESUS is as powerful saying it on the inside as

September 2023
Theme: Grace & Mercy
Awareness month for: Alopecia, Childhood Cancer, Gynaecological Cancer

saying it aloud? (This was a one-on-one consultation with the Almighty). I kept calling JESUS, JESUS, JESUS and I felt my heartbeat start regulating (slowing down) and kept calling on Jesus. A nurse came running with an ECG machine (she did not belong to that ward), and by the time they strung me up and pressed the button, the nurse looked at me in shock and said: *"But the heartbeat is normal!".* GOD DID IT AGAIN!

Sisters, not only did my heartbeat regulate, I felt strength in my limbs, and later that evening I got up and went to the bathroom by myself. What a GOD!

On 4 March 2022, at 3:50am, this could have been my sunset - BUT GOD! I was awoken by an excruciating pain on the left side of my head, and suddenly I felt a gush and it was blood running in back of throat and through my nose. This was frightening! I pressed the button and the nurses came running. One of them put my head in a downward position. I said, *"God what is this?".* And I heard, **"YOU SHALL NOT DIE"**! It was then I realised that I am in warfare. I spent the rest of that morning repeating Psalm 118:17: *"**I shall not die, but live and declare the works of the LORD**"*, with my hands hovering over my head. I was bleeding from my nostrils and coughing up blood. Two doctors who were on duty came and saw me and all they said was that the ENT specialists were aware of what has happened, and they will be here in the morning.

Three doctors arrived later that morning and took me to another ward for further assessment. They cleaned the left nostril and then placed a camera in the right nostril. I felt a clogging in my throat and I tried clearing it by coughing but nothing happened. I told the doctor and she inserted a long (suction) tube and what came up was blood clots.

GOD IS A GOOD GOD! I said: "Thank you, JESUS!", (in my hoarse voice).

The doctor told me that if the bleeding didn't reduce, they would have to take me back to the theatre. I replied, *"The devil is a liar!".* She also said; if the blood is light red this meant it was still bleeding and if it was dark red it was old blood. With this information I knew what to look for. They took me back to the ward and I kept on praying.

The nurse checked my blood pressure it had reduced. I was so happy. When they later checked, it was elevated. Subsequently the doctor told me that I would have to stay another night due to the bleeding and elevated blood pressure.

On Saturday morning, I noticed that my blood was both light and dark red in colour and so I continued praying and trusting GOD for healing. A young doctor came and told me that I should be going home that morning. I looked at him in shock because my blood pressure was still high and the bleeding hadn't stopped. However, that afternoon another doctor came and said I will have to spend another night.

Suddenly I remembered that my pastor, Bishop Dexter Edmund, was having a Leadership Conference, so I messaged my husband to tell Bishop to pray. Deuteronomy 32:30 says: *"One shall chase a thousand and two put ten thousand to flight"*, and I knew that there were more than two in attendance and they prayed and God answered our prayer.

Saturday evening one of the nurses who was with me the previous Friday morning asked me how I was feeling. I replied that I was feeling much better, so she proceeded to say they would probably keep me for one more night, I replied: *"Nope! I'm leaving tomorrow"*. Sunday morning came and they discharged me.

On 11 April, I got my results back. Everything was NEGATIVE. NO CANCER! TO GOD BE ALL THE GLORY!

Sister Fiona Blackwood

SATURDAY 23rd

According to His mercy He saved us - Titus 3:5

I AM FORGIVEN - Reading: St Matthew 27:21-35; Ephesians 4:31-32; Titus 3:4-7

Often when we think about forgiveness, we think about those who have hurt us. Forgiving someone can feel like such a challenge, but today let's change the focus and remember how it felt to be forgiven.

From the moment that you accepted Christ as your personal saviour, you were forgiven. You were made free from the penalty and bondage of sin. The door to forgiveness was opened and you were made free.

Sometimes, when we think about the things we have done in our past, it seems a little too simple to say: *"I am forgiven".* But know and accept that you have been made free! You no longer need to carry the weight of your sins each day!

Today step out in confidence knowing that by faith and God's grace you are and have been forgiven! Reflect the joy and liberty of being forgiven, and use this feeling to affect the way you treat others.

Christine Knight

Let us therefore come boldly unto the throne of grace - Hebrews 4:16

HIS GRACE *IS* AMAZING - Reading: Hebrews 4:14-16

In recent years, I have been led to a prayerful contemplation of the Apostle Paul's words to the Ephesians: *"For by grace you have been saved through faith, and that not of yourselves; it is the gift of God, not of works, lest anyone should boast."(Ephesians 2:8-9 NKJV).* In this I have discovered that His grace is truly amazing.

While many of us know the simple definition of grace, *"unmerited favour",* it is critical to understand that, first and foremost, grace speaks of the initiative of God. To bring me into covenant relationship with Himself, to ransom my life from being the hostage of sin, God always makes the first move. He died, *while* I was still a sinner.

Why does He do this? *"But God, who is rich in mercy, **because of His great love with which He loved us**, even when we were dead in trespasses, made us alive together with Christ (by grace you have been saved)"(Ephesians 2:4-5 NKJV).* Out of an abundant wealth of mercy, and simply because He loves me, He withholds the punishment my sin *does* deserve (mercy) and, in exchange, He extends to me the favour I *don't* deserve (grace). Unsolicited and unconditionally.

This initiative shocks us. Why? Because we *know* we don't deserve it. It disorients us. In the world we live in, we are groomed not to trust this idea of 'something for nothing'. However, God takes the initiative, by grace and out of mercy, to establish a relationship with people who absolutely do not deserve to be in relationship with Him. This is amazing grace.

What does He ask of me in return? Faithful obedience. He extends His hands towards me, invites me to take His hands and walk with Him, and away from sin. Then, to work out His purpose and good pleasure in my life, He invites me to continuously access His rich supply of grace and mercy.

*"For we do not have a High Priest who cannot sympathize with our weaknesses, but was in all points tempted as we are, yet without sin. **Let us therefore come boldly to the throne of grace, that we may obtain mercy and find grace to help in time of need."** (Hebrews 4:15-16 NKJV)*

Sis A Todd, ON, Canada

**International Daughters Day*

MONDAY 25th

I will not put forth mine hand against the LORD'S anointed – 1 Samuel 24:10

DON'T TAKE REVENGE - Reading: 1 Samuel 24:1-22; Romans 12:19-21

There isn't anybody reading this page today who has never been hurt by a trusted individual. Not all hurt is deliberate, but sometimes it is. Plots and schemes can be planned to slow you down, or to bring you down altogether.

We read about the jealousy of Saul towards David. Jealousy led to hatred and then attempted murder *(1Samuel 18:11; 19:10)*. Saul's feelings were not hidden - if someone throws a javelin at you, it's easy to work out the rest!

So how should you deal with knowing that someone doesn't like you or hates you, knowing that they've tried different methods to destroy you? What would you do if an opportunity for revenge presented itself to hurt them as much as they had hurt you?

David cut a small piece of Saul's robe, and showed Saul how close that he had come to him without killing him. Sparing Saul's life was noble, but it's quite possible that the decision to do the right thing was not really the first thing that came into David's mind; I think that David cutting Saul's garment proves that. The right thought is not always the first thought that comes into my mind either, and I'm sure that's true for you too: *"Evil is (always) present with me" (Romans 7:21).*

Nonetheless, David told himself: *"I will not put forth my hand…" (1 Samuel 24:10).* And there are situations when, as godly women, we too must tell ourselves: *"I will not…"*. Don't try and justify why you should; restrain yourself and say: *"Although I could, I will not…"!*

JEJ

*TUESDAY 26th

He giveth more grace - James 4:6

RECEIVING GOD'S DIVINE UNMERITED FAVOUR - Reading: James 4:1-10

James 4:6 is very important. So important that it is featured in Proverbs 3:34, and repeated twice in the New Testament, i.e., 1 Peter 5:5 and James 4:6.

This Scripture has taught us that *"God giveth more grace. Wherefore he saith God resisteth the proud but giveth grace to the humble "*. Grace is unconditional love and favour towards a person who does not deserves it (Ref: Paul Zahl).

According to the Scriptures: *"All have sinned and come short of the glory of God" (Romans 3:23-24)*, and equally all need the grace of God to bring us to repentance and acceptance of Salvation. *"For the grace of God that bringeth salvation hath appeared to all men" (Titus 2:11).*

Pride is a deep pleasure or satisfaction and confidence in oneself, a feeling of being better than others (Miriam-Webster .com.). Every person has pride problems because the sin-nature is self-centred, wanting only to please itself.

Pride causes us to replace our trust in God with trusting in our own selves, leaning on our own understanding. But humility is an act of selflessness and kindness, that exhibits patience, gentleness, and is concerned about others.

Jesus was the perfect example of humility and came to save sinners who were lost. Jesus taught us: *"And whosoever shall exalt himself shall be abased; and he that shall humble himself shall be exalted" (St Matthew 23:12).*

We must remember and strive to humble ourselves before Almighty God. We must have a heart of humility, brokenness and contrition to receive Jesus Christ as Lord.

Missionary M Fraser

*World Dumpling Day

WEDNESDAY 27th

You, Lord, are good, and...and plenteous in mercy - Psalm 86:5

WHAT DOES YOUR MERCY LOOK LIKE? (PART 1) - Reading: Psalm 86:1-5

As we look at God's forgiveness and His mercy, may we also consider our own. We sometimes have difficulty in extending forgiveness and mercy to others; forgiveness is not always easy.

Note: it is not possible to show mercy if we can't forgive. When we have truly released someone from our heart, in our prayers we ask God to bless them in the same way that we would want Him to bless us. We don't wish that God would allow bad things to befall them.

See that the psalmist says God is *"plenteous"* in mercy; God's compassion is abundant, not sparse! I'm glad about that and so should you be. We will never know how often in our lifetime that we have offended God, really grieved Him to His heart, and yet, amazingly, He still loves us.

Forgiveness and mercy should not be reliant upon receiving an apology from your offender; you may never get one! As Stephen was being stoned to death, he did not pray for God to send a bolt of lightning to kill his tormentors. In the midst of the painful assault on his body: *"Stephen calling upon God said Lord Jesus receive my spirit. And kneeled down, and cried with a loud voice, Lord lay not this sin to their charge"* (Acts 7:59-60).

Today, let us pray a prayer of mercy for those who have hurt us.

JEJ

THURSDAY 28th

A Samaritan, came where he was: and had compassion on him - St Luke 10:33

WHAT DOES YOUR MERCY LOOK LIKE? (PART 2) - Reading: St Luke 10:25-37

Have you ever been wounded and needed healing, but instead received another bruise?

Or have you ever made a serious mistake, known that it was a mistake, and whilst trying to deal with it you were constantly reminded by others that it's your own fault why your life is in a mess?

The Good Samaritan may have wondered why the man was on the Jericho Road alone. That road was notorious for bandits and danger to the extent that it was sometimes called: 'The Way of Blood'. But the time for that conversation, or for asking of questions, was not while this man lay there half dead and still haemorrhaging. It was time for the Samaritan to try and save the victim's life, to come off his beast, do basic First Aid, and quickly get him to the nearest hospital for professional health care.

Real mercy sees needs first, and faults later: *"How can I help?"* or *"What can I do?"*. Thank God that when we've needed Critical Care for our bleeding situations, self-inflicted or otherwise, Jesus willingly came down from where He was to where we were and said: *"I am come that (you) might have life, and that (you) might have it more abundantly" (St John 10:10).*

In mercy Jesus speaks life into us first, knowing that conforming us into His image is a patient work-in-progress.

JEJ

September 2023
Theme: Grace & Mercy
Awareness month for: Alopecia, Childhood Cancer, Gynaecological Cancer

*FRIDAY 29th

The LORD is merciful and gracious, ...and plenteous in mercy - Psalm 103:8

THE MERCIES OF GOD - Reading: Psalm 103:1-11

The psalmist here describes God's character as merciful and finishes the verse saying that He is plenteous in mercy. He aptly describes God's mercy as great, endless; it's higher than the heavens above and deeper than the deepest sea.

When recently studying through the women of the Bible, one of my aims was to learn how God showed His grace, His love and His mercy to those women and to all of us individually. My study was indeed an eye-opener! God is certainly still doing the same for us today as He did for women in Bible days.

No matter what I go through, great is His mercy towards me. Song writer A. B. Simpson describes God's mercy as: *"An ocean divine, a boundless and fathomless flood...O, let us be lost in the mercy of God 'til the depths of His fulness we know"!* Beloved be encouraged today to launch out and lose yourself in God's mercy.

Knowing these mercies are with me wherever I go builds my faith, and gives me confidence. Goodness and Mercy are following me.

Marriette Bell

*Macmillan Cancer Support World's Biggest Coffee Morning

SATURDAY 30th

His mercies and compassions are new every morning – Lamentations 3:22-23

GOD GIVES US HOPE IN AFFLICTION - Reading: Lamentations 3:18-26

In the midst of affliction there is hope!

Many songwriters have been inspired to write positive, optimistic songs declaring the faithfulness of God and His ability to console and uplift in times of distress. Given the season that we are in, this is a reassuring and encouraging message. There is hope, indeed, there is comfort available for the children of God in times of distress, trials and turmoil.

It is significant that Jeremiah, the 'weeping prophet' introduces us to the *"Balm in Gilead" (Jeremiah 8:22)*. The reference here was to a cure for spiritual sickness that was rejected by a people consumed by sin. Nonetheless, our 'take away' is that God was willing, and is always willing, to heal soul, spirit and body.

The third chapter of Lamentations is directed to exiled Judah, shortly after the fall of Jerusalem (586 BC). Chapters 1 and 2 deal with the grief and broken-heartedness of the prophet who recognised that God punishes sin. God had reminded Judah previously that there were consequences for sin, yet in spite of that, God wanted His people to know that there was hope!

In the midst of this lament there is a glimmer of hope. Why? Because we have a God who is intrinsically good, a God who is faithful, merciful and who is full of compassion. He meets us at our point of need, offering solace, comfort and being a balm to our sin-sick, weary souls. Despite the sorrows that we have endured, the Scripture declares: *"It is of the LORD's mercies that we are not consumed, because his compassions fail not. They are new every morning: great is thy faithfulness"*. We are encouraged to trust in God even when we cannot 'trace' Him.

We can bank on the fact that each morning we have access to new mercies. A compassionate and merciful God is moved to act on our behalf. Whatever trials we are going through, our God is moved by love to vindicate us, to support us, to be our *'bridge over troubled waters!'*.

Lady Shirley Hamilton

ALOPECIA

Are you losing your hair, or has your hair thinned as you have got older? Mine certainly has. I've noticed a significant thinning in my front hairline, extending to the middle of my head.

It is normal to lose hair. We can lose between 50 and 100 hairs a day, often without noticing. Hair loss is not usually anything to be worried about, but occasionally it can be a sign of a medical condition. Some types of hair loss are permanent, like male and female pattern baldness. This type of hair loss usually runs in the family, and you will probably be aware of it.

Alopecia areata is more than thinning, it is actual areas of hair loss leading to balding. It occurs when the immune system attacks hair follicles and causes the follicles to stop producing hair. Anyone can get this condition: men and women are equally affected. Children may also be affected, but it tends to be a condition that affects older people. It can be progressive, or gradually improve. There are many treatments available, but they are not always effective.

Hair loss may be due to non-immune causes such as stress, illness, iron deficiency, or cancer treatment.

If you are losing hair in clumps, have bald patches, or your scalp is itching or burning, please see your General Practitioner. They may arrange a telephone consultation first of all but, explain your symptoms, and they will then arrange a face-to-face consultation to examine your scalp.

Hair loss can reduce your self-esteem and sense of worth. Tell your GP if you are concerned about your hair loss, and ask which treatments are available. Don't keep your concern or anxiety about hair loss to yourself. Talk about it.

Dr Jo Brooks FRCPCH
Consultant Community Paediatrician

October

The Word of God

*SUNDAY 1st

For the word of God is alive and active - Hebrews 4:12 (NIV)

THE WORD OF GOD - Reading: Hebrews 4:1-13

There is no one since the beginning of time who has inspired men to write seamlessly, apart from the Holy Ghost (2 Peter 1:21). Producing 66 books, all with precision and clarity through divine inspiration.

The gospel writer St John was divinely inspired to write: *"In the beginning was the Word and the Word was with God and the Word was God" (St John 1:1).*

The power of the breath of God inspired divine inspiration through man. In Hebrew the Spirit or 'Ruach' by itself is known as the breath of God. The Apostle Paul in his letter to Timothy, inspired by the Spirit, says: *"All Scripture is breathed out by God".* This has multiple benefits for believers, e.g., learning, correction and training in God's righteousness to ensure we are equipped with the tools for ministry (2 Timothy 3:16).

God meets us in His Word and the Holy Spirit works powerfully though the Word of God. Therefore, the Word of God is multi-facetted. Example: The Word of God, is known as the Sword of the Spirit (Ephesians 6:19).

In the book of Hebrews, we are introduced to the double-edged sword which is able to cut and heal simultaneously. This Sword does not kill man like a natural sword. The Word of God is sharp like a surgeon's scalpel, where it cuts deep, and is precise in diagnosing the condition of the heart. It exposes our weaknesses, doubts, bitterness and unforgiveness; it reveals our spiritual health. This brings man to confession and repentance.

The double-edged sword does a quick work in restoration and healing. God's Word means what it says. Nothing and no one can resist the Word of God.

Missionary Audrey Simpson

*Grandparents Day UK

MONDAY 2nd

Thy word is a lamp unto my feet, and a light unto my path - Psalm 119:105

LEAD ME LORD - Reading: Psalm 119:105-112

God wants us to be totally dependent on Him, even with the smallest of decisions. We sometimes end up in deep waters due to our making choices which are not in accordance with God's Word.

Some of us have never had to depend upon a lamp for light; the time and place where we were born means that we've always known electricity. But in ancient times, those venturing out at night had to carry a lantern to shed light on their path so that they would not stumble or fall in the darkness.

Likewise, the light of God's Word gives us direction. It illuminates the holes and uneven patches which we would not see when walking in our own wisdom. It tells us when to stop and when to go; when to say yes and when to say no.

We will avoid much heartache and trouble if we see the Word as a lamp and a light, a compass and an atlas. It is the very Mind of God. Ladies, let's put away our independence and say: *"Lead me Lord through your Word".*

JEJ

October 2023
Theme: The Word of God
Awareness Month for: Breast Cancer, Cholesterol, Domestic Violence, Lupus, Menopause, Mental Health

TUESDAY 3ʳᵈ

The word of our God shall stand for ever - Isaiah 40:8

GOD'S WORD IS SURE – GOD'S WORD ENDURES - Reading: Isaiah 40:1-10

According to St John 1:1, *"In the beginning was the Word, and the Word was with God and the Word was God".*

In St Matthew 24:35 we read*: "Heaven and earth shall pass away but my words shall not pass away".* God's Word is Himself, therefore if His Word was to pass away, then God would also have to pass away and no longer be the Sovereign Eternal God that He is.

Grass is temporary and so are flowers. The sun shone and they dried up and perished. Even the hardest of blooms only last for a very short while. Yet amidst the frailty and instability of life, there is one thing that remains forever, that is the Word of God.

We are here today and tomorrow we are gone. We are temporary, but God's Word is forever: *"Forever O Lord your Word is firmly fixed in heaven" (Psalm 119:89).* According to 1 Peter 1: 24: *"All flesh is as grass and all the glory of man as the flower of grass".* Whatever heavenly glory we possess is soon gone, but if our hope and salvation are based upon the solid rock of God's unfailing Word, our future is secured forever.

Because you are everlasting, your promises are sure. We can trust you Jesus.

Missionary M Fraser

WEDNESDAY 4th

The entrance of thy words giveth light - Psalm 119:130

THE LIGHT OF GOD'S WORD – Reading: Psalm 119:129-136

Most of us hear many Scripture lessons taught and sermons preached each year.

Yet it is not the amount of Word that we hear that brings change, it is the entrance or absorption of the Word that yields results.

We sometimes seem to misunderstand the purpose of the Word. Although hearing and reading it may bring excitement and thrill our souls, that is not its primary objective. If the Word only excites and thrills, and does not enter the heart, we continue to live in darkness. Darkness in this context means that we believe wrong and it will therefore naturally follow that we also live wrong. We live according to what we believe.

When the Word gains entry into our heart, what a difference! It is like someone who was blind and has received their sight; they no longer stumble or walk uncertainly.

Make time to not just read the Word but study it, read it slowly in your own time. Invest in or download study aids, e.g., Blue Letter Bible, a good Study Bible. Or if you don't understand what you've read, ask someone to explain.

How about having a Bible study partner? Join up on the phone or online to help each other to explore and understand God's Word.

JEJ

October 2023
Theme: The Word of God
Awareness Month for: Breast Cancer, Cholesterol, Domestic Violence, Lupus, Menopause, Mental Health

329

*THURSDAY 5th

As newborn babes, desire the sincere milk of the word - 1 Peter 2:2

AN APPETITE FOR THE WORD - Reading: 1 Peter 2:1-10

There is a misleading concept which says that once we have accepted Jesus Christ as our personal friend and Saviour, that's enough.

This is very far from the truth. We must always crave and have an appetite for the Word, just like how newly born babies crave for their mother's milk. I remember my mother telling us to add Farley's Rusks to the milk when our children appeared to be unsatisfied after having a bottle. The rusk was added to make them feel full for longer.

In the same way that a newborn baby depends on milk to live and grow, the Word of God is nourishment and essential for every believer. We must intake it regularly, chew and meditate on the Word. Feasting on the Word will develop our faith and spiritual development. In contrast, just as children who are not correctly nourished 'fail to thrive', believers who have no appetite for God's Word will be stagnant or regress.

I am reminded of a song that we used to sing in Sunday School by an unknown author: *"If you read your Bible pray every day, you'll grow, grow, grow. Don't read your Bible, forget to pray, you will shrink, shrink, shrink"*. Let us stay in the Word.

Evangelist Diane Campbell

*World Teachers Day

*FRIDAY 6th

Thou art my hiding place…I hope in thy Word - Psalm 119:114

LORD, I AM HIDING IN YOU - Reading: Psalm 119:113-120

Do you remember as a young child playing Hide and Seek? We made sure that we hid in places where we thought we wouldn't be found. Sometimes we were successful, and other times we were disappointed to learn that the place which we thought was so secure, was easily discovered.

As time went by, we learned through our Christian Walk, that our security is not based upon being able to do things for ourselves or our families, or creating our own 'bubble' of protection, but it's about being totally dependent upon the Living Word of God.

Psalm 119:114 states: *"Thou art my hiding place and my shield: I hope in thy Word"*. What is God's Hiding Place? It's the place where I experience peace, joy, love, protection. It's a place where I am covered. It's also a place where I can say: *"No weapon formed against me shall prosper…" (Isaiah 54:17).*

Moses asked God to show him His glory, but God said: *"There shall no man see me, and live. But I'll hide you in the cleft of the rock and cover you with my hand, you will see my back parts when I'm passing by" (Exodus 33:18-23).* After seeing God's hinder parts, Moses' face glowed with the glory of God.

God's Hiding Place is where we can experience His glory. Everything that we need is in that Hiding Place so Lord, help me to give you all of me, for when it came to my salvation, you spared nothing! You spared nothing!

Evangelist Deveen Smith

*World Smile Day

October 2023
Theme: The Word of God
Awareness Month for: Breast Cancer, Cholesterol, Domestic Violence, Lupus, Menopause, Mental Health

331

SATURDAY 7th

My word shall accomplish that which I please - Isaiah 55:11

A NON-NEGOTIABLE WORD - Reading: Isaiah 55:1-13

I do remember when we were being raised as children often hearing in our house: *"It's not you raising me, it's me raising you!".* You may have heard that line too! The idea behind that discipline was to establish parental authority, and an understanding to us as children that we were not our parents' equal.

In Isaiah 55, God reminds us of His authority concerning His Word. Before we get to our focus verse, God tells us clearly in verses 8 and 9 that we are not on the same level as Him: *"My thoughts are not your thoughts, neither are your ways, my ways".* In verse 11 there is no wavering of God's single control, nor any suggestion that we may be able to negotiate with His Word. God says: *"So **shall my Word** be that goeth forth out of **my** mouth: **it shall not** return unto me void, but **it shall** accomplish that which I please, and **it shall** prosper in the thing whereto I sent it".*

Children know when there's a bit of 'wriggle-room' with what their parents say, but there should also be no doubt when an answer is a firm *"No",* or *"Not today"*! We have become used to negotiating, debating in meetings and conferences. We are invited to share our ideas and opinions to reach a compromise to accommodate all parties, and sometimes we also have that same mindset towards God: But, *"Who has directed the Spirit of the LORD, or being His counsellor has taught Him?" (Isaiah 40:13).*

God is not negotiating His Word with us. We must obediently do as we are told.

JEJ

October 2023
Theme: The Word of God
Awareness Month for: Breast Cancer, Cholesterol, Domestic Violence, Lupus, Menopause, Mental Health

SUNDAY 8th

As for God, his way is perfect; the word of the LORD is tried - 2 Samuel 22:31

GOD'S WAY IS PERFECT - Reading: 2 Samuel 22:20-33

This Scripture speaks of the character and divine power of God who is perfect; He is truth and without blemish. Our Lord is the self-existent one, there is no other God. His Word has been tried and proven to be faithful and trustworthy.

In ancient times a buckler was a small shield that fitted on the wrist of a solider, and was used for protection in battles. This analogy is used to describe God as our shield and protector. He is a present help in time of trouble.

Saul armed David with his armour, but David took it off because he'd never tried it before. David proved God for himself when the Lord delivered him from the lion and the bear. So instead, David went into battle in the name of the LORD of hosts and killed Goliath.

How long will you continue to fight your Goliath and fail? Put on the whole armour of God so you can withstand the attacks from the enemy. The Word of God is sharper than any double-edged sword. God's way is 100% bullet-proof, and His faithfulness never comes to an end.

Put your trust in God, His way is perfect and He will protect you from your enemies.

Rachel Lewin

October 2023
Theme: The Word of God
Awareness Month for: Breast Cancer, Cholesterol, Domestic Violence, Lupus, Menopause, Mental Health

333

MONDAY 9th

The law of the LORD is perfect, converting the soul - Psalm 19:7

A PERFECT LAW - Reading: Psalm 19:7; 119:65-72

Who appreciates the law?

Man's law keeps authority and lines of safety. It demands things to be so. It defines right from wrong but cannot make good from wrong. Some run from it, break it or live in fear to abide by it.

Yet God's law converts, i.e., 'changes', 'inverts', 'substitutes', mutates and 'metamorphoses'. It does not only show us where we are wrong, but the complete law of God's love is able to take us who were born in sin, and transform everything about us. There is no other law which has the power to remake the guilty!

The law of the LORD makes us new when we delight in it. It translates us from death to life, it gives us beauty and takes away our ashes.

God's law is indeed perfect. It brings light and uprightness to dark saddened conditions when we adhere to, submit and delight in it. What deep thing in your life seems impossible? His law has power beyond our own limitations.

What hopeless heart needs the joyous laws of God to make it new? Lord, re-teach us, renew us, repair and reconnect us to your law. It is indeed sweet and perfect in this imperfect world. We trust in your perfect law.

My life may seem in places hopeless, but your law can cause what was not to become true in my life. Teach me daily to love your law. In Jesus' name.

Joy Lear-Bernard

October 2023
Theme: The Word of God
Awareness Month for: Breast Cancer, Cholesterol, Domestic Violence, Lupus, Menopause, Mental Health

334

*TUESDAY 10th

Call His name Emmanuel, which means, God with us - St Matthew 1:23

GOD IS WITH US - Reading: St Matthew 1:23; St John 1:1-18

This passage of Scripture starts with *"Behold"* which means: *"Look"* or *"WOW"!* The writer is trying to tell us something important.

It is not about a virgin having a baby, although that is amazing, but it's about the baby. The baby is no ordinary child, this is The Lord Jesus Christ! As we investigate God's Word, we realise that Jesus is God manifested in flesh. What does this mean for us? Well, God Himself wanted and still wants to live among us.

The God who made heaven and earth, God of the Universe, God of Creation, He wants to help us daily with everything that pertains to our lives. Yes! Every decision that we make, whether it is mundane or important. God does not want to be on the side-lines of our lives but right in the middle, dwelling within us, guiding us, and most importantly making us more and more like Himself each day.

Let us commit ourselves to Him daily, trusting Him with everything.

Marie Chisnall

World Porridge Day & Mental Health Day

WEDNESDAY 11ᵗʰ

Be ye doers of the Word, not hearers only - James 1:22

DO THE WORD - Reading: James 1:19-27

In his writings, James makes the point that hearing the Word of God, and not obeying them, it is deceiving one self.

James declares that Christians should be doers of God's Word. A doer is a person who acts rather than just speaking or thinking (Mirriam-Webster.com).

David in Psalm 119:9-10 asked the question: *"Wherewithal (how) shall a young man cleanse his way?"*. He answers by saying: *"By taking heed thereto according to thy word "*. Hearing the Word, and putting it into practice, is what Jesus and James advocate.

Jesus has likened the person who hears His words and obeys them unto someone who is wise and builds their house upon the rock. The floods came and the wind beat upon it, but the house withstood the storm (St Matthew 7:25).

God's Word demands a change in our lives by producing evidence, i.e., bearing good spiritual fruits (St Matthew 13:39). The results of spiritual fruitfulness are that God is glorified, we grow, and others come to know Jesus. Obedience to His Word *"is not grievous" (1 John 5:3)*; Jesus said that: *"If you love me, you will keep my commandments" (St John 14:15)*, and *"to obey is better than sacrifice" (1 Samuel 15:22)*.

Therefore then, as a final reminder, hear the Word but also make sure that you do what you hear.

Missionary M Fraser

THURSDAY 12th

I esteem the words of His mouth more than my necessary food - Job 23:12

THE TREASURE OF GOD'S WORD - Reading: Job 23: 1-17

How many meals a day do you consume? And then do you 'pick' in between meals?

Some women have a weekly meals chart, especially if they are trying to follow a strict diet. It forward plans what they will eat at mealtimes on each day of the week.

If you were to consider how often during the day you feel hungry for the Word, enough to reach for another helping, how would that compare with your appetite for natural food? Do you have set times to spend studying the Word? And perhaps like a daily menu, have you set out particular subjects or Bible characters that you would like to study?

No matter how busy we are, we always find time to eat. None of us will go from morning until night without having at least one meal, but we are sometimes too busy to read the Word.

As we contemplate Job saying that he treasured and valued the words of God more than his daily bread, let us throughout the next week keep an honest Word Diary, i.e., make a note of how many times each day we read the Word or how often we have meditated upon His Word.

JEJ

October 2023
Theme: The Word of God
Awareness Month for: Breast Cancer, Cholesterol, Domestic Violence, Lupus, Menopause, Mental Health

337

FRIDAY 13th

Receive with meekness the Word which can save your souls - James 1:21

LAY IT ALL DOWN - Reading: Galatians 5:19-26; James 1:19-21

Dear Ones, as we sit and meditate on the above Scripture, we are reminded to put to death anything that does not please our Holy God. What are these things then that we must put away?

Sins such as: shameful desires, sexual sin, impurity, lust, greed. Sins of speech, anger, malicious behaviour, slander, dirty language and lying.

How do we as mere mortals do this? Well, we cannot on our own, but thank God, He has sent His son Jesus Christ to help us. Psalm 119:9 tells us that it is the Word of God that cleanses us. Jesus also told His disciples: *"You are already clean because of the Word I have spoken to you" (St John 15:3).*

We know from studying the Scriptures that Jesus is The Word of God, so let us empty ourselves before Him and allow Him to fill us.

Marie Chisnall

October 2023
Theme: The Word of God
Awareness Month for: Breast Cancer, Cholesterol, Domestic Violence, Lupus, Menopause, Mental Health

338

SATURDAY 14th

Blessed are they that hear the Word of God, and keep it - St Luke 11:28

DID YOU HEAR? - Reading: St Matthew 7:24-27; St Luke 11:28

Hearing must be followed by actions based on what we've heard, otherwise we have not really heard. To hear is more than just receiving sounds through the ear canal.

We see in the book of Revelation that the conclusion of each of the letters to the seven churches in Asia, ended with: *"He that hath an ear, let him hear what the Spirit saith unto the churches".* Meaning, if you've heard, then do what the Spirit said.

What is a constant frustration with parents and their children? It's that the child, although not physically deaf, by their actions demonstrates poor hearing by not doing what they have repeatedly been told.

The hearer who keeps/does what they hear is described in today's focus verse as *"blessed"* or *"happy"* or *"favoured"*. There's a blessing and peace that comes with obeying the Word.

Jesus, in teaching about the house built upon the sand and the one built on the rock, again makes the point about doing what we hear. The intended learning outcome of that parable is, if we don't keep God's Word we will fall when storms come, just like a house built upon sand (St Matthew 7:26). But when we hear and live the Word, we can echo the psalmist in Psalm 125:1, *"They… shall be as mount Zion, which cannot be removed…".*

JEJ

October 2023
Theme: The Word of God
Awareness Month for: Breast Cancer, Cholesterol, Domestic Violence, Lupus, Menopause, Mental Health

339

Let the Word of Christ dwell in you richly in all wisdom - Colossians 3:16

WORDS OF A DEAR FRIEND - Reading: Colossians 3:12-17

God's Word to me is like a letter from a dear friend. Here are some of my favourite verses:

Deuteronomy 33:25
…….. as thy days, so shall your strength be

Proverbs 11:25
…… he that watereth shall be watered also himself

Proverbs 25:11
A word fitly spoken is like apples of gold in pictures of silver

Romans 8:18
For I reckon that the sufferings of this present time are not worthy to be compared with the glory which shall be revealed in us

Hebrews 13:14
For here we have no continuing city, but we seek one to come

James 1:5
If any of you lack wisdom, let him ask of God, that giveth to all men liberally, and upbraideth not; and it shall be given him

God is in control.

Evangelist Cherry Smith

MONDAY 16th

For ever, O LORD, Thy Word is settled in heaven - Psalm 119:89

THE FOR EVER WORD - Reading: Psalm 119:89-96

I always feel a sense of peace when reading today's focus verse, I can't even fully explain why.

Perhaps it's because life is so uncertain, nothing lasts forever, people are changeable and can also be gone in a moment, the world is almost unrecognisable to the one which I grew up in. Nevertheless, in the midst of every type of fluidity, God's Word remains the same.

James 1:17 says that in God our heavenly father: *"there is no variableness, neither shadow of turning".* The constancy of God's Word far surpasses the rigidity of the law of the Medes and the Persians (Daniel 6:12) which, although not meant to be altered, had to be changed. It contained a flaw because it was written by man. But the Bible, which is more than just a good book, it is the mind of God Himself, is without fault and settled in a place where nobody can reach it to make adjustments; it's confirmed in heaven. God's Word never needs updating! The written Word is inspired by Him who was, and still is, and is yet to come (Revelation 4:8).

I've learned and am continuing to learn that whenever I want the comfort of 'sameness', I will only find it in the immutable Word of God. Anything else can change.

JEJ

October 2023
Theme: The Word of God
Awareness Month for: Breast Cancer, Cholesterol, Domestic Violence, Lupus, Menopause, Mental Health

TUESDAY 17th

I shall not die, but live, and declare the works of the LORD - Psalm 118:17

MIRACLE WORKER! - Reading: Psalm 118:16-24;

I give God thanks for his goodness and mercies towards me. I am blessed and highly favoured. According to medical science, I should have died 23 years ago but God allowed me to live as my work on earth is not finished.

As a result of infertility and severe pains in my abdomen, my doctor carried out some investigations which led to a diagnosis of endometriosis. The findings led to other issues. The doctors therefore suggested that my husband and I consider adoption. The Lord spoke to Pastor Raymond in a dream confirming that, despite what the medical report said, we would have a child and we should name her Alexandria.

The years went by and I began to seriously think about adoption. But then I became pregnant and, on our 7th wedding anniversary, I was blessed to give birth to Sister Alexandria. Then two years later we were blessed to have another daughter, Sister Hannah.

After another two years, I was blessed again to become pregnant; the pregnancy was confirmed at eight weeks. One morning I woke up feeling slightly strange within myself. I was not feeling unwell as such, it's very hard to explain how I felt. I arrived at work and during my lunch break I mentioned the strange feeling to my manager but instead of being sympathetic, she was very unhappy with me because there was a high level of sickness absence. The government department in which I worked was very stressful especially dealing with customers and so my manager thought that I was hinting that I needed to take some sick leave!

However, after work when I arrived home, I was still feeling strange. The next day I woke up and there were obvious signs of a miscarriage so I attended Accident and Emergency at my local hospital. A doctor examined me and sent me home but she asked me to visit the hospital again on Monday morning for further examination.

I updated my family regarding the situation. My younger sister, Nurse Sandra, advised that at the hospital I should insist that I be given an ultrasound scan. Her reason for saying this was that if I was miscarrying, I should be thoroughly checked for other possible complications as well.

When I arrived at the hospital, the nurse asked me what I thought I was currently experiencing. I responded that I was having a miscarriage but all is well. She told me that there was nothing more they could do so I would be discharged. It was then that I suddenly remembered the instructions from Nurse Sandra! I asked my nurse to

October 2023
Theme: The Word of God
Awareness Month for: Breast Cancer, Cholesterol, Domestic Violence, Lupus, Menopause, Mental Health

342

kindly perform an ultrasound before letting me go. She agreed and a scan was done immediately.

The nurse was shocked by what she saw and started to shake. She told me that my baby was in my fallopian tubes. Now I was shaking too and couldn't look at the scan. I was distressed and in shock, and suddenly went into a trance. Somewhere in the distance of my semi-consciousness, I could hear the nurse saying that she would have to get a wheelchair to transport me upstairs to the ward. She said I would not be allowed home that day because the foetus was growing daily and it was quite big. If the embryo touched the large blood vessel which was near to where it was positioned, I would die. She said they would have to prepare me for emergency surgery later that day.

Suddenly, I was on a ward. I came out of the trance and tears were running down my face. I knew that Pastor Narme planned to collect me so I sat up in the bed and rang my mom, Mother Bell. She was very calm and reassuring, as usual, and encouraged me that Jesus never fails and said she was praying and believing God would take me through. She was already claiming the victory and speaking in Holy Ghost tongues.

My husband arrived to take me home as planned that morning and was very shocked to see me on a hospital ward and in bed! We prayed together on the ward and left everything in God's hands. I then informed our family. I could feel the prayers. The surgery was successful.

I was off work to recover for a while. During that time my manager visited me at home. I reminded her how I felt the last day at work before I was admitted into hospital. She apologised for her attitude but I said to her that she was under pressure so I understood her position.

I eventually returned to work. I have a scar to remind me that our God is the God of all flesh, and there is nothing too hard for Him (Jeremiah 32:27).

I am here today because God is still working miracles.

Evangelist Janette Narme

October 2023
Theme: The Word of God
Awareness Month for: Breast Cancer, Cholesterol, Domestic Violence, Lupus, Menopause, Mental Health

343

WEDNESDAY 18th

Speak the Word only, and my servant shall be healed - St Matthew 8:8

SPEAK THE WORD ONLY - Reading: St Matthew 8:5-13

Usually, from today's key verse, we speak about: the miracle of the Word which Jesus sent to the centurion's servant who was sick at home, the centurion's faith, and the servant's instant healing.

For a change, let's consider: *"speak the Word only"*. The time in which we're living means that there are many teachers and preachers who struggle to: *"speak the Word only"* for fear of offending their audience. But as legislations change in our world and oppose the Word, and in the face of heretical teachings, it is necessary now more than ever to *"speak the Word only"* in its raw form.

Paul predicted in 2 Timothy 4:3 (NLT): *"The time is coming when people will no longer listen to sound and wholesome teaching. They will follow their own desires and will look for teachers who will tell them whatever their itching ears want to hear"*.

Despite the spiritual climate of the age, we all carry the responsibility not to add to or subtract from God's Word, but to divide it rightly (2 Timothy 2:15). It is the purity of the Word that makes it potent and effective.

It was the *"Word only"* that John the Baptist preached in the wilderness of Judaea and to Herod and Herodias, Jesus taught it on the Sermon on the Mount, Peter preached it on the Day of Pentecost, and it caused Stephen to be stoned to death. With or without an *"Amen!"*, it is that same undiluted *"Word only"* which we are charged to speak today.

JEJ

October 2023
Theme: The Word of God
Awareness Month for: Breast Cancer, Cholesterol, Domestic Violence, Lupus, Menopause, Mental Health

344

THURSDAY 19th

The words that I speak unto you, they are spirit, and they are life - St John 6:63

WHAT'S MY APPETITE? - Reading: St John 6:60-71

The crowds chased Jesus relentlessly across Capernaum after He multiplied loaves and fish for them. Jesus told them: *"You don't want the miracle that convicts you of who I am, you're chasing me for food to temporarily fill your bellies!" (St John 6:26).*

Does that sound familiar? Could it be that our prayers and activities so often display our desire for temporary things? A quick fix? A temporary high? A feel-good sermon? This humble Jesus did not fit their expectations. Does He fit ours? Does the rugged cross still appeal to us enough to take up our own? Does the eternal bread of Truth satisfy us, or are we still hungry and thirsty for others things? Do we chase Him until we feel good or until we're made 'good' in His sight?

You see, it's a question of appetite. There ought to be a hunger for His Spirit and to be fed and filled by Him. And that same Spirit, being the force that will call us home when He comes back, is what our heart truly needs.

In St John 6:63 Jesus taught telling them the truth is: *"I am that Bread of Life" (St John 6:35).* That was a hard truth for them to swallow. Paraphrased, He said, *"You won't respond to this if you're in the flesh, 'quickening' will only come if you're truly of God".*

What drives my appetite? Is it God's Spirit or a temporary quenching of my own wants?

Here is an opportunity to respond afresh to the Spirit of God. To prove: *"Lord I'm hungering and thirsting after you, chasing your Word and not only your works".*

Let's pray the hymn beautifully penned by Judson W. Van De Venter:

"Come to my soul, blessed Jesus,
Hear me! O Saviour divine!
Open the fountain and cleanse me,
Give me a heart like Thine"

Joy Lear-Bernard

October 2023
Theme: The Word of God
Awareness Month for: Breast Cancer, Cholesterol, Domestic Violence, Lupus, Menopause, Mental Health

*FRIDAY 20th

Thy Word have I have hid in my heart, that I might not sin - Psalm 119:11

A GUIDING WORD - Reading: Psalm 119:9-16

This Scripture verse should be a key verse for all Christians.

To be a Christian means to be a follower of Christ. The Bible is the written Word of Christ and His instructions, and guidance for us to be the kind of Christians He wants us to be. Therefore, we must have the Bible close to us at all times so that we can live our lives according to those words.

What better place to keep God's Word than within our heart? If we do keep the Word close to us then it will keep us on the right path, away from sin, so that we do not sin against God. He hates sin.

We don't have to rely on our own decision-making because God left us His words as a guide, and it has everything that we need to follow Him.

Isabel

*World Osteoporosis Day

October 2023
Theme: The Word of God
Awareness Month for: Breast Cancer, Cholesterol, Domestic Violence, Lupus, Menopause, Mental Health

346

*SATURDAY 21st

The Word of God liveth and abideth for ever – 1 Peter 1:22

THE BIBLE STANDS - Reading: 2 Peter 1:10-21

1. The Bible stands like a rock undaunted
   'Mid the raging storms of time;
   Its pages burn with the truth eternal,
   And they glow with a light sublime

   Refrain:
   The Bible stands though the hills may tumble,
   It will firmly stand when the earth shall crumble;
   I will plant my feet on its firm foundation,
   For the Bible stands

2. The Bible stands like a mountain towering
   Far above the works of men;
   Its truth by none ever was refuted,
   And destroy it they never can

3. The Bible stands and it will forever,
   When the world has passed away;
   By inspiration it has been given,
   All its precepts I will obey

4. The Bible stands every test we give it,
   For its Author is divine;
   By grace alone I expect to live it,
   And to prove and make it mine

Haldor Lillenas

*National Apple Day

October 2023
Theme: The Word of God
Awareness Month for: Breast Cancer, Cholesterol, Domestic Violence, Lupus, Menopause,
Mental Health

*SUNDAY 22ⁿᵈ

The seed is the Word of God - St Luke 8:11

A PERFECT WORD - Reading: St Luke 8:4-15

Those who love gardening know that when planting seeds, as well as preparing the ground, you must be patient.

Jesus teaching a parable concerning the Sower and the Seed mentions four types of soil which He then compares to four types of hearts. The seed was perfect, it was the ground that was by the wayside, or rocky, or thorny, but thankfully there was good ground too.

Likewise, the seed, i.e., the Word of God, is perfect. It does not need to come in different packages for the different kinds of hearts - the Word of God fits every heart type. It works on the inside first where the Word's effect cannot initially be seen.

None of us can determine who is a *"good ground"* hearer. There are some who have heard the one-size-fits-all Word as a prostitute, a gambler, a drug baron, a liar or a thief. They did not give their heart to the Lord immediately, but that did not mean the Word didn't fall on good ground.

The seed, the Word, works best in dark places, a sinful heart being one of them. It can take a little while for the seed to swell and burst and send down roots before a shoot becomes visible above the soil. So don't write-off anyone or your dark seasons when the seed of the Word has been sown. Be patient and let the seed work!

JEJ

*International Stammering Awareness Day

October 2023
Theme: The Word of God
Awareness Month for: Breast Cancer, Cholesterol, Domestic Violence, Lupus, Menopause, Mental Health

348

MONDAY 23rd

Now faith is the substance of things hoped for - Hebrews 11:1

GOD IS A HEALER - Reading: Hebrews 11:1-6

To God be glory, majesty and power always and ever more.

God is always available to those who believe and have faith. The Bible tells us in Hebrews 11:1 that: *"Faith is the substance of things hoped for, the evidence of things not seen"*. This tells me that I need to have faith in God, this is a must for my Christian walk.

I have seen God work in my life to help me with a health condition which the doctors said could only be treated with medication. The medication was actually not helping my body and was presenting other health risks. I asked God for guidance to help me make a decision whether I should continue or cease to take the medication. With much prayer and total focus upon God and the Word I stopped taking the medication. One day I heard God tell me to believe that He is able to heal my body. I just believed God would come through for me and he would make a way.

*I stopped my taking my medication and informed the doctors that I was no longer taking my injections. Following this, during my last blood screening, I was told that my liver function was normal and there was no evidence of any problems with kidney function.

Thank God that He has healed me from my condition and my body once again feels healthy. Hallelujah! Thank you, Jesus!

Name withheld

*This is a personal testimony of faith. Please continue to take your prescribed medication unless advised to stop by your GP or other professional medical advisor

October 2023
Theme: The Word of God
Awareness Month for: Breast Cancer, Cholesterol, Domestic Violence, Lupus, Menopause, Mental Health

349

TUESDAY 24th

Remember the Word unto (me) which hast caused me to hope - Psalm 119:49

HOLD ON TO THE WORD - Reading: Psalm 119:49-56

A while ago I stood behind a mother and her young daughter as we waited to cross the road.

The mother had many bags in her hands so I saw her point to the edge of her blouse as she said to her child: *"Hold on and don't let go"*!

There is a song written by Kurt Carr: *"I Almost Let Go"*. The first verse starts with: *"I almost let go"*; the second verse begins: *"I almost gave up"*. Almost, i.e., I could have but didn't; I very nearly but not quite. We've all had at least one of those *"I almost..."* experiences. Honestly, we almost let go. Let go of what? Almost let go of our joy, our peace, of our hope, our faith and nearly let go of our praise.

Sometimes when we're faced with what appear to us to be giant circumstances, hope seems pointless (Luke 8:49) or our faith seems so small. But faith the size of a mustard seed is still powerful (Matthew 17:20).

Rahab asked for a true token as evidence that the spies would come back for her before Jericho was utterly destroyed. She put the scarlet line not only where they could see it when they returned, but also in easy-view for herself. Every time that she glanced at her window, that cord reminded Rahab of the promise: *"We won't forget you"*!

To every reader who feels that their strength is almost gone because of non-stop pressure and personal floods, now is the time to take another look at your true token, i.e., the Word that God has given to sustain you until your storm has passed.

Keep: *"I had (I almost) fainted unless I had believed to see..."* (Psalm 27:13) in your heart so that you can find it when you need it. Then hold on and **don't** let go!

JEJ

October 2023
Theme: The Word of God
Awareness Month for: Breast Cancer, Cholesterol, Domestic Violence, Lupus, Menopause, Mental Health

WEDNESDAY 25th

O earth, earth, earth, hear the Word of the LORD - Jeremiah 22:29

SERMONS BY SIGNS - Reading: Jeremiah 22:1-30

God knows how to get our attention.

In today's world church attendance is on the decline, churches are closing down and there are more people than ever before who say that they are an Atheist, they do not believe in Almighty God.

Humankind wants to get on with life and, they think, sustain themselves. Since people refuse to make time for God and hear His audible spoken word, God is delivering many of His messages by signs. We may join with the world and use certain terms to explain some of the unusual events happening around us, but really it is the outpouring of God's wrath and the beginning of the end.

We see and hear the Word of God in action as gradually all of the world's central systems fail, as nations revolt against governments worldwide, as the value of world currencies fall, there are wars and rumours of wars, in the alarming surge in every kind of evil, in the love for God in many becoming cold.

Still people as it were put their fingers in their ears to shut out the sounds of the signs. Noah preached for 120 years before the flood came. God in His mercy will always give time to heed His warning. It is not His will that anyone should perish. Signs of the times are everywhere, that means that there are mini visual sermons everywhere.

JEJ

THURSDAY 26th

I say the Word, and will perform it, saith the LORD GOD - Ezekiel 12:25

WORD OWNERSHIP - Reading: Ezekiel 12:1-28

Group discussions and brainstorming sessions can be interesting and stimulating. Great ideas come forth as we speak at length and picture in our minds the end result. Sometimes minutes are written as evidence of what was said.

However, a downside of these debates can be finding someone who will take ownership to bring into being matters discussed. To find a volunteer to take responsibility for completing can be difficult, hence why many meetings have repetitive text, i.e., the same subject is talked about over and over again whenever that team meets.

God doesn't have this problem. He does not operate by the ideas of others, neither does He need any of us to decide when or how to perform His plans.

When God speaks, whether it's a blessing or a curse, it will come to pass. That is certain because He executes His Word Himself.

JEJ

FRIDAY 27th

Man shall not live by bread alone but by every word…- St Matthew 4:4

A WORD IN RESERVE - Reading: St Matthew 4:1-11; Ephesians 6:10-18

There are some products which I ensure that I never run out of; I always have at least one spare 'just in case'.

I do believe that each of us should have our own reserve or collection of Scripture verses which we memorise. If you're not able to remember well, then perhaps write them on a sticker and put in places where they will be seen, e.g., above your bedroom door handle, on the bathroom mirror, on the dashboard in your car, on the fridge door, on your desk at work, etc.

In the same way as when you're being assessed, taking a test or exam, and your mind suddenly goes blank although you know your subject, this can also happen when you're catapulted into a situation by surprise, or one that you were already in somehow got worse.

Depending on your case, you may not be able to read a Bible for days, and it's a Word in reserve that your soul will live on just like when Elijah, fleeing from Jezebel, *"went in the strength of that meat for forty days and forty nights"* (1 Kings 19:8-9).

So choose some Scriptures that reaffirm who you are and who God is. Pick verses to remind you to continue to bless the LORD. Look for words of reassurance that God is with you and in control. Make up a powerful personal arsenal of Word that when the enemy is attacking you from every angle, you're ready to fight back with: *"The sword of the Spirit, which is the Word of God"* (Ephesians 6:17).

JEJ

SATURDAY 28th

Sanctify them through Thy truth: Thy Word is truth - St John 17:17

SANCTIFY THEM - Reading: St John 17:6-19

"Sanctify them…". This was the High Priest's prayer on the night before death.

Jesus in deep anguish, interceding on our behalf. He petitioned on our behalf, topics such as the necessity of the Word, sanctification, truth. The Logos Word fervently prayed that believers must receive the spoken Rhema inspired Word to be sanctified. Believers ought to be 'set apart', indeed, also be cleansed, *"Sanctified and washed by the Word" (Ephesians 5:26).*

We are cleansed through His spoken word (St John 15:3). His Word is true; only with truth can we be sanctified. False doctrine cannot save, neither can man's opinion. Man's wisdom, thoughts or tradition cannot make us clean. The power unto salvation is the WORD, i.e., His Word. God spoke the Word in creation *"… and it was done, commanded and it stood fast" (Psalm 33:9).*

Jesus spoke to the wind, waves, demons, sicknesses. Even death obeyed His Word! Likewise, He commands us to be sanctified by His Word. To be washed and set apart for His purpose. Let us live sanctified lives; live the Word.

Sis Jx

October 2023
Theme: The Word of God
Awareness Month for: Breast Cancer, Cholesterol, Domestic Violence, Lupus, Menopause, Mental Health

354

*SUNDAY 29th

Is not my Word like a fire? saith God: and like a hammer? - Jeremiah 23:29

THE EFFECTIVE WORD - Reading: Acts 7:1-60

The Word of God is powerful and effective. It is immutable, i.e., it cannot change. The Word of God is not like liquid which takes on a different form depending on the vessel in which it is being carried. It is fixed and forever settled in heaven.

Interestingly, God's Word impacts its hearers in different ways. Some will joyfully ask: *"What shall we do?" (Acts 2:37)*, yet others will seek to take revenge on God's mouthpiece (Acts 7:54-60). What is soothing and inviting for one, brings discomfort and vexation to another as the Word reveals their heart's condition.

The Word is like a fire. What does fire do? It purifies but can also destroy. It spreads quickly and consumes anything in its path. No wonder many will testify that they didn't go to church to get saved, but *"something got hold of them"*. That 'something' was the fire of God's Word.

The Word of God is like a hammer. What does a hammer do? It is an instrument used to drive or pound a nail into a hard resistant surface. Some of us before our conversion tried to resist Christ but, under the Hammer of the Word, like Saul on the Damascus Road, we had to surrender our will and cry: *"Lord, what do you want me to do?"*. And after conversion, when we are going in the wrong direction, the Word pounds again to break our stubborn will and redirect us into divine submission.

JEJ

*Clocks go back UK

MONDAY 30th

O taste and see that the LORD is good - Psalm 34:8

JUST A LITTLE PIECE (AND MORE) – Reading: Psalm 34:8-11; Proverbs 11:30

I am sure that there are some good cooks reading this page! When you cook, the whole house is filled with the aroma of seasonings and spices you add to the pot. The smell brings with it anticipation of a delicious meal, but it is the taste that is important. The taste must be at least as good as the smell, if not better.

I remember a while ago my mom cooked some pieces of chicken for the following day, and left them on top of the cooker to cool while she went upstairs. I went into the kitchen later and saw the tray. I stood looking at the various chicken pieces, wrestling (not for too long) between my conscience and my appetite. I noticed a crispy part on one of the pieces which I thought, if I just picked that bit off, would leave the rest of the chicken leg intact for dinner tomorrow.

But I hadn't taken into consideration the taste! It was only a little bit from the edge, yet that gave a desire to try a little bit more. As I stared at the same chicken leg, I saw another juicy-looking bit and tried to pull it off delicately. Finally, I concluded after all the pickings I'd taken, that I might as well finish the whole piece! With the chicken bone now in the bin, I understood why David said: *"O taste and see that the LORD is good"*.

As we try to win wisely souls for Christ, may we introduce Him to them in small, bite-sized pieces. They will then, from the taste, want more.

JEJ

October 2023
Theme: The Word of God
Awareness Month for: Breast Cancer, Cholesterol, Domestic Violence, Lupus, Menopause, Mental Health

356

TUESDAY 31st

My words shall not pass away - St Matthew 24:35

REMEMBER JESUS' WORDS! - Reading: Hebrews 13:5-8

The words of God are pure. They are likened unto silver which is tried in a furnace on the earth and refined seven times. The grass withers, the flowers fade. The first heaven and first earth will one day pass away, but the Word of our God will stand fast forever, they will endure for ever and ever.

"The law of the Lord is perfect, restoring the soul. The testimony of the Lord is sure making wise the simple. The precepts of the Lord are right, rejoicing the heart. The commandments of the Lord are pure, enlightening the eyes. The fear of the Lord is clean, enduring forever" (Psalm 19:7-8).

The promises of God are 'Yes and Amen' in Christ Jesus, they will never ever fail. Praise the Lord!

Thank you, Jesus, for dying on the cross with me on your mind so that I can walk free. No matter what trials or tribulations that I may face, I pray I will continue to hold fast to your Word of Truth which can never fail.

I agree with the songwriter who wrote: *"Through it all I've learned to depend upon His Word".*

Sister Esther Miller

November

Thanksgiving, Praise & Worship

*WEDNESDAY 1ˢᵗ

Praise waiteth for thee, O God, in Sion - Psalm 65:1

MEDITATIONS – Reading: Psalm 65:1-13

The setting of Psalm 65 was a celebration of a bountiful harvest produced after much rain; this was seen as the crowning of the year. The children of Israel were anticipating the coming of the King to Zion (Sion), preparing a welcome celebration of praise.

In the height of praise there is a build-up of speechless wonderment of Almighty God. A worshipful silence of His terrible, wonderful, presence. Prophet Isaiah saw the Lord's train fill the temple (Isaiah 6:1)! Therefore, a literal translation would be: *"Praise is silent for thee"*. Regular words fail when God shows up. His presence causes silent surrender of our frail state.

Zion was a location, a high point or hill in the city of Jerusalem, which was captured from the Jebusites of Canaan by King David. It became the headquarters, the city of David, for praise and worship; a stronghold of Victory.

When He came to Zion, His people did not recognise Jesus Christ as The Messiah. We are blessed for, although we were not physically there when He came to Jerusalem, we believe. By grace we are saved through faith in the finished work of Jesus' death on the cross.

A storehouse of banked-up praises for Jesus' coming is building up in the saints to at last see the one in whom we have believed and hoped, for so long; Creator of heaven and earth, our Sovereign King.

We pause to applaud the majesty of God.

Charmaine Boora

Stress Awareness Day

THURSDAY 2nd

In every thing give thanks for this is the will of God - 1Thessalonians 5:18

THANKS FOR EVERYTHING - Reading: Psalm 92:1-15; 1 Thessalonians 5:18

Today we are being admonished to give God thanks in all things.

This verse sort of reminds me of Romans 8:28 which says: *"And we know that all things work together for good…"*. It can take years to see the positive outcome of what God is working together for good. Likewise, by faith we thank God in all things, when we know that we are living inside His will.

Sometimes I've felt as though the only reason why God allowed certain things to happen to me was so that I could help someone else when it happened to them! Whilst in deep contemplation of this possibility, I decided to thank God for trusting me with those kinds of trials, to go in and come out faithful.

I'll agree that it may take several attempts to do this, it will not always come naturally, but do encourage yourself to give God thanks in every thing. Thank Him for lessons learned, experiences gained, and that you're still standing.

JEJ

FRIDAY 3rd

O come, let us worship and bow down - Psalm 95:6

TIME OUT - Reading: Psalm 95:1-11

I'm sure that I'm not the only one who feels there are not enough hours in a day, often wondering: *"Where has the time gone?"*.

But even as I'm typing that there isn't enough time, I'm also correcting myself. In creation and the dividing of times and seasons, God decided that seven days were sufficient for one week to the extent that there was a day on which He rested. We too need to make time to rest - to replenish spiritual and physical strength.

Despite being busy, we continue to cram in more tasks and activities, and hardly ever decline an invitation. But today, we're going to say and do: 'Time Out'! If we look at the focus verse in full, we will see that we cannot action in haste what the writer has said we must do: *"O come, let us worship and bow down: let us kneel before the LORD our maker"*.

Here is a call to *"Come!"*. Put down what you're doing, cancel what you had planned for this evening, switch off your phone, and *"come"*. To labour the point, and place greater emphasis on why we must *"come"*, the unnamed psalmist tells us that we are going to present ourselves before *"the LORD our maker"*! If I wanted to decline an invitation through being busy, I wouldn't refuse this one, not with wording so deliberately styled! It's probably more of a summons to *"come"*, than an invitation really.

Although we can rush through thanksgiving, or even hurry a praise, we have got to take Time Out to worship!

JEJ

SATURDAY 4ᵗʰ

Thanks be to God, which giveth us the victory - 1 Corinthians 15:57

SO THANKFUL - Reading: Ezekiel 37:1-14

Our God is real! **We are children of a miracle-working, truly wonderful, amazing God**! I am so very thankful that He is a God that can and will; He is able!

It has been two-plus years since I was admitted as an emergency into the intensive care unit, and placed in an induced coma with Covid-19, and all its related respiratory symptoms and the effects. This was an extremely difficult and challenging time for my family, and a concerning time for my brethren. Nevertheless, sincere prayers were sent up from all over the UK and abroad, and God heard and answered those prayers.

I remained in the coma for almost six weeks before God decided to wake me up. Although I was obviously unaware of what had been going on, my family was able to tell me. I know that the days and weeks I was in the coma put a great strain on my loved ones.

I opened my eyes, not knowing where I was and found I was lying in a bed unable to mobilise myself. I could not move my legs, had little movement in my arms/hands, my vision was impaired, and was faced with several other medical issues. To move me, the nursing staff would have to strap me up to a hoist. I very soon found that all the things that I used to do daily (before Covid), and absolutely took for granted, I could no longer do. BUT thanks be to God - with His help and His working through the doctors, physiotherapists, occupational therapists, nurses, and so lovingly my family, over many weeks I was gradually restored to a reasonable level of health, strength and mobility.

Two years on, and although I still carry some medical problems which I am told will be lifelong, God is keeping me. I have my personal independence once again, and am able to do most things that were taken away from me during my illness. My relationship with the medical profession is ongoing but God has been and still is working on me. Because of Him, I am still here.

What I have learnt and been reminded of in all of this is nothing that most of us don't already know, but things have now certainly been reinforced.

I have been reminded that - it is only because of God that my eyes are opened every morning. Only because of Him that I have breath. Only because of Him that I can move and carry out the duties of daily living. I really only need to deal with one day and its contents at a time. The many things that I consider important, and apportion time to, are really NOT that important at all. Refuse to take on or carry any unnecessary upsets, hurts or heavy weights. Totally lean, depend, and trust in the Lord. Love, even the unlovable.

So, sisters, when I wake up in the morning I give God thanks – thanks for opening my eyes, thanks for giving me family and friends, thanks for all the precious saints of God, thanks for the use of my hands, my feet, my eyes, my mouth. So many things to thank God for, the list is endless. He has done far more for me than I deserve. No amount of words that I can speak will ever be enough.

I am thanking everyone for all the prayers, the support, the encouragement and the kindness shown to me but most of all, I am thanking God for who He is and for not treating me as I deserve. I am only still here because of His love for me. What a truly amazing God is He!

Sister Gale Miller

SUNDAY 5th

Praise him for his mighty acts and his excellent greatness - Psalm 150:2

CERTAINLY A MOVE OF GOD - Reading: Psalm 150:1-6

Years ago, my husband and I decided to open a West Indian bakery shop.

There was nothing of that sort in the area so the City Council heralded our plans and were as excited about the project as we were. They were excited enough to voluntarily offer us a grant of £7,000 and provided us with two Project Workers to support us. They took pictures and showed them in their City Council magazine; we were given very good reviews and encouragement.

The business started and did fairly well initially, but it is fair to say that after a while, it was not doing well any more. We both had ideas of what was wrong, e.g., high overhead costs with the property, etc., but we could not find the extra funds to progress it further. Potential partners wanted half, or even more than half, of the business which would leave us with the bare bones.

The Council instructed that the business be closed. Of course, we were very sad and disappointed, full of anxiety and stress. Closing the business was never part of the plan. We prayed and others prayed for us. The decision was made and, as the Council had given us a generous grant, we had very little say in the matter.

My anxiety became unbearable. I was worried most of the time about what to do which prevented me from sleeping or eating properly. I was overwhelmed by this feeling of failure and helplessness. *"How could this happen to us?"* was one of the questions I would frequently ask myself.

One night, I had a dream that I was walking down a corridor with a loaded rucksack on my back. A person came to me and told me to get down on my front, lie down on the floor and go under the door bottom with the rucksack on my back. I said: *"You know that this is not possible!"*. He demanded that I lie down and do exactly what he said, so I got down on my front and started to wriggle my body towards the door bottom. *"There is no way this was going to happen"*, I repeatedly muttered. I started screaming: *"Help! Help! Somebody, please help me! Jesus, please help me!"*.

I woke up and realised that I was in bed and this experience was just a bad dream. Somehow, I had a sense of relief, and my anxiety was not causing my heart to palpitate. I felt at ease and started to divert my thinking that nothing is impossible with God. I mentioned the dream to my husband but we had no idea what it meant. So, persevering as usual was what we had to do.

Then we received a letter from the City Council to come to see them as soon as possible. My heart palpitations came back and it was extraordinary; it was like my heart was jumping out of my chest! I thought, worst-case-scenario, they are going to ask us to sell our house to pay back the £7,000 which they had given to us as a grant. The Council had never asked to see us before because we had Project Workers.

We attended the meeting with two men from the Council and one of our Project Workers. The men said that they would get straight to the issue. Again, my heart was pumping so fast, I could hear it in my chest!

They advised us that they had received good reports from our Project Workers, that we had worked very hard indeed to make the business work, that we were not being blamed for the failure of the business.

They then said: *"So we have decided to write off the bill!"*. My response was: *"I won't believe you unless you write what you've said in a letter"*. One of the men answered: *"Yes, of course we will send you a letter to confirm, but we just wanted you to know in person before we send the letter"*.

I repeated myself: *"Until you send it in writing I won't believe you"*. Then it was like my dream came straight back to me, asking Jesus or anyone to help me. This was our help! The City Council was writing off the bill! The feeling was surreal; I cannot explain something that looks unreal.

I stood up and shook the men's hands and left their office. A few days later we received the letter confirming the conversation with the City Council.

We just thanked God, and I've never forgotten what He did for us. I was strengthened and relieved from the burden which was the large sum of money coupled with intense stress and anxiety. I will always remember that what is impossible with men is possible with God. I have proven the Almighty God.

This was: *"certainly a move of God"*. Thank you, Jesus!

Missionary M Fraser

MONDAY 6th

They that worship (God) must worship him in spirit and in truth - St John 4:24

A SEARCH FOR TRUE WORSHIPPERS - Reading: St John 4: 19-26

The woman at the well is a text where Jesus prophesises about her life and actually reveals who He is to this woman for her salvation.

Their conversation marks the many things we tend to identify with in order to secure who we are. Our history, who our fathers were, our customs and where we go to worship, our relationship status and our lifestyle. Jesus deflated her statements one by one, challenging her to look more deeply at herself.

It is important to recognise our fleshly inclination just as hers was to 'be' something. Pride calls for us to 'own' or 'be' something for our identity to have value, and if we are not keen for the things of God, we may bring these values into His house.

Could it be that we are being reminded to focus on what we know less, and more on if we are known of God in quiet contemplation and prayer? We can learn a beautiful lesson from Jesus in this text. God is a Spirit and He is always seeking. Jesus was not won over by this woman's temporary conditions and what she knew about her culture and customs. He wanted a worshipper, and one that worshipped in spirit and in truth.

He is still seeking such to worship Him with all our sensibilities, desire and thinking submitted to Him and His Truth. This is the very word of God: *"counting it all but dung" (Philippians 3:8)* unless it is of value to Christ.

Joy Lear-Bernard

TUESDAY 7th

Seven times a day do I praise thee - Psalm 119:164

ALL DAY PRAISE - Reading: Psalm 119:161-168

The writer of today's focus verse was clearly a Praiser. I can imagine that they were on praise-repeat all day which would have stemmed from maintaining a godly focus and grateful heart.

Of course, circumstances will always arise to blow out your praise and place you on mute, but even then, you can praise your way through. Praise needs to be a discipline which is not circumstantial: *"His praise shall continually be in my mouth"* (Psalm 34:1).

Set an atmosphere of praise in your home, in your car (you will be a better and calmer driver!), and anywhere you go. Replace gossip and complaining with praises. A praise atmosphere lets God know that He is welcome to stay with you; *"Seven times a day"* simply means that your praise never stops!

"All day long, I've been with Jesus
All day long, my lips have uttered praise
All day long my heart, my soul's been lifted in worship
All day long, I have been with Him

No way could I ever honour you enough
For all you have done for me
So I will offer up thanksgiving from my heart
And praise continually"
(All Day Long sung by GMWA Women of Worship)

JEJ

WEDNESDAY 8th

Not unto us, O LORD, not unto us, but unto thy name give glory - Psalm 115:1

GOD CARRIED ME THROUGH - Reading: Psalm 115:1-18

It was autumn 2015.

I had been experiencing increasing stomach pain, inability to digest food, and weakness. A sudden bout of sickness on school grounds while collecting my younger child, and the increased stomach pain was unbearable.

My GP diagnosed that I had food poisoning. The days went by, the pains grew worse, I couldn't keep anything down. Some nights my inside felt like it was being torn up and burning. Pain would shoot up into my head, I would be on the floor, or leaning against the bathroom door retching, for what seemed like hours. I couldn't call out as I didn't want to panic my children.

At the insistence of my mom, I was taken to A&E. Once examined, the triage doctor explained the X-ray result. My infection markers were high, and I had to be sent to another hospital. There, a drip was inserted, I was allowed nil by mouth and taken by ambulance from the A&E that night.

Following various tests, it was discovered that I had Necrotising Pancreatitis. The consultant sat by my bed as he told me the test results. They wanted to operate immediately. The procedure meant keyhole surgery and attaching a drain for a while before determining next steps. I tried to mentally process their findings; I didn't know what it would mean. I prepared a Will, just in case! I remained in hospital for a short period as they observed my response to the surgery. The consultant on ward rounds looked at my scan post-op and then at me. He noted that the scan didn't match how I looked. My answer to him was: *"It's because of God!"*.

Things were happening too fast to be afraid; I had to leave the unknown to God. I realised He was carrying me through. Through the following months of sleeping upright supported by pillows, Jesus stayed with me. Through the challenge of having to daily drain off the damaged tissue, the weekly visit to clinic to remove and replace the wound drainage bag and re-attaching it to my side, Jesus stayed with me. Through the pain, to even when a consultant removed the tube from my side without anaesthetic the following year, ...uhm...my God, my God, yes, Jesus was with me!

The LORD is beautiful for situation. Even now I wonder how I came over that hurdle, God has been my buffer. I've proved Him for myself, and I know Jesus never fails. Glory!

Our Great Physician is Jesus Christ, He forgives all our iniquities and heals all our diseases. I can never forget what great things he has done!

Charm

THURSDAY 9th

I will extol thee, my God, O King... for ever and ever - Psalm 145:1

OVERCOMING LIMITATIONS - Reading: Psalm 145:1-21

The year 1982 was a year of sorrow.

The normality of our everyday peaceful life became chaotic. Why? Because my 12-year-old son who was a beautiful, healthy, sports-loving caring boy, advanced for his years, suddenly became sick.

My son complained of feeling unwell. His head was hurting and he could not stand, he just collapsed. The hospital diagnosed that he had viral tuberculosis and meningitis. Investigations were carried out to find out how my son had contracted the disease. It was discovered that one of the pupils at his school had returned to school too soon after having tuberculosis. The school was administering the child's medication and had not informed any of the parents until my son became ill.

My son was in the hospital for six months on very strong medication; he was delirious for two of these months. His speech became impaired, and he had to undergo speech therapy and physiotherapy and wear special boots. He had to learn to write again.

My son was eventually discharged but had to attend the school at the hospital daily. His health gradually improved and he became able to do all of the things that he had been unable to do for himself.

We, as a loving family, contributed to his care. His siblings helped him with his reading and taught him to write letters; they were very loving and protective of their brother. When my son was in hospital, my other children would still set his plate at our dinner table. The first Christmas that my son was in hospital, his brother and sister cried and would not eat anything; they wanted to be at the hospital so I had to take them there.

My son was resilient. He helped himself and became independent. God's hand instilled strength and courage in him such that I, as a mother, was amazed; but I did not try to hinder my son or question what he was doing.

He returned to secondary school and went on to college, and passed his exams. He began to teach at the hospital's school. He then worked for the council in Education setting up computer programs for schools around the country.

Then in 1973 he became wheelchair-bound and worked in a primary school teaching until he retired after 30 years. He has refused to have carers and attends to his needs. He travels abroad on his own and said: *"What will be, will be".*

We have been told that my son will eventually become a paraplegia. But I know that God is a healer, a miracle worker. We do not live in fear but in hope. God has brought us from a mighty long way. We talk about the Lord and about the saving of his soul. As his mother, I will always pray for my son's soul, that God will bring him out of darkness and he will come to know who Jesus is. I am always telling my son and other unsaved family members but the Word of God has to enter into their heart.

Pray for us. We all have a story to tell of God's goodness, His mercy and His grace and the world needs to know, considering the challenges that we all are facing in these dark and last days. Be blessed in Jesus' name.

Sister Norma Greene

FRIDAY 10th

He…entered with them into the temple…leaping, and praising God - Acts 3:8

LET OUT YOUR PRAISE - Reading: Acts 3:1-11

Drivers reading this page know that we can't start to drive a vehicle in 5th gear.

Here we have a man who, immediately after being healed, hit a level of thanksgiving and praise that caused the temple congregants to *"wonder"* and be *"amazed"*. He had been lame from his mother's womb; he had never been privileged like most people to be able to walk.

He did not need to go through any of the 'warm up' preliminaries which we sometimes have in our services to set the atmosphere for the day's Praise and Worship. He had a heart overflowing with gratitude, and everybody knew about it!

Nobody should have to force us to praise God; the stimulant for praise is our memory. Just recall some of the things which God has done throughout your lifetime, that should be enough to trigger thanksgiving or a praise. David wrote: *"Marvellous are your works and my soul knows it very well" (Psalm 139:14).*

This first-time visitor came into the prayer service leaping (jumping) and praising God! You see, he had been immobile all of his life so couldn't do 'Reserved Praise'! Perhaps they had assembled for a quiet time of prayer as usual, but it was time to change the order of service: *"All the people saw him walking and praising God" (Acts 3:9).* I think that he was shouting: *"You don't know like I know, what He's done for me!".*

JEJ

*SATURDAY 11th

The LORD has done great things for us; whereof we are glad - Psalm 126:3

THIS MUST BE GOD! - Reading: Psalm 126:1-6

I was in my 40s. My day started as normal; I was getting ready for work and then I fell to the floor. I'd had a massive bleed on my brain, and a heart attack at the same time, and I was at home on my own.

I lay on the ground from 8am until 3pm before my manager came to see why I had not come into work and called for an ambulance. I was in hospital for three months. One day the physiotherapist asked me to try and lift my leg. When I lifted it, he was amazed and, although he was not a Christian, said: *"This must be God, this is nothing to do with us, i.e., the medical team!".* The whole ward was talking about my miracle!

The prognosis given was that I would be bed-bound and not walk again; I was told that I would be in a wheelchair for the rest of my life. But that's not what God said! I can now walk with a stick, I go for walks around 'the block', I swim, I do my own shopping and housework. And from taking eleven different kinds of medication each day, I now only take two.

God has been more than good to me.

Evangelist Deveen Smith

(Adapted from: I Arise – 2022)

*Armistice Day

November 2023
Theme: Thanksgiving, Praise & Worship
Awareness Month for: Prematurity, Diabetes, Mouth Cancer, Family Caregivers

374

SUNDAY 12th

Worship the LORD in the beauty of holiness - Psalm 96:9

BEAUTY AT ITS BEST - Reading: Psalm 96:1-13

Women, we are beautifully made by God and should enjoy who God has made us to be! Yet we're made most beautiful when we affirm David's imploring to all creation for us to ascribe, to the only true God, all glory and honour.

Limitation of earthly beauty tells us to work on ourselves. Holiness tells us to focus more on God. All creatures, all eyes, are to be set on Him, on His holiness which speaks of His sacred nature and to us to be in pure connection with Him in our personal call to that holiness. The Scripture describes this as beautiful. This reconnection with wholeness and purpose is what our Creator calls beautiful. Our reverence and humbling existence being turned back to Him is the most beautiful and complete positioning we could ever come to; it is why we live.

We will forever cry out for 'true' beauty when we seek aesthetics and what others call external beauty; and plans that surge with brilliance but are sometimes without a fear and reverence for the beauty of His Holiness.

Why was David's appeal so urgent in Psalm 96? Because our Maker created us to worship only Him. David announces to us to get back to worship *"for he cometh, for he cometh to judge the earth" (Psalm 96:13)*, and desires to see what He planned fulfilled in you and me. That is for us to be poised in holy worship to Him. This will be beauty at its best.

Joy Lear-Bernard

*MONDAY 13th

Dawn 'til sunset the name of the LORD deserves to be praised - Psalm 113:3

PRAISE IS WHAT WE MUST DO! - Reading: Psalm 113:1-9 (CEV)

We serve an awesome God, and it is our duty to praise him, for who He is, and what He has done; we were made to give God glory!

We must praise Him regardless of how we feel and what we are going through. Currently, we are living in unprecedented times, difficult times, but we must still praise God.

Psalm 34:1 says: *"I will bless the LORD at all times: His praise shall continually be in my mouth".*

When we reflect upon the goodness of God in our own individual lives, out of a very grateful heart we can conclude:

"And all my life you have been faithful
And all my life you have been so, so good
With every breath that I am able
Oh, I will sing of the goodness of God"
(Goodness of God by Bethel Music, sung by Jenn Johnson)

Sis Beverley Lewin

*World Kindness Day

November 2023
Theme: Thanksgiving, Praise & Worship
Awareness Month for: Prematurity, Diabetes, Mouth Cancer, Family Caregivers

376

TUESDAY 14th

And Noah builded an altar unto the LORD - Genesis 8:20

BUILD AN ALTAR - Reading: Genesis 8:1-22

The altar is a sacred place; God's throne of grace, a place of repentance, and where we make a sacrifice unto God. All that Noah offered had to be clean and without blemish because God expects nothing but the best.

We are now under the New Covenant in that we are to: *"present (ourselves) as a living sacrifice holy, acceptable unto God" (Romans 12:1)*, and God is seeking worshippers who will worship Him in spirit and in truth (St John 4:24).

Sometimes people worship God in spirit but not in truth, like Cain who offered a sacrifice unto God but his heart and lifestyle were not right before God. We must examine ourselves as we enter into the presence of God. For example, the brazen altar is where we meet God and are washed by the blood of Jesus for the remission of our sins, and at the brazen laver we are washed by the Word of God.

The burnt offering speaks of a complete surrender unto God, and repentance from sin. Only then can we enter into the Holy Place and worship God in spirit and in truth.

My prayer is that: *"The very God of peace sanctify you wholly; and I pray God your whole spirit and soul and body be preserved blameless unto the coming of our Lord Jesus Christ" (1 Thessalonians 5:23)*.

Rachel Lewin

WEDNESDAY 15th

In every nation, those who fear God, are accepted of Him - Acts 10:35

ACCEPTED IN THE BELOVED - Reading: Acts 10:34-48

There are some 21 Christian nations in the world, and many others where Christians are in the minority.

No matter what our national state, we are all *"accepted in the beloved" (Ephesians 1:6)*. All over the world, Christians have a personal relationship with God. Fearing God helps us to understand who He is and give Him the reverence due to His matchless name.

We don't cower from Him, we shower Him with worship, praise and adoration. *"All of our righteousness is as filthy rags" (Isaiah 64:6)*, but we have been given a new name and a new robe washed in the blood of the Lamb.

We cannot earn our salvation by works of righteousness, but our works are the fruit of our faith (James 2:18). Let us thank God that, in the time we live in, there is a refuge and an anchor for all.

Beverley V. Galloway

THURSDAY 16th

And we know that all things work together for good…- Romans 8:28

EVENTUALLY - Reading: Psalm 119:65-72; Romans 8:28

"**A**nd we know"…but at what stage?

Although we may not understand immediately how everything will work together for good, we join with Apostle Paul and make this statement by faith. The *"together for good"* may not even happen in our lifetime but we believe that God is always in control. He has a plan drawn for each of us.

We see in the Scriptures many occurrences which, for the individuals involved, did not have an obvious divine purpose or be *"good"*: Joseph was ill-treated and sold by his brothers and ended up far away from home in Egypt. Jochebed placed her baby son (later named Moses) in a basket on the River Nile. Naomi and family moved to Moab because there was a famine in Bethlehem-judah. Caesar Augustus suddenly called for the world to be taxed in their city of nativity. See if you can understand why these examples have been chosen to support *"work together for good…"*, and do add more, there are many.

Then there must surely be your own experiences which will come to mind; a sequence of life events that you may even have blamed on the devil until much later in your story.

The Message translation of Romans 8:28 puts it this way: *"…we can be so sure that every detail in our lives of love for God is worked into something good".* So, thank Him!

JEJ

*FRIDAY 17th

I will praise thee, O LORD, with my whole heart - Psalm 9:1

YADAH THE LORD - Reading: Psalm 9:1-20

David understood deliverance and thus he mastered Praise!

As a man of war, David knew who was responsible for giving him the victory over his enemies, to which the only appropriate response was to 'Yadah' the Lord, that is, to praise but with extended hands. Not only with his lips but in sincerity of heart.

Like David, we can pause and recall to our minds and trace throughout the course of our lives, even unto this day, the countless victories that God has won for us. We can see His faithfulness, constant mercies and steadfast love through the public and private battles, the deliverance through trials, the hardships, the losses He comforted us through, the sicknesses that He healed.

Beloved, only a sincere, whole heart, entire being, hands-thrown-in-the-air kind of praise is the right response to honour an awesome God whose works surpass our comprehension!

So, praise passionately, praise with sincerity, praise intentionally, and declare both among the world and the saints the marvellous works of God in your life! He alone is worthy!

Name withheld

*World Prematurity Day

SATURDAY 18th

O give thanks unto the LORD, for he is good - Psalm 107:1

FROM TEST TO TESTIMONY - Reading: Psalm 107:1-8

Writing my journey of becoming a mother has been a cathartic experience for me. I have such gratitude to God for blessing me with the opportunity to be a mother, a gift that I do not take for granted. So where do I start?

I was told six weeks before I got married that I had fibroids (several of them in fact), and that my chances of conceiving naturally were slim. I got married at 37 years old and already had the societal pressures on me that my 'body clock' was ticking. However, I had faith that if it was God's will for me to be a mother, then it would come to pass.

I got married and within three months I became pregnant. Clearly, I had no problems conceiving. For the first ten weeks of pregnancy all seemed okay. However, eleven weeks into the pregnancy I bled and so was rushed into hospital. All checks were done and baby was fine and developing well, so I was discharged from hospital. I had a painful pregnancy and had constant pains in my stomach and groin area. Despite the discomfort, I put on a brave face and smiled through it as I felt it was important to just be grateful to be pregnant. The fibroid pain was excruciating and I was given no support or advice from the community midwife as to how I could manage the pain. I continued to bear it.

Fast forward to 29 weeks of pregnancy, I bled again, and was rushed into hospital. The bleeding was heavy and there was no obvious cause. Scans were undertaken, the baby was fine and there were no concerns with the baby's development. However, doctors were concerned about the bleeding and suggested that I be given a steroid to strengthen my unborn baby's lungs, should the baby need to be delivered early. I had the injection and after two days my bleeding stopped and I was discharged.

Two days later, I was bleeding again, in immense pain and back in hospital. During hospital monitoring, the midwife said that my waters had broken, and I was having contractions. The contraction pains were the pains that I had felt from around twelve weeks into pregnancy, and so that pain was normal for me. This was my first pregnancy so I had no idea that the pain I was experiencing wasn't normal.

At 29 weeks and 5 days the bleeding was persistent, and the doctors decided that my baby should be delivered early. They said that they would do everything to ensure mine and the baby's safety. My husband, family and church family were prayerful, and this gave me a peace like no other. As I prepped for surgery, my mom saw a sister from church who happened to be preparing to be in the same theatre I was going to be in. Sis J said to my mom that she and her colleague would pray for me before they went into theatre. Wow Lord! You strategically placed people of God around me in a time I needed you the most. Isn't God good! Staff in the theatre could not believe how calm I was, but I knew that God was with me and I had an inner peace.

I was born at 30 weeks gestation and my mom had miscarried three times before she had me. She was an incredible source of support for me.

My baby was delivered weighing 2lb 14oz at 29 weeks and 5 days gestation and rushed to the ICU. I got to see him for one minute before he was taken away which was really hard and upsetting. But I was grateful that he was alive and doing well. The doctors informed me that had they not delivered him when they did, then there could have been a negative outcome for us. The bleed was attributed to my fibroids pressing on and eroding the placenta.

After a couple hours, my husband and I were allowed to see our son. He was in the incubator, all wired up and on a small amount of oxygen. It was difficult seeing him so small and helpless in the incubator, and I had such a sense of guilt that he was born early because of my body's failings. As grateful as I was that he was alive and doing well, I was sad that I wasn't able to incubate him for longer. However, I trusted that God would strengthen my baby, and that one day he would be out of the incubator and in my arms. After a couple of days, my husband and I were able to hold him. That was such an incredible and emotional moment.

Our son was a little fighter, and he went from strength to strength. He was in hospital for six weeks, and was on small amount of oxygen for five weeks. God placed an amazing midwife on my maternity ward, who allowed me to stay on site at the hospital for a few weeks in a flat for parents who had babies in ICU. What a blessing this was, as I don't think I could have coped emotionally with having to leave my baby in hospital in the first few weeks of his birth. My son was a greedy baby and thrived in hospital. Despite reflux, he had no additional needs or complications and was discharged from hospital after six weeks.

Now, at 3 years old, he is a boisterous little boy with lots of energy, tall for his age and continues to thrive. My Miracle Baby is such a blessing to our family's lives. It wasn't an easy time by any means, but I am incredibly thankful to God for carrying us through. Be assured that in your time of testing, God will give you strength so that your test becomes your testimony.

GG

SUNDAY 19th

With my mouth will I make known thy faithfulness - Psalm 89:1

KEPT FROM BEING A FATAL STATISTIC - Reading: Psalm 121:1-8

Stop and let me tell you what the Lord has done for me!

It was the morning rush hour during the schools' exam period of May 2019. I planned to drive the children to school and make the routine drop offs. As I drove away from home, and headed for the motorway, I heard a loud banging sound. I had checked the car the night before but didn't see anything. I pleaded for Jesus' protection by His blood, praying throughout the journey across town.

My eldest daughter was in the front passenger seat reading her revision notes, my other children were at the back. The banging was getting louder. I wondered what it could be as I continued to drive, feeling the vibration of the vehicle and the pulling of the steering wheel. I had no idea of how grave a danger we were all in. I prayed that I could reach my last school stop in time for my daughter's exam. Once the children were all at school, the banging was causing the car to shake from side to side. Gripping the steering wheel, and with the hazard lights on, I drove slowly. I asked God to just help me to get the car to a safe place to stop.

Another driver drove alongside offering to help. It so happened that he lived on the road where I'd stopped my car. I couldn't have driven another minute's distance! When he looked at the car, he explained what the problem was. The lugs (bolts) in the car wheel – three were missing and only one was left holding the front passenger side wheel on and that had almost come off!

Amazingly, this man was also a mechanic. He left shortly and returned with some car wheel lugs to secure my wheel. He said: *"Someone must love you"*. I shared with him that I am a Believer and had been praying as I was driving the children to school. I felt weak with gratitude, knowing that God had protected not only me but my children too. We could have been dead but for the safe protection of our Lord Jesus!

I had to testify of His protection, for what marvellous things He has done. The children realised the loving care of Jesus towards us. They understood how we could have been a road accident statistic, but God would not have it so.

Charm

MONDAY 20th

Sing ye to the LORD, for he has triumphed gloriously - Exodus 15:21

WHAT IS YOUR SONG IN THE MIDST OF YOUR CRISIS? Read - Exodus 15:1-21

As we go through life, there will be ups and downs; and as Women of God, we have to be faithful throughout our Christian walk.

It is true that: *"life is a journey"*. There will be bumps in the road, the wind may blow and the storms will come so forcefully. But it is for us to have a song, not only in the day, but in the night also.

If we look in Exodus 15:1, Moses led the children of Israel with a song: *"I will sing unto the LORD, for he has triumphed gloriously: the horse and his rider has He thrown into the Sea"*. This is a song of celebration. God had parted the Red Sea and the children of Israel crossed over safely. But as time went by, they experienced Marah, bitter waters; and the Lord delivered them.

We see in verse 21, Miriam, the sister of Moses, leads the women in praise and worship: *"Sing ye to the LORD, for he has triumphed gloriously…"*. This was confirmation of Moses' song.

Our lives are filled with challenges and celebrations, but: *"Let us not be weary in well doing for in due season we shall reap, if we faint not"* (Galatians 6:9). What will be your song in the midst of your crisis?

Missionary Maxine Barclay

TUESDAY 21st

One of them, when he saw that he was healed, turned back - St Luke 17:15

ONE OUT OF TEN - Reading: St Luke 17:11-19

Thank you is one of the first expressions that a parent will teach their child to say.

They'll sometimes take things back from their child, or stand there awaiting the child's response, if verbal appreciation is not given. *"What do you say?"* is a common question to children.

In times of desperate need, we often spend hours and days in fasting and prayer, beseeching God to intervene on our behalf. God, with fatherly lovingkindness, grants our request, but do we always remember to say: *"Thank you"*?

In today's lesson, ten men were lepers. All ten *"lifted up their voices, and said: Jesus, Master, have mercy on us"*. He heard and healed them all. How then did only one have a thankful heart? When that leper saw the miraculous change which Jesus had wrought in his body, he couldn't do anything but go back in humility and fall at Jesus' feet glorifying Him.

Has Jesus done something(s) for you and you've not yet thanked Him? You asked the church to pray, fast and believe God with you, and He did even more than what you had hoped for. In your excitement of being delivered, you've never returned and said thanks. You may have told others what Jesus did, but that's not enough! Have you thanked Him, the one who brought your desire to pass?

Today, be that one out of ten. Go back and say: *"Thank you!"*.

JEJ

WEDNESDAY 22nd

I will worship towards thy holy temple, and praise thy name - Psalm 138:2

INTENTION TO WORSHIP - Reading: Psalm 138: 1-8

There is a resounding theme of intention and decision that makes the psalms so personally convicting.

Psalm 138:2, like countless others, uses that powerful word *"WILL"*. David marked the temple, physically reverencing, by turning towards it in order to praise God. He knew God's strength and honoured Him by his behaviour. We can hardly ever follow through with something wholeheartedly without a full conviction.

David infamously made bad decisions too that led to sinful acts, and yet here he makes good ones with equal full intention: *"I will!"*.

As true believers, our decision to worship God must be a few things as reflected in Psalms:

• It must be based on conviction by experience, i.e., our testimony

• It must be unapologetic; turning boldly towards a worthy God with full praise and honour, no matter who sees us

• It must leave no room for other gods in our lives

• It must see the magnified Word of God as the focus for all submission

• It must be wholehearted

Today, we are reminded that the mandate we have to swim against the tide is simply a marking of how Sovereign and worthy our God is of our wholehearted surrender. For a moment in meditation, let's describe our own act of worship towards God. Are there words like: *"wholehearted"*, *"turned towards"*, *"will"*?

If we are plagued with mediocrity and can describe our Christian walk with *"sometimes"*, *"maybe"*, *"feel"*, then here's a challenge to change!

We can truly cry again to God and hear His answer to: *"I will worship towards thy holy temple"*, and turn full face with no apology!

Joy Lear-Bernard

*THURSDAY 23rd

Thus far the LORD has helped us - 1 Samuel 7:12 (NKJV)

A DAY OF THANKSGIVING - Reading: 1 Samuel 7:1-17

"Then Samuel took a stone, and set it between Mizpeh and Shen, and called the name of it Eben-ezer, saying, Hitherto hath the LORD helped us." (1 Samuel 7:12 KJV)

In the context of this passage, God had provided the children of Israel a miraculous deliverance from the armies of the Philistines. They earnestly sought God's help and He answered them miraculously. Samuel set up a memorial stone to commemorate this great event.

As we reflect over the past 2 ½ years - the hardships we endured being locked down, some experienced discouragements, disappointments, the pain of losing loved ones and not being able to celebrate their lives. Others experienced depression and anxiety. Had it not been for the Lord on our side we could have been overwhelmed and felt hopeless.

But our God, who is rich in mercy, by His grace we can say with authority: *"This I recall to my mind, therefore I have hope. It is of the LORD'S mercies that we are not consumed, because His compassions fail not. They are new every morning: great is thy faithfulness" (Lamentations 3:21-23).*

By the grace and help of the Lord we have come this far, so we have confidence and hope for our future because God is with us. With a heart of gratitude and thanksgiving we can say: *"Till now the Lord has helped us, and he will lead us safely home"!*

Lady Winsome Saunders, Baltimore, USA

*Thanksgiving Day USA

FRIDAY 24th

Stand up and bless the LORD your God for ever and ever - Nehemiah 9:5

TO GOD BE THE GLORY FOR WHAT HE HAS DONE - Reading: Neh. 9:1-15

Our God is great!

I give honour to the spirit of God who holds my life together during my journey of faith. I have remained under the protection of God all my life. He has taken me out of so many dangers, snares and traps put in my way to destroy me.

I recall one such trap in 2009. My colleague and I, we were regular walkers in the area where our offices are based. We would walk during our lunch breaks, there is a golf course and football pitch surrounding the building. We often walked along the golf course because it is tranquil and naturally beautiful.

This particular day was warm, still and tranquil but for some reason I felt the need to avoid the golf course, so suggested to my colleague that we should walk towards the football pitch instead. I told her that this had dropped into my spirit and I would obey.

We walked for about an hour and on our way back from the walk we encountered a police cordon! We were told that a serious assault had taken place at the entrance of the golf course an hour before. Because our office is the only building in that area, the people working there were asked if they had seen anyone suspicious hanging around.

The police told us that we had had a lucky escape. I know that this was not about luck, this was God's doing! He had steered us away from the golf course and danger.

Name withheld

November 2023
Theme: Thanksgiving, Praise & Worship
Awareness Month for: Prematurity, Diabetes, Mouth Cancer, Family Caregivers

388

SATURDAY 25th

His praise shall continually be in my mouth - Psalm 34:1

I WILL BLESS THE LORD - Reading: Psalm 34:1-2; Hebrews 13:15

How do we give thanks and praise to our GOD for His excellence? Just thinking about Him should bring out the fruit of our lips…

When we consider the fact that He woke us up this morning, He set us on our way, we give Him thanks. But the psalmist is encouraging us to go a little deeper; to consider Him as God and God alone. Not for anything that He does or anything that we need, but just because He is God. Our words are to glorify, to magnify and to extol Him because He is worthy! Hallelujah.

At all times, whether or not things are going our way, whether we are experiencing sickness, unemployment, bereavement or brokenness, He is still God.

Let our mouths continually have that theme of praise from a grateful heart.

Beverley V. Galloway

Enter into His gates with thanksgiving - Psalm 100:4

MY 4LB-&-A-BIT BAG OF SUGAR - Reading: Psalm 100:1-5

At nine weeks pregnant I had a threatened miscarriage; I was put on bed-rest and told that if I carried to my sixteenth week, the pregnancy stood a good chance of continuing.

After this, life carried on cautiously. I was unsaved at the time but had a prayerful mum and dad. Understandably, I worried constantly. At 35 weeks, one morning my waters broke and I knew I was in labour! My baby was not due until early May and we were still in March.

He arrived at 4.35pm, weighing 4lbs:10ozs. I was allowed a brief look at him before he was taken to the Neonatal Premature Baby Unit. It was love at first sight. He was perfectly formed but oh so tiny and in need of much feeding up. He had to be placed on a pillow to be fed, and we spent seven days and nights in hospital.

I remember feeling scared to take him home. My husband and I wondered how normal nappies were going to be usable as he was so tiny. In hospital, disposable nappies were used but were not yet readily available to buy. A lovely midwife taught us how to shorten a terry towelling nappy to fit him.

I used to (and still do) refer to him as my 4lb bag of sugar (he was such a sweet baby). Whilst the pregnancy and early delivery were stressful, I believe God kept this child safe. This little bundle of joy grew up to become Elder Nicholas Myers.

Sis Shirley Myers

MONDAY 27th

You shall have no other gods before me - Exodus 20:3 (NIV)

ONLY GOD! - Reading: Exodus 20:1-26

As I look at this passage of Scripture the word: *"You"* jumps out at me.

I am looking at myself: have I put other gods before Almighty God? It's easy to do! We have such busy lives, and we are always looking for *"down time"* to relax. Maybe it's a god of watching TV for hours each day, or your favourite celebrity, social media, or a book that you would prefer to read rather than reading your Bible when it's time to study the Word.

Another thing we could be guilty of is putting a loved one before God. Let's think about who God is and how much He loves us. He tells us that He is jealous for us. That's not in the same sense as we associate jealousy, but when we go after worldly things He knows where that can lead, it can be a slippery slope into trouble.

God only ever wants the best for us. If we look to Him we will have peace, and an abundant life which is the greatest adventure.

Marie Chisnall

TUESDAY 28th

I will praise thee; for I am fearfully and wonderfully made - Psalm 139:14

THANK HIM! PRAISE HIM! - Reading: Genesis 2:22-23; Psalm 139:13-16

As I meditate upon Psalm 139, I am reminded of how great our God is. He has everything under His control.

This Great God that fills the heavens and the earth, who is the God of creation, the God of the universe, He chose to create and love us. Yes, we are loved! He fashioned every part of us because He knew what our purpose would be.

If you have ever studied the human anatomy, you will have realised how intricate it all is. Just think about it for a moment, the way that every part of your body does what it needs to do without trying to function as another body part. The hand doesn't do what the foot does, the eye doesn't do what the ear does. And to know that God sings over us because He is pleased with His creation!

Let us thank Him for this wonderful life that He has given to us. Praise Him for the incredibly beautiful body He has given us. Oh, let us worship Him for who He is, for there is no one like our God. Hallelujah!

Marie Chisnall

November 2023
Theme: Thanksgiving, Praise & Worship
Awareness Month for: Prematurity, Diabetes, Mouth Cancer, Family Caregivers

392

WEDNESDAY 29th

My soul longeth, yea, even fainteth for the courts of the LORD - Psalm 84:2

LONGING FOR GOD - Reading: Psalm 84:1-12; Hebrews 10:25

This verse reflects a heart with a zeal and a passion for the house of God. It's the place where the spirit of the Lord is, a place of restoration, healing, revival and anointing.

In Hebrews 10:25, we are reminded not to forsake (forget) the house of God; it is a place where I can meet the only wise, living God and my soul be fed and satisfied.

It is a privilege to enter!

Sis Rose Morrison

THURSDAY 30th

Let every thing that hath breath praise the LORD - Psalm 150:6

PRAISE GOD! - Reading: Psalm 150:1-6

The psalmist David encourages his audience to praise the LORD. Praise is an expression of approval and commendation.

David instructs that God should be praised with all different types of musical instruments such as the trumpets, harps, timbrels, cymbals - all of which make a different sound. Likewise, each of God's people's voices of praise don't sound the same.

The Pharisees were displeased when the crowd shouted out joyful praises as Jesus entered Jerusalem. But: _"(Jesus) answered and said unto them, I tell you that, if these should hold their peace, the stones would immediately cry out" (St Luke 19:40)_. This shows how worthy God is to be praised.

David suggests that we praise God in dancing, with singing, in words. He calls us to express the excellency of God, His beauty, His greatness, and His power. In Psalm 148, David commands numerous examples of creation to join in praise to God their Creator, e.g., the sun and moon, stars of lights. The heavens, mountains, hills, dragons, and all deeps. The hail, snow, even the mountains, hills, and fruitful trees.

As humankind, created in God's own image, why should we not praise Him? _"He inhabits the praises of His people" (Psalm 22:3)_. We capture God's attention, and He will show up, when we praise Him. It doesn't need to be a large crowd; you can be alone or with only two or three and Jesus has promised to be in the midst (St Matthew 18:19-20).

In Psalm 150:6, David concludes his reflections with: _"Praise ye the Lord"._

Missionary M Fraser

MOUTH CANCER

Mouth cancer, otherwise known as oral cancer, includes cancer of the mouth, tongue and the part of the throat at the back of our tongue. It is more common in men than in women and 1 in 75 men, and 1 in 150 women, will be diagnosed with mouth cancer at some point in their life. Most people diagnosed are over 60 years of age.

In terms of the mouth (not the tongue or throat), approximately 55% of people survive 5 years or more after diagnosis*.

Early detection is vital and greatly improves outcomes for treatment, and so we recommend regular dental check-ups as your dentist will be looking for anything suspicious in your mouth, and will refer you for urgent further testing if necessary.

Signs of mouth cancer can include, but are not limited to, a mouth ulcer that will not heal, abnormal red or white coloured patches on the skin inside your mouth or a lump in the neck. If you find anything in your mouth that doesn't seem normal, or worries you, ask your dentist or doctor for help and advice.

Smoking and alcohol increase your risk of developing mouth cancer. Although you may not partake yourself, others around you may do and you can encourage them to stop or reduce these habits and reduce their risk of developing oral cancer.

Treatment of oral cancer depends on where the cancer is, how large it is, and your general health. The specialist will discuss with you your options, how treatment will affect your quality of life and the side effects.

Dr Nadine Miller BDS MFDS RCS Ed

References

www.cancerresearchuk.org

M.A O. Lewis (2018) Mouth Cancer: presentation, detection and referral in primary dental care, *British Dental Journal* volume 225, pages 833–840

*People diagnosed in England between 2009 and 2013

December

The Gift of Jesus Christ

FRIDAY 1st

For God so loved the world that He gave His only begotten Son - St John 3:16

A GIFT FOR EVERYONE - Reading: Ezekiel 16:6-9; St John 3:16-17

Imagine that you were so poor you had absolutely nothing! You had no home, no clothes - only the rags that you were wearing, and you were starving.

Because of all of this, your body was covered in sores and you smelled so bad. Then one day, a stranger came up to you and said: *"I am going to change your life because I love you"!* He then gave you the most beautiful home and furnished it, a wardrobe full of clothes, fine food to eat.

But you still had sores and your body smelled really bad. He then said: *"I am going to clean you and heal you. I love you and you are mine. You will never want again; all I ask is that you love me".*

This is just what Jesus Christ has done for us. We were wearing filthy rags and sin had made us smell so awful; but then Jesus called us by our name, and told us that we are His! He continues to cleanse us each day as we trust and walk with Him.

Marie Chisnall

SATURDAY 2nd

The Lord himself shall give you a sign - Isaiah 7:14

A VIRGIN SHALL BEAR A SON - Reading: Isaiah 7:1-15

King Ahaz was told through the prophet, who was God's mouthpiece, to ask for a sign but Ahaz flatly refused.

Despite this, God gave Ahaz a sign and within a few years his enemies were put down. Not only was God speaking to Ahaz, He was also speaking to the House of David. He was instructing them to look for a specific sign, i.e., a virgin pregnant with child.

This verse also has a far-reaching prophecy. St Matthew 1:23 speaks of His title, Immanuel, which means "God with us" and refers to His deity and closeness to man.

How then can God be with us? 1 Timothy 3:16 affirms that Jesus Christ manifested Himself in the flesh; God, who is a spirit, took on human form. This is known as His incarnation. St John1:1, and St John 1:14, clearly confirm that Jesus is God. Note that God has always existed, even before Genesis 1 where He created the heaven and the earth. Today He is with us through His spirit which leads and guides believers in Christ into all truth.

When Jesus was ascending back to heaven, He said to His disciples: *"Nevertheless I tell you the truth, it is expedient for you that I go away, for if I go not away, the Comforter will not come unto you, if I depart, I will send Him unto you"* (St John 16:7).

This is why it is essential that believers in Christ experience the New Birth in two parts, i.e., baptism in water in the name of the Lord Jesus and baptism of the Holy Ghost.

Missionary Audrey Simpson

*SUNDAY 3rd

Bethlehem Ephratah,... out of thee shall he come forth - Micah 5:2

CAN ANY GOOD THING...? Reading: Micah 5:1-4

Micah prophesied the direct location of this Judean town, named twice: Bethlehem, commonly and popular named. Ephratah's first reference is in Genesis 35:16.

Smaller of the cities of Judah, insignificant, not renowned. Yet God, before time, ringfenced the 'House of Bread'. Rulers would come from her. Kings would be born and buried in that City of David, so called in Scriptures (St Luke 2:4).

It was the birthplace of Israel's greatest king. David's lineage and genealogy are rooted there; and God made an everlasting covenant with David to build Him a dynasty and establish David's throne forever (2 Samuel 7:10-16). Jacob's Messianic prediction, i.e., *"The Sceptre shall not depart...until Shiloh comes" (Genesis 49:10)* foretold the kingly tribe and region.

Bethlehem in Judah, emerged from obscurity, then became notable and regal as prophecies fulfilled. The world watched while heavenly and earthly visitors ascended to the little town of Bethlehem. Divinely orchestrated, the authorities commanded everyone returned to their original hometown for census. Being from David's lineage and native home, as appointed, a virgin delivered on time.

A Holy Child was born. The Ultimate Ruler. Eternal King and Saviour of the world. The Lion of the tribe of Judah and Captain of our Eternal Salvation.

Sis Jx

*International Day of People with Disabilities

MONDAY 4th

This is the sixth month with her who was called barren - St Luke 1:36

WHAT WERE YOU CALLED? - Reading: St Luke 1:34-37

Elisabeth *"who was called barren"*, now six months pregnant! God's divine plan and purpose were taking place in her.

We may be seen as or called many things in this life, but what does God call us? What is His plan? Imagine for a moment how Elisabeth felt being called *"Barren..."*. Now imagine her joy at being six months pregnant!

Mary knew not a man, but the angel declared, *"The Holy Ghost shall come upon thee"*. Mary would see God at work in Elisabeth whilst His Word was accomplishing what He had designed for Mary too. When God calls us and moves in us, amazing, miraculous, life changing things will happen.

Our amazing God will always get the glory when we make ourselves available, and surrender to be used by Him. The names won't matter; He'll use what we're being called in our favour. Age is not a barrier to God - young, middle-aged or senior, He has a purpose for us all.

Sis Rose Morrison

The Word was made flesh, and dwelt among us - St John 1:14

BORN LORD OF ALL - Reading: St Matthew 2:1-2; St John 1:14-16

The Magi brought Him quality gifts, not any old thing; these were precious gifts, gifts fit for a King.

They had followed the star in the east, which led them straight to the place where Jesus was. They had come to worship this King who, when born, was first found by the shepherds wrapped in swaddling clothes and lying in a manger.

Imagine now the scene, the sounds and the smell. What an unexpected surprise for these new parents to have beheld: here their young child being gifted with gold, frankincense and myrrh.

Even with no room in the inn, from such humble beginnings, the heralded entry of this infant would ignite the story of God's unfolding love in a most unlikely way. Isaiah the prophet spoke of it: *"Unto us a child is born, unto us a son is given...his name shall be called Wonderful…" (Isaiah 9:6) - "Immanuel, God with us" (Isaiah 7:14, St Matthew 1:22-23).*

Some recognised that He was no ordinary child from the beginning, although born to ordinary parents. They were led bravely into the unknown, simply trusting their God and receiving the truth they were told.

Today, so many believe by faith in this Son of man, and Son of God who lived, ruled and is still saving lives today. He was born with clear purpose, a life destined for greatness, a King born to die, who fulfilled His reason why. What a mystery, foretold throughout history right up until today. A baby, born King and Saviour, spoken of down the ages. What a beautiful mystery that has been unfolding throughout history covering pages telling of an Eternal Love story...

We too bow down and worship Him, our Lord of All.

Evangelist Viv Lear

**International Volunteer Day*

WEDNESDAY 6ᵗʰ

Ye were sealed with that holy Spirit of promise - Ephesians 1:13

FOR WHAT WE ARE ABOUT TO RECEIVE - Reading: Ephesians 1:13-14

"In whom ye also trusted, after that ye heard the word of truth, the gospel of your salvation: in whom also after that ye believed, ye were sealed with that holy Spirit of promise,
Which is the earnest of our inheritance until the redemption of the purchased possession, unto the praise of his glory".

Once upon a time we heard the great news of salvation, and believed and trusted in the Word of Truth. Because of that, we were thrust into eternity whilst being right here on earth!

The Holy Spirit sealed us, put His mark of ownership upon us, and became our entry ticket into Glory. That's not where the story ends; the Holy Spirit's sealing also becomes our guarantee for what we are about to and are guaranteed to receive on the other side of eternity.

Let us be conscious of the fact that we are so precious to God that He went to great lengths to make us His. Every time that we enjoy the presence of the Holy Spirit, we have been given a foretaste of what is to come, so may we always be truly thankful.

Minister Kay Dawkins

THURSDAY 7th

The Spirit of the Lord GOD is upon me - Isaiah 61:1

THE MEASURE OF SUCCESS: YET NOT I - Reading: Isaiah 61:1-11

We have, as individuals, a pandemic of reckless proportions. One that surges through our churches and similarly to our secular communities. It does not take the physical life but indeed leaves us lifeless. It is the 'I' mentality.

Whilst we are encouraged to garner good self-esteem somewhere, as it does, carnality has infected us wrapping itself around ministry, service and Christian living. It whispers to us that it is about the 'I' in success that matters.

To know our gifting is a wonderful thing. But rather know from where it came and for what purpose; this is what we all need in order to be sober and spiritually effective. This virus shows up in language like: *"I am me"*, rather than *"Christ in me"*.

But let us consider Jesus and esteem. In St Luke 4:18-19, Jesus refers to Isaiah 61:1. He speaks of the Spirit of Lord as the source of His anointing, and the broken as His focus for ministry. Jesus, as God manifested in flesh, knew fully His power and purpose, yet the confidence He displayed was only to please God. The pinnacle and success of ministry was the cross and an empty tomb.

Jesus died to Himself 40 days in the wilderness, hungry and tempted. He died to Himself as He mourned His cousin's execution for the gospel's sake. He died to Himself in the garden of bitter tears. Dying to self is what gives the greatest aptitude for anointing.

If we truly want to know success in life, true value and boldness, it is Christ's beautiful example of daily dying and brokenness to self that bring God's Spirit to the glorious fore so that we can truly say: *"The Spirit of the Lord GOD is upon me...".*

Joy Lear-Bernard

FRIDAY 8th

My kingdom is not of this world - St John 18:36

HE STILL CAME - Reading: St John 18:28-40

1.He left the splendour of heaven
Knowing His destiny
Was the lonely hill of Golgotha
There to lay down His life for me

Refrain:
If that isn't love then the ocean is dry
There're no stars in the sky
And the sparrow can't fly!
If that isn't love then heaven's a myth
There's no feeling like this
If that isn't love

2. Even in death He remembered
The thief hanging by His side;
He spoke with love and compassion
Then He took him to Paradise

(Author unknown)

SATURDAY 9th

(They) pierced his side and came there out blood and water - St John 19:34

BLOOD & WATER - Reading: St John 19:28-37

God gave His only begotten Son, Jesus Christ, to pay the ultimate price for sin.

When Jesus came to earth, He surrendered Himself as a willing sacrifice to shed His blood and die for the remission and forgiveness of our sins (Hebrews 9:22). John describes Jesus as: *"The Lamb of God which taketh away the sin of the world" (St John 1:29).*

A spear was thrust into Jesus' side as He hung on the cross. Oh, what cruel hands did to our Saviour although He was sinless and guiltless! Blood and water gushed out of His side as evidence of His death.

Just as the Passover lamb could have no broken bones (Exodus 12:46), Jesus, as prophesied in Psalm 34:20, died before any of His bones could be broken (breaking of bones was customary to help hasten death at crucifixion).

Blood and water often precede birth in the natural. At Calvary, the blood and water preceded birth of The Church on the day of Pentecost when the Holy Spirit first fell in Jerusalem, fifty days after Passover.

Christ gave His life to give us eternal life. He gave His life a ransom for many, for *"whosoever believeth in Him"* so that we *"should not perish but have everlasting life" (St John 3:15-16).*

The Gift of Salvation has been received by the Ekklesia, i.e., the called-out ones, meaning the Church.

Sis Jx

SUNDAY 10th

We have seen… and are come to worship him - St Matthew 2:2

LOOK HOW FAR YOU'VE COME - Reading: St Matthew 2:1-12

It may not read this way, but the period of time between when the star appeared to the wise men (Magi), and their reaching the house where Jesus was with His parents, was more than one year.

We know this because in St Luke 2:12-16, Jesus is described as being a babe lying in a manger, but is described in St Matthew 2:9-11 as a young child in a house when He was found by the wise men.

It was nothing less than determination which kept the wise men focused as they travelled through the heat and cold to worship the King of kings. See that they made preparation to worship before leaving home. They knew that they could not present themselves before a king empty-handed (such a thing would be irreverent), so they brought gold, frankincense and myrrh.

They preserved their gifts on the long journey, they lost nothing on the way. After months of anticipation and travelling to Bethlehem, the Magi were bursting to worship! As soon as they entered the house where Jesus was, they fell down, worshipped, opened up their treasures.

Just reflect now how far you've come on your Christian journey. Think of the insults, ridicule, financial hardship, failed relationships, false statements, abuse, grief and rejection along the way, and you haven't turned back. You *know* that it's only a made-up mind that presses on to see Jesus.

You've come this far by faith. It's time now to open up your treasures of gratitude! Worship and bow down.

JEJ

MONDAY 11th

The babe leaped in Elisabeth's womb - St Luke 1:41

LEAPT IN HER WOMB - Reading: St Luke 1: 39-56

The meeting of Mary and Elisabeth is one of my favourite Bible stories.

Reading it I'm reminded of a worship service where we were invited to pray in pairs. A sister turned to me (at the time weary and isolated) and invited us to pray. As we held hands an unrestrained, unpredicted burst of prayers and tears overwhelmed us in mirroring fashion. We felt a cave of burden that neither of us had expressed verbally. Gushes of lament and pain surged out of us until our knees buckled and our faces were wet with release.

The young expectant Mary had to journey some way to the pregnant Elisabeth in Scripture, and the sameness of purpose in them leapt in unison. Just like them, we as two women, found ourselves knitted together by experience with the power of prayer and connection defeating the wiles of the enemy, unloading the heavy backpack and sharing a powerful moment.

Connection is important, imperative. It is why we have community. It is why we do and should seek out safe 'Elisabeths' in our sphere. 'She' needs us as much as we need her. Maybe she is older and needs you as she navigates the terrain of her own season.

Maybe you feel alone today, take confidence that someone has you on her mind, in their prayers and before God's throne. You are not alone. Reach out. Ask God for your Elisabeth and watch the burdens lift.

Joy Lear-Bernard

TUESDAY 12th

He was wounded for our transgressions, bruised for our iniquities - Isaiah 53:5

HE TOOK MY PLACE! - Reading: Isaiah 53:1-12

The Eagle Eye prophet reported and detailed the account of the Passion of Jesus Christ.

The Son of God would suffer to secure our salvation: *"It pleased the LORD to bruise Him" (Isaiah 53:10)* as was covenanted in Genesis 3:15 *"And I will put enmity between thee and the woman, and between thy seed and her seed; it shall bruise thy head, and thou shalt bruise his heel"*, all because of God's love for humankind (St John 3:16).

The punishment for sin is death. There is no remission or forgiveness for sin without shedding blood. Animal blood was used under the Old Covenant but proved ineffective to remit sin appropriately. Therefore, the Sacrificial Lamb was slain, i.e., Jesus Christ. His flesh was pierced and mutilated for us who had rebelled against God. Yet, Jesus took the blows that crushed and humbled Him, took them for us who were guilty of evil doings.

We deserved to be punished but our deliverance rested upon Him. Hence, He endured and learned obedience unto death. He was disciplined and tortured, and opened not His mouth. Instead, He willingly took the shame so that we could *"have peace with God" (Romans 5:1)*.

Nevertheless, after all the beatings and pierced broken flesh, crushed and humbled, finally came His death on a cross. It wasn't for nothing, no! Through His suffering we were made whole and cured from the bondage of sin.

Sis Jx

WEDNESDAY 13th

Joseph of Arimathaea craved the body of Jesus - St Mark 15:43

AN HONOURABLE CRAVING - Reading: St Mark 15:42-47

Joseph of Arimathea was a learned respectable man, a counsellor.

He was able to boldly go before Pilate, and knew well the Scriptures. Distinguished, you might call him. This versus the battered, broken, unrecognisable body of Jesus. What honour would this lifeless body hold to Joseph's credibility? But Joseph knew something about the kingdom of God, and had seen something in Jesus that he saw fit to honour.

We are modern day counsellors, learned and versed, but we too are challenged to be bold enough in our present world to say: *"I want Jesus!".*

Nothing of our faith speaks louder than when we say: *"I crave to hold Jesus close. I need to honour His death and burial and to be partaker in His resurrection. I believe in Him!".*

Do we crave Jesus? Do we hunger for Him regardless of how the world sees Him? I'm desperate for what the cross means, and denounce my own reputation to seek it. To behold Him is my duty and to love His love for me.

Joseph's story is a testament to us to crave, yearn, wholly desire to be close to Jesus and His blood. To worship Him and deny all else today takes a heart which says: *"I crave Jesus!",* and to boldly receive Him with honour.

Joy Lear-Bernard

THURSDAY 14th

Mine eyes have seen thy salvation - St Luke 2:30

ORDINARY WITH AN EXTRAORDINARY PROMISE - Reading: St Luke 2: 22-35

Today we're looking at Simeon who, from what I can tell, was an 'ordinary' man. The Bible says that Simeon was: *"in Jerusalem, just, devout, waiting for the consolation of Israel (i.e., the Messiah)"*. Much more than that we do not know.

Yet this man, who carries no lengthy written profile, had at some stage received a divine promise that he would not die until he had seen the Lord's Christ, i.e., Jesus. What a promise!

Have you noticed a pattern in Luke's recordings in chapters 1 & 2, i.e., ordinary people chosen for extraordinary promises and privileges? Unassuming people being moved from the back row to the front: Mary, Joseph, Simeon, Anna. The kind that, when their names are called, people might say: *"**Who?**"*!

I wonder if there is an extraordinary promise which God has given to a reader of this page, although she considers herself to be: *"just an ordinary woman"*, or *"little old me!"*:

"There was a man…whose name was Simeon…"; Simeon's credential – *"a righteous man"*! Your credential: *"a righteous woman"*! Because you feel so ordinary, you can't understand why God picked you out for such an extraordinary promise or purpose. Can you keep on believing until the promise comes to pass? Our God is not ordinary, neither are His promises, yet He keeps them all!

JEJ

FRIDAY 15th

They saw fish laid thereon, and bread - St John 21:9

GOD HAS ALREADY PROVIDED - Reading: St John 21: 1-25

Peter was a fisherman when Jesus called him. Without much persuasion, Peter left his fishing career to follow Him (St Luke 5:1-11).

We almost have a feeling of déjà vu reading St John 21. Just as in Luke 5 where Peter and his fishing partners had unsuccessfully toiled all night and caught nothing, we see a repeat of the same in today's reading.

When God wants to close a chapter in our lives, He can make things which used to be easy suddenly become difficult. Peter was an expert at fishing, yet in Luke 5 he had an unproductive night doing what he'd been doing for years.

We see that after Jesus had risen and appeared to His disciples, Peter one day decided to return to the familiar, and go fishing again. Like the day when he met Jesus, once more Peter and the others laboured all night and caught nothing until Jesus turned up and said: *"Cast the net on the right side"*, and they miraculously caught 153 fishes.

However, when the disciples dragged their net of fishes to the shore, they saw that Jesus had already prepared breakfast for them using **nothing** from what they caught (St John 21:9). Jesus invited His disciples to: *"Come and dine"*.

Are you trying to make something work which has passed its expiry date because you're afraid to let it go? You hold on because you're wondering about provision: *"How will I manage?"* – *"What if?"* Please read Luke 5 and John 21 for your answer. It is easy to focus on the disciples eventually having a draught, but then completely miss the point that they did not need what they toiled all night to get!

You will always struggle when outside of the will of God, when you go back to or continue with the familiar, when you try to re-open a door which God has shut rather than moving forward into God's Unknown. Yes, you may have a measure of 'success', eventually, through your own efforts, but God has already provided for you on the other side!

JEJ

SATURDAY 16th

She opens her mouth with wisdom - Proverbs 31:26

WISE WOMEN, WISE QUOTES - Reading: Proverbs 31:10-31

1. *Our walk with God is a journey, not a destination* **(First Lady Yolanda Edmund)**

2. *Believe and receive; doubt and do without!* **(Mother Ethlyn Simmonds)**

3. *God is a bridge over troubled water!* **(Mother Chloe Dunn)**

4. *Go down in prayer, and rise to meet your day!* **(Mother Sweedie Edmund)**

5. *Hold on to your faith and don't be fearful!* **(Pastor Verna Wynter)**

6. *Don't wait to be discovered, discover yourself!* **(Overseer Joy Henry)**

7. *Avoid unnecessary temptation!* **(Mother Gloria Fearon)**

8. *No matter how you feel, pick yourself up, wash your face, fix your hair, and face your day!* **(Mother Sweedie Edmund)**

9. *If in doubt, check it out!* **(Dr Una Davis)**

10. *Tell yourself: "I am beautiful. I am valuable. I am God's peculiar treasure". Affirm yourselves through God's Word!* **(Overseer Joy Henry)**

11. *Always let your failures be your teacher, not your undertaker!* **(Mother Margaret Lena Brown)**

12. *Don't let your children grow up believing in Father Christmas or a Tooth Fairy. Tell them that you bought the presents, and you gave them the money!* **(Mother Icilda Hall)**

13. *The whole Word of God is my favourite, from beginning to end!* **(Mother Vivelyn Sheppey)**

14. *A pure heart will show in your thoughts, words, choices, attitudes, and more!* **(Mother Gloria Fearon)**

15. *Keep walking in victory!* **(Dr Una Davis)**

Adapted from 'I Arise' 2022

SUNDAY 17th

Anna served God with fastings and prayers night and day - St Luke 2:37

OPEN DOORS THAT GOD PROVIDES - Reading: St Luke 2:36-38

Look at Anna's personal circumstances – she was married for seven years, and a widow for eighty-four years. She had been a widow much longer than she had been married.

Did her circumstances cause her to walk away from God? Did she apportion blame to someone else for her singleness? Did she remain in a state of mourning? Anna never ceased her relationship with God; she stayed faithful in building and maintaining her spiritual life. Anna's consistent and continual dedicated lifestyle allowed her to quickly recognise and proclaim Jesus as the Messiah - an open door that God provided.

Has life given us some tough, hard knocks? Get up, although our knees may be weak and our hearts are racing. Is there no one around to be our biggest cheerleader? Get up – use our knees to cry out to God, verbalise our thoughts and feelings to Him. Just keep that line of communication open.

Our spiritual influence flows from a spiritual lifestyle, not just from the presence of our spiritual gifting. Let our spiritual lifestyle give us the ability to discern the things of God swiftly and rightly, especially when He opens doors.

Evangelist Sheridon

MONDAY 18th

They... platted a crown of thorns, and put it (on) his head - St Mark 15:17

THE MOCKERY OF MAJESTY - Reading: St Mark 15: 16-20

Mark 15:17 depicts details of Jesus' tortuous tormenting impending death at the hands of Jewish leaders. Blows whilst blindfolded, demanding prophecy, jeered by His creation.

What Jesus went through was excruciating. It is appropriate to preserve the word 'agony' to describe such pain.

Mockingly they robed Him, they put a thorny crown on Him. Sinners seemed to be His boss, and He their prey. Yet here is the convicting wonderment that brings the believer to tearful surrender: their worst humiliating act of aggression was by His own permission and design. He allowed every single bloodied blow. He permitted Himself to be debilitated, holding back His own power. They only thought that they were in charge, but He was always in control!

He let them mock His majesty because He was majestic! He wore the purple robe with purpose. His sovereignty would be proved to thrive not just survive over death.

He tolerated each skin-tearing stripe, He meekly bore them because we needed him to. He resolved not to come down even as they mocked Him to. He stayed on the cross because we needed Him to, and to complete His reason for coming to earth.

Jesus was not caught powerless. He could easily lay down His life and raise it up again (St John 10:18). He endured the cross on purpose, and that purpose was you and I.

Surely when He was on the cross, we were on His mind. What majesty.

Joy Lear-Bernard

TUESDAY 19th

He said...a body hast thou prepared for me - Hebrews 10:5

THE FAITHFULNESS OF GOD - Reading: Isaiah 7:14; Hebrews 5:1-13

When I reflect on the birth of Jesus Christ, I praise my Lord and Saviour for His faithfulness and the fulfilment of His promise.

Throughout Scripture, we see over and over, God's constant desire to be with His people and to have fellowship with us.

The birth of Jesus marks the coming of the promised Messiah. He who would save us from sin, the punishment of sin, and grant us access to salvation, restoration, freedom and right relationship with God. All of this because of God's unwavering love for His people.

What an honour that the holy and Almighty God would throughout the ages pursue me! That He would take on flesh to restore and redeem me! Even though His people turned their backs to Him, He remained faithful to His Word, and His promise of Salvation.

I thank God for the birth of Jesus Christ and the awesome expression of God's love and grace for you and me.

Christine Knight

WEDNESDAY 20th

This shall be a sign...you shall find the babe...lying in a manger - St Luke 2:12

THE KING IN A MANGER - Reading: St Luke 2:8-20

There are many rich people who live in ordinary houses in non-exclusive areas.

They don't all drive the most expensive of cars, neither do they always wear exclusive clothes. They're rich and recognise that their affluence is not about location or having costly possessions. They are confident and secure to live way below their means because they know who they are.

The birth of Jesus was like that. The maternity ward for Mary was a stable, and Jesus' Moses Basket was a manger. A manger is a trough or box from which horses and cattle feed.

We can understand why the angel of the Lord would explain to the shepherds that, despite the place and surroundings, when you see a baby lying in a manger, that's Him!

What do I mean by 'Him'? Well, this is Him of whom Isaiah spoke in 7:14 and 9:6-7. This is *"A light to lighten the Gentiles, and the glory of His people Israel"* (St Luke 2:32). In the trough is *"God clothed in flesh"* (St John 1:14) dressed in His overalls/working clothes, come to minister and die to save humankind from their sins. In that feeding box *"He made Himself of no reputation"* yet, one day, *"Every knee shall bow and every tongue confess that He is Lord"* (Philippians 2:6-11). The baby in the stable that has a bad smell is Jesus Christ who *"Although He was rich, for your sake became poor"* (2 Corinthians 8:9).

Shepherds, don't be confused by the stable, the manger, or that the baby is wrapped in strips of cloth. It's definitely Him!

JEJ

THURSDAY 21st

Emmanuel interpreted is, God with us - St Matthew 1:23

HOPE IN THE MIDST OF DARKNESS - Reading: St Matthew 1:18-23

The world celebrates 25th December as Jesus' birthday. Whether right or wrong, one thing is certain: that God clothed Himself in flesh and appeared to us as Jesus Christ, and was born of the virgin Mary. What a glorious hope Jesus' birth represents!

However, wherever God gives hope, Satan endeavours to bring sorrow and hopelessness. So much so that, despite Jesus' glorious birth, today we live in a world spinning out of control, a world in turmoil. People are experiencing personal tragedies, financial crisis, the tragic loss of loved ones to a menacing virus, fuel deprivation, all whilst trying to come to terms with the cost of living which is rocketing sky high! Broken, bewildered and feeling forsaken, many are left asking: "Where is God in all of this?". But regardless of the state of world, God has not forsaken His people. The prophet Isaiah reminds us that He is: *"Emmanuel, which is being interpreted as God with us" (St Matthew 1:23).*

Indeed, I am reminded of the many times that God has laid heavily on my heart to encourage my Sunday morning Facebook Live broadcast, 'Morning Manna – Voice of Hope', listeners with hope. For, despite the uncertainty of these challenging and perilous times, Christmas will always be a reminder to Christians that Jesus was born to give us a window of hope, through which we can look into eternity, and one day inherit it. For just as the old saying goes: *"Where there is life there is hope".* Hope is confidence, it is a positive expectation that something good is going to happen. Hope enhances life.

Be reminded today that we have a lively hope in Christ Jesus. Thus, we celebrate today and every other day, for He is our hope!

Rev. Dr. Una M. Davis

FRIDAY 22nd

Fear not, Mary: for thou hast found favour with God - St Luke 1:30

APPOINTMENT BY DIVINE RECOMMENDATION - Reading: St Luke 1:26-33

Mary was not known by a title when she found favour.

The Bible records that she was: *"a virgin espoused to a man..."*. This reminds us to keep ourselves spotless because we never know when God will send us a message that we are *"highly favoured...and blessed among women"*.

I say to us as women of a great God, our response should also be: *"So be it unto me according to thy word"*. It was a move from fear to favour that allowed Mary to give birth to a son named Jesus. God wants to birth in us both the spiritual and the natural.

Favour confirms that we are a chosen vessel used by God to shift and change the spiritual atmosphere in the lives of those we meet. Many women are frequently subjected to other people's perceptions of who they are and who they should be. This word reminds us that we are 'favoured', i.e., recommended!

I encourage all women to stand in hope, and with great expectation that our aspirations and dreams will be realised through Divine Recommendation by God.

Sister Vivean Pomell

SATURDAY 23rd

With God nothing shall be impossible - St Luke 1:37

THE INFINITE GOD - Reading: St Luke 1:26-38

God is only limited in our mind. Outside of our mind, He has no limit. God is infinite. Why then do we struggle to believe that with God, nothing is impossible?

Do we really believe that Jesus was conceived in the womb of a virgin by the Holy Ghost? Do we truly believe that Jesus was dead for three days, and then arose with all power? Do we absolutely believe that one day soon we are going to be caught up in the air to meet Him and, *"So shall we ever be with the Lord"?*

If the answer is yes to all of the above, there should be no uncertainty that God can do on our behalf things which are far less 'complex' in comparison.

We refer to Sarah who laughed when she overheard that she was to become a mother in her winter years. We speak also of Mary who initially queried the message from Angel Gabriel of her forthcoming pregnancy: *"How shall this be, seeing that I am a virgin?"*.

But here lies something marvellous: a harlot called Rahab believed God 'first time' against the odds. She asked no questions, instead, by faith, she simply said: *"According to your words, so be it" (Joshua 2:21)*. So, ironically, the writer of Hebrews 11 includes the harlot in his Gallery of Faith, and excludes the virgin who became the mother of the Christ-child.

God wants some first-time believers. Believers who don't need persuading like Sarah or Mary that He can do what He says. He is The Infinite God!

JEJ

SUNDAY 24th

(Mary) wrapped him in swaddling clothes - St Luke 2:7

THE PRESENCE IN OUR PRESENT - Reading: St Luke 2:1-7

Oh, that initial joy of delivering a child after the preparation and excitement in looking forward to the event!

But I wonder if at the time of delivery Mary realised the significance of wrapping her most special first baby in swaddling clothes, of laying Him in, possibly, the most humble position she could have, or the reality that she had delivered a King-child!

There's a saying: *"If I knew then what I know now…"*. Having the benefit of biblical hindsight and revelation means that we are in a privileged position to know that our sovereign King of kings and Lord of lords humbled Himself to entertain coming down into a world of sin. Here He died a most horrible death, so that we could live and reign with Him!

How wonderful is love like this!

Sister Elaine

MONDAY 25th

(Christmas Day)

For unto us a child is born, unto us a son is given - Isaiah 9:6

EXCITEMENT & EXPECTATION - Reading: Isaiah 9:1-7

A child's birth brings excitement. The expectation for the child is healthy growth and success in whatever they choose to do.

Well, over 2,000 years ago, heaven rejoiced when God gave us a special child. The expectation was that He would be received on earth as our Saviour. Unfortunately, only the minority discerned the significance of the gift.

A new birth brings excitement in naming the child which often depicts its character. Isaiah 9:6 foresaw God's gift with excitement and expectation by prophesying the characteristics and symbolism of the name:

Wonderful Counsellor: Excitement - we have someone who will listen, understand and provide a solution to our problems without judging; there's no limit to the number of free counselling sessions we can have. He's our personal psychologist with the expectation He will counsel, guide and lead us in the direction and ways of God.

Mighty God: The excitement is that this child is God manifested in flesh. Our expectation is that He will free us from our burden of sin by His power and ability to fight and win our battles.

Everlasting Father: Our natural father will only live for a period of time; the excitement here is that this child will be the father who dies, resurrects and lives for evermore. Our expectation is that He will give us eternal life.

Prince of Peace: Ever felt troubled, anxious, angry, afraid and more? How exciting to know that this child will bring peace between God and man, and has the ability to give us inner peace to cope with the storms of life, not just at Christmas.

Wow! What an expectation that one child would have all these qualities. This child is JESUS. I invite you to join me in celebrating the fact that Jesus was born on a date of which we are uncertain. However, we must give thanks to God for giving us His son, Jesus.

The excitement is that He came to give us life more abundantly with the expectation that it can be forever if you choose Him today.

Lady Pam Lewin
Ishah to Ishah (Woman to Woman)
A ministry of Bethesda Apostolic Eagles International

December 2023
Theme: The Gift of Jesus Christ
"Let earth receive her King"

TUESDAY 26ᵗʰ

(Boxing Day)

Thou shalt call His name JESUS - St Matthew 1:21

GOD'S GREATEST GIFT - Reading: St Matthew 20:27-28

Mary was told by God that she was going to have a son, and that His name would be called Jesus. And more than that, that He would save His people from their sins.

Mary was a young virgin girl, espoused or promised to a man called Joseph. They would have had plans for their forthcoming marriage; maybe they would have discussed where they would live, how many children they might have and all the hopes and dreams of a young couple. But God had other plans for them!

We are told in this passage of Scripture that the child she was carrying would save His people. God knew that we needed a Saviour, even though we did not recognise we were dying in our sins. So, He gave the greatest gift of all, His only begotten Son, Jesus Christ.

We must acknowledge our sins, just like an addict has to come to the awareness of their addiction and ask for help. As we acknowledge and come to Him, He holds out His arms to embrace and receive us.

Marie Chisnall

WEDNESDAY 27th

If thou be the Son of God, come down from the cross - St Matthew 27:40

STRENGTH IN SUFFERING - Reading: St Matthew 27:40-44

Imagine this: Jesus Christ – God manifested in flesh and Creator of man – left subject to their ridicule, goading and abuse. He was lied about, beaten, mocked, and scorned. He had enough right to defend Himself. Further, He had the ability to escape, to manifest His full strength and destroy His accusers with one breath! But He didn't. He stood as a sheep before its shearer, dumb.

After living righteously and boldly declaring who God is, we can find ourselves in a position of suffering or unwarranted abuse from others. We can feel the need to defend and justify ourselves, wanting God to appear immediately and vindicate us.

God's Word encourages us when in similar experiences to those of men like Job and David; both remind us that *they that trust in the Lord will never be ashamed.* Their chronicles ground us in the knowledge that our *Redeemer lives.* Jesus, our greatest example, endured the cross and despised the shame because He knew His purpose and the joy that would come from His suffering.

The account of the Resurrected Christ that follows in Matthew 28 is a stark contrast to the darkness and sorrow we see in Matthew 27. Everything is different in the following chapter! Continue to trust God through your affliction; He will give you the strength to bear it. Be faithful, be encouraged: things won't be the same in your next chapter.

Beulah McKenzie

THURSDAY 28th

It is finished - St John 19:30

LET THE CHURCH SAY "AMEN!" - Reading: St John 19:28-30

28 After this, Jesus knowing that all things were now accomplished, that the scripture might be fulfilled, saith, I thirst.

29 Now there was set a vessel full of vinegar: and they filled a sponge with vinegar, and put it upon hyssop, and put it to his mouth.

30 When Jesus therefore had received the vinegar, he said, It is finished: and he bowed his head, and gave up the ghost.

Our LORD and Saviour Jesus Christ was a man on a mission; He knew exactly what He came to earth to do.

From His birth to His death, Jesus was fulfilling prophecy and purpose. The penultimate loaded statement to leave His mouth before He died was: *"I thirst"*. The vinegar conveniently placed nearby was given to Jesus on a sponge upon hyssop, so He could now utter the immortal phrase: *"It is finished"*. The mission was accomplished, humankind's sin was purged. He had paid the ultimate, once-in-a-lifetime, eternally atoning, sacrifice for sin.

When we say: *"Amen"*, it means: *"truly"*, *"so let it be"*, *"it is done"*. So, for what Jesus Christ accomplished at Calvary, and what that means for us, let the Church say "AMEN"!

Minister Kay Dawkins

FRIDAY 29th

I must be about my Father's business - St Luke 2:49

A CALL TO REMEMBER - Reading: St Luke 2:41-52

As I read this Scripture verse, I noticed that Jesus' response to His mother was in the form of questions.

He did not give her a direct answer, and neither was He being disrespectful. In fact, Jesus was showing kindness and consideration by helping Mary to remember the reason for His birth, to understand that despite being her earthly son, His heavenly Father had primary place in His life. She had no cause to worry, particularly, if she remembered her encounter with the angel Gabriel (St Luke 1:26-38), and Simeon's prophecy (St Luke 2:25-35).

This event was not coincidental, it was orchestrated to bring Mary and Joseph back in line with God's plan, to remember that Jesus' main purpose was to accomplish the will of God, hence the reason for His virgin birth. Mary was being prepared to let go and to allow Jesus to be who He came to be.

Like Mary, we too must remember the reason for which Jesus came, to save and transform lives. Jesus' response to His mother is a reminder to us to know our heavenly Father, and be conscious of His calling on our lives. Let us arise and do our Father's business diligently.

J Henry

SATURDAY 30th

Mary kept all these sayings in her heart - St Luke 2:51

SILENTLY PONDER - Reading: St Luke 2:41-52

Mary was indeed blessed among women, picked out to be the mother of Jesus Christ.

She was chosen not only because she was a virgin but because of her character. She was called for a purpose, not to elevate or exploit her position. A woman of humility who at no stage do we read of bragging about her son, Jesus, nor do we read of her behaving in a superior manner to the other women of her time.

We see in St Luke 2:19, that Mary pondered the series of occurrences in her heart. In verse 51, again Luke notes that Mary *"kept all these sayings in her heart"*.

An indicator of maturity is knowing when to speak and when to think only. We often rightly applaud Joseph (Jacob's son) for his exemplary character and behaviour in Potiphar's house and then in prison. But one of Joseph's 'mistakes' was that the dreams which he should have pondered in his heart, he shared with his whole family. There was no obvious need to tell them. Whilst we understand that God's will had to be done through a sequence of happenings to get Joseph to Egypt, hopefully you'll grasp what's being said in its context.

Sometimes we 'talk out' everything that God tells us, promises which He's disclosed for our lives, and God only gave us a preview so that we could ponder and prepare. It was not to be announced!

Let us be Wise Women. Be mature, don't show off the Divine Peep into your future. Keep that Personal Word from the Lord personal, and ponder.

JEJ

SUNDAY 31st

(New Year's Eve)

I came so everyone would have life, and have it fully - St John 10:10 (CEV)

JESUS, THE SAVIOUR OF THE WORLD - Reading: St John 10:1-14

To have witnessed the birth of our three children is a memory that I will carry with me for a lifetime. Each of them is now an adult and pursuing their respective dreams and ambitions, but they began their lives as gifts to us through the miracle of birth.

The month of December is a time of giving and receiving, a time to be grateful and, for many, a time to lament. Yet we are thankful for the birth of Jesus Christ, the most precious gift that came into the world to be a ransom for us. He came to love, heal and forgive, to restore, renew and revive.

Thank God for Jesus, the Saviour of the world: *"He is my strength in time of weariness and a light when shadows fall. Jesus is my all in all".*

May the love and light that comes from Jesus, and His grace and favour, fill each of our days with hope and our minds with peace. May each day of the New Year remind us that He is Lord, and that our praise and worship are perfect gifts to give Him because He has given to us so much!

Bishop Dexter Edmund
Presiding Bishop, Bethel UK

Some things that I did not know about getting older…

I did not know…

- that just as some old people walk slow and not straight, I am doing the same thing now, with a walking stick. But I now stop and let the young pass

- I am afraid of technology, but I am bold in other things e.g., I went into the bank to update an account. The clerk asked me what I was saving for. I said for my funeral. She answered by saying that she had not heard anything about my death yet, so I didn't have to worry!

Evangelist Cherry Smith

- that although I am mentally active, people would deal with me based on my frail external appearance

- that people would often talk about me to people around me as though I can no longer hear, think or answer for myself

- that I would still feel young inside although my body is decaying

- how much I would look forward to seeing Jesus more and more as I know that my years remaining here are not many

- that I would shrink in height, I used to be so tall!

Name withheld

SUPPORT DIRECTORY

Please contact one of our professionally qualified Bethel UK Counsellors if you have been emotionally affected by any of the subjects covered in *"I Arise"* 2023: **Bethel Counselling Initiative 07783 046250.**

Alternatively, please see the list below which includes independent agencies in the UK who will be able to offer you support:

Child Bereavement UK
https://www.childbereavementuk.org/
Helpline: 0800 02 888 40
Email:helpline@childbereavementuk.org

Provides support for children and young people up to the age of 25 who are facing bereavement, and anyone impacted by the death of a child of any age. They offer support sessions for individuals, couples, families and children and groups for families, parents and young people. Also provides a helpline and guidance for professionals.

Cruse
https://www.cruse.org.uk/
Helpline: 0808 808 1677 (Monday to Friday 9am to 9pm)
Email:helpline@cruse.org.uk
Cruse Chat live online chat also available

A national charity offering bereavement support, information and campaigning. Cruse offers up to six sessions of one-to-one counselling support, usually on the phone / online, as well as a free helpline and chat support. The website includes guides to understanding grief that are written by bereavement specialists, and information about what to do after someone dies.

Dementia UK
Tel: 0800 888 6678
Carers Direct - helpline for Carers: 0300 123 1053
John's Campaign: 01245 231898 (support to be able to sit with /support loved ones whilst in hospital). Contact Julia Jones julia-jones@talk21.com or Nicci Gerrard nicci.gerrard@icloud.com
Admiral Nurse Dementia Helpline 0800 888 6678
Age UK National Helpline 0800 6781602

Hope Again (Cruse)
https://www.hopeagain.org.uk/
Tel: 0808 808 1677 (Monday to Friday 9.30am to 5pm)
Email:hopeagain@cruse.org.uk

Trained volunteers are available to speak on the free helpline or by email. The website includes parental / guardian advice, videos and resources for families on how to support a child or young person who is grieving.

MIND
http://www.mind.org.uk/
Info line (Tel.): 0300 123 3393 (open 9am to 6pm, Monday to Friday)
Legal line (Tel.): 0300 4666463 (open 9am to 6pm, Monday to Friday)

Mind's Info line provides information and signposting about mental health problems, where to get help, treatment options and advocacy services. Legal Line is a telephone service offering legal information and general advice on mental health related law e.g., on being detained under the Mental Health Act ('sectioned'), mental capacity, community care, discrimination and equality.

National Association for People Abused in Childhood (NAPAC)
https://napac.org.uk/
Tel: 0808 801 0331 (helpline open Monday to Thursday: 10am to 9pm, Friday: 10am to 6pm)

Email:support@napac.org.uk

A registered charity providing support and information for adult survivors of any form of child abuse.

National Domestic Abuse Hotline
https://www.nationaldahelpline.org.uk/

Tel: 0808 2000 247 (free and 24/7)
Live chat also available through the website Monday to Friday, 3pm to 10pm.

Run by Refuge, this national helpline provides emotional and practical support, including helping individuals to find a refuge or other place of safety and access specialist services in their locality.

National Stalking Helpline
Tel: 0808 802 0300
https://www.suzylamplugh.org/am-i-being-stalked-tool

The National Stalking Helpline is run by Suzy Lamplugh Trust. They provide information and guidance on topics including:
•The law in relation to stalking and harassment in the United Kingdom
•Reporting stalking or harassment
•Effective gathering of evidence
•Ensuring your personal safety

Rape Crisis
https://rapecrisis.org.uk
Tel: 0808 802 9999
Live chat available through the website.

Rape crisis is a charity working hard to end sexual violence and abuse. They provide support after rape, sexual assault, sexual abuse or any form of sexual violence.

Relate
https://www.relate.org.uk
A national charity offering support for marriages in crisis

Shelter
https://england.shelter.org.uk/
Helpline: 0808 800 4444
Live chat available through the website.

National charity providing one-to-one, personalised help with housing issues and homelessness, a free emergency helpline and free legal advice for people who have lost their homes or who are facing eviction.

Silverline
www.thesilverline.org.uk
Helpline Tel: 0800 4 70 80 90

Silverline is a national, free, confidential helpline for older people offering friendship, advice and information. It is open 24 hours a day for anyone who feels alone or wants to talk about something. As well as the helpline, they offer telephone friendship (a weekly 30-minute call between an older person and a Silver Line Friend volunteer), Silver Letters (a fortnightly exchange of a letter between an older person and a volunteer), Silver Circles (a call between a group of older people on a shared interest or topic, taking place each week for 60 minutes) and Silver Line Connects (help with informing and connecting an older person with national and local services).

The Daisy Chain Project: Domestic Abuse Legal Advice Charity
https://www.thedaisychainproject.com
Email:info@thedaisychainproject.com

A charity based in Worthing with a UK-wide reach that aims to help fight domestic violence by providing pro bono legal advice, educating people about what constitutes domestic abuse. The Daisy Chain Project legal team consists of qualified and regulated barristers and solicitors who offer free legal support to men and women experiencing, or fleeing, domestic abuse. All barristers and solicitors are regulated by the Bar Standards Board and Solicitors Regulation Authority respectively.

Victim Support
https://www.victimsupport.org.uk/
Helpline: 0808 1689 111 (24/7)
Webchat available through the website

Provides free and confidential support for people affected by crime and traumatic events, regardless of whether they have reported the crime to the police. Services include information and advice, immediate emotional and practical help, longer term emotional and practical help, advocacy, peer support and group work, restorative justice, personal safety services, help in navigating the criminal justice system.

Young Minds Crisis Messenger
https://www.kooth.com/
For urgent help text YM to 85258

Provides free, 24/7 crisis support across the UK if you are experiencing a mental health crisis. All texts are answered by trained volunteers, with support from experienced clinical supervisors. Texts are free from EE, O2, Vodafone, 3, Virgin Mobile, BT Mobile, GiffGaff, Tesco Mobile and Telecom Plus.

If you would like to share a testimony or be one of the writers for: *"I Arise"* 2024, please send an email to: bnwcinspirations@gmail.com

Contact us at: bethelwomen@betheluniteduk.org.uk

Printed in Great Britain
by Amazon

11862357R00249